CW01024503

Oral World and Written Word

LIBRARY OF ANCIENT ISRAEL

Douglas A. Knight, *General Editor*

Oral World and Written Word

Ancient Israelite Literature

SUSAN NIDITCH

First published in Great Britain 1997
Society for Promoting Christian Knowledge
Holy Trinity Church
Marylebone Road
London NW1 4DU

First published in the USA 1996
Westminster John Knox Press
Louisville, Kentucky

Copyright © Susan Niditch 1996

All rights reserved. No part of this book may be reproduced or transmitted in any form or by any means, electronic or mechanical, including photocopying, recording, or by any information storage and retrieval system, without permission in writing from the publisher.

Scripture quotations from the New Revised Standard Version of the Bible are copyright © 1989 by the Division of Christian Education of the National Council of the Churches of Christ in the USA and are used by permission.

All translations are the author's own unless otherwise noted.

Book design by Publishers' WorkGroup

British Library Cataloguing-in-Publication Data
A catalogue record of this book is available from the British Library

ISBN 0-281-05059-7

This book is printed on acid-free paper, ANSI Z3948 standard. ∞
Printed in the United States of America

Contents

Foreword

The historical and literary questions preoccupying biblical scholars since the Enlightenment have primarily focused on the events and leaders of ancient Israel, the practices and beliefs of Yahwistic religion, and the oral and written stages in the development of the people's literature. Considering how little was known about Israel and indeed the whole ancient Near East just three centuries ago, the gains achieved to date have been extraordinary, due in no small part to the unanticipated discovery of innumerable texts and artifacts.

Recent years have witnessed a new turn in biblical studies, occasioned in large part by a growing lack of confidence in the "assured results" of past generations of scholars. At the same time, an increased openness to the methods and issues of other disciplines such as anthropology, sociology, linguistics, and literary criticism has allowed new questions to be posed regarding the old materials. Social history, a well-established area within the field of historical studies, has proved especially fruitful as a means of analyzing specific segments of the society. Instead of concentrating predominantly on national events, leading individuals, political institutions, and "high culture," social historians attend to broader and more basic issues such as social organization, conditions in cities and villages, life stages, environmental context, power distribution according to class and status, and social stability and instability. To ask such questions of ancient Israel shifts the focus away from those with power and the events they instigated and onto the everyday realities and social subtleties experienced by the vast majority of the population. Such inquiry has now gained new force with the application of various forms of ideological criticism and other methods designed to ferret out the political, economic, and social interests concealed in the sources.

This series represents a collaborative effort to investigate several specific topics—politics, economics, religion, literature, material culture, law, intellectual leadership, ethnic identity, social marginalization, the international context, and canon formation—each in terms of its social dimensions and processes within ancient Israel. Some of these subjects have not been explored in depth until now; others are familiar areas currently in need of reexamination. While the sociohistorical approach provides the general perspective for all volumes of the series, each author has the latitude to determine the most appropriate means for dealing with the topic at hand. Individually and collectively, the volumes aim to expand our vision of the culture and society of ancient Israel and thereby generate new appreciation for its impact on subsequent history.

The present volume takes up the old and elusive problem of the origin of the literature preserved in the Hebrew Bible. Too often modern scholars have sought documentary sources, oral traditions, and literary editors from the viewpont of our own literate world or our romanticized fantasy of antiquity. In so doing, Susan Niditch argues, we have moved far from what is needed: a full appreciation of the aesthetics of an oral culture. Disputing the commonly held assumption that literacy had the same meaning then as now and that the mere existence of written texts must necessarily suggest a widely literate culture, she presents a nuanced and dynamic picture of the growth of the various writings in our possession. As she shows, the aesthetic characterizing most written material from ancient Israel, both canonical and epigraphic, points decidedly to an oral world. For the Israelites, writing often had a magical, symbolic, or monumental character, although over time it increasingly adapted itself to pragmatic, everyday needs. Yet the oral mentality among the people maintained itself and affected their attitudes toward writing. Orality and literacy should thus not be pictured as strict opposites or alternatives but as ends of a continuum, with various specific types of literature to be placed at one point or the other along the spectrum. Comparative evidence from other cultures reinforces this view of the interplay between the oral and the written—oral aesthetics infuse the written form, and orality typically continues even after a text is recorded in writing. All extant Israelite literature is based on this continuum. Sensing the power of both the spoken and the written word in Israel's social world should, she demonstrates, lead to a fundamental reconsideration of our understanding of the literary character of the Hebrew Bible.

Douglas A. Knight
General Editor

Preface

This book was researched with assistance from a 1995 grant from the National Endowment for the Humanities. I thank the Endowment for its invaluable support. Smaller grants from Amherst College assisted with preparation of the manuscript, and I thank the Trustees of Amherst College for their help.

Pieces of my work were presented in earlier form as lectures in various settings: Portions of the introduction, chapter 3, and chapter 7 formed the 1994 Bonnie Pedrotti Kittel Lecture at Yale University; a version of chapter 1 was the 1995 Lord-Parry Lecture delivered at the Center for Studies in Oral Tradition, University of Missouri, and was published in *Oral Tradition,* volume 10; portions of chapters 5–7 contributed to the 1994 Presidential Address at the New England Regional Meeting of the Society of Biblical Literature; a form of chapter 8 was presented to the Colloquium for Biblical Research in Cambridge, Massachusetts, in August 1995. On each of these occasions, members of the audience or participants offered useful comments and criticisms that helped to shape the book.

A number of colleagues provided bibliographic assistance or read chapters of the work, offering valuable suggestions: Frank Moore Cross, John Miles Foley, John S. Holladay, Peter Machinist, Carol Meyers, Robert R. Wilson, and Douglas A. Knight, the able editor of this series.

The manuscript was prepared by Diane Beck with her usual grace, patience, and expertise. I thank my dear husband, Robert Doran, for helping me to sort out my ideas, as always, and for his constant and good-humored support. I thank my daughter Rebecca for her genuine interest in my work and for the beautiful music that stays with me as I write. I thank my daughter Elizabeth for reminding me that too much work is a bad thing and for teaching me the conga.

Introduction

We think of the Bible as a book, neatly bound, printed, read silently or quoted or studied, a set text. If we are readers of English, we may prefer the King James Version or the Revised Standard Version. The New Revised Standard Version may come to mean Bible to a new generation of readers who make its text their own.

Turning our ancestors into ourselves, we call the Israelites "people of the book" and reinforce this proverbial image of a community well versed in the skills of literacy with scholarly treatments of the last century that seek to explain the genesis of the Hebrew Bible and to explore the relationships between the literature and actual Israelites. For example, behind the documentary hypothesis associated with Julius Wellhausen but still influential today is the assumption that written layers or sources—the earliest dating back to the Davidic monarchy of the tenth century B.C.E.—underlie large portions of scripture. These written sources, it is suggested, were woven together and edited in a cumulative process of writing. Other more recent studies emphasize "intertextuality" in the Bible, one writer's quotation of another's written, fixed text. Other scholars regard large portions of scripture as the product of modern-style literati or of ancient historiographers, all of whom rely upon the resources or reflect the values of an essentially literate culture.

Neglected in all these approaches is the importance of the oral world for understanding the Bible's written words. Interesting exceptions to the dominant trends in scholarship are found in the work of various exemplars of the so-called Scandinavian school of scholarship (e.g., H. S. Nyberg, Ivan Engnell, Eduard Nielsen). While some of their suggestions are now dated and others are idiosyncratic, they did emphasize the importance of oral traditions for understanding the literature and culture of ancient Israel. [1]

This study approaches anew the idea that large, perhaps dominant, threads in Israelite culture were oral, and that literacy in ancient Israel must be understood in terms of its continuity and interaction with the oral world.

What do we mean by oral culture? What do we mean by literacy in the ancient world?

Even adherents of a documentary hypothesis or proponents of a single historiographer's theory might agree that behind the written work of the Hebrew Bible are oral compositions. Images of these oral contributions to the biblical tradition, however, tend to be condescending or romanticized and frequently include an evolutionary notion whereby oral means early, primitive, and unsophisticated—prebiblical. We suggest rather that the oral world lives in the words of scripture, but not necessarily the oral world as described by Hermann Gunkel.

Influenced by the Brothers Grimm's own artificial portrait of the German folk, Hermann Gunkel, the father of biblical form criticism, provided generations of biblicists with romantic portraits of an Israelite folk and the oral culture in which they participated:

> In the leisure of a winter evening the family sits about the hearth; the grown people, but more especially the children, listen intently to the beautiful old stories of the dawn of the world which they have heard so often yet never tire of hearing repeated.[2]

In his great commentary on Genesis,[3] in *The Folktale in the Old Testament*,[4] and in other works, Gunkel portrays the participants in an Israelite oral culture as naive—even literally, as in the above, young—rural, either pastoral or agrarian, living in a world of family-centered societies without kings or bureaucracy. Influenced by Axel Olrik's 1908 study "Epic Laws of Folklore,"[5] Gunkel perceived the material to which these Israelite folk listened to be poetic, repetitive, simple, and single-stranded in plot. Finally, he suggested that these oral compositions and their oral cultures predated the Bible, having been reworked and transformed in the written sacred traditions of Israel that became the Bible. Indeed he asks:

> However—and the reader will have certainly long since asked the question—what has the Bible to do with folktales? Is it not an attack on the prestige of the holy book to seek in it products of the imagination? And how can the lofty religion of Israel—to say nothing of the New Testament—contain material filled with what may be creative, yet nevertheless entirely subordinate, belief? These questions must be answered, first, by saying that the Bible hardly contains a folktale anywhere. . . . The elevated and rigorous spirit of biblical religion tolerated the folktale as such at almost no point and this near total eradication from the holy tradition is one of the great acts of biblical religion.[6]

Scholars used to place an oral stage for the Bible or for its separate compositions in a premonarchic phase of Israelite history, be it nomadic or patriarchal—notions of Israel's early history that have increasingly fallen into disrepute. Nowadays scholars describe participants in a highland culture practicing subsistence agriculture and write of the village- and kinship-based decentralized world of Israel's origins. These scholars, however, agree with their precursors that the monarchy brings a state, urbanization, schools and writing, courtly records, recorders, and literate authors imagined to be of various kinds. Gerhard von Rad's phrase was "Solomonic Enlightenment."[7]

This diachronic approach to orality and literacy is, however, misguided, devaluing the power of oral cultures and misconstruing the characteristics of orally composed and oral-style works. Such an approach ignores the possibility that written works in a traditional culture will often share the characteristics of orally composed works. It misrepresents ancient literacy as synonymous with literacy in the modern world of print, books, and computers and draws too artificial a line, chronological and cultural, between oral and written literatures.

Orally composed and oral-style works can be rural or urban, unsophisticated, rustic, and parochial or sophisticated, aristocratic, and cosmopolitan, concerned with farm or court, village or city, composed by men or women. There is no one oral genre or oral culture in a society but a range of sorts of compositions, styles, contexts, and composers. Orally composed and oral-style works need not be short and simple but may, like the *Iliad* and the *Odyssey,* be lengthy and filled with complex characters and subplots.[8]

Seemingly more rural works need not be imagined in Israelite social history as confined to "early times." Even once there are kings in ancient Israel and a state—which some would say begins with David or Solomon in the tenth century B.C.E., others not until the eighth century B.C.E., well into the northern and southern monarchies—the vast majority of people continue to lead agrarian lives. They work the land, live in villages led by elders, and continue to tell stories, preserve custom and law, and cite proverbs orally. Some people were probably regarded by their communities as especially good weavers of narration or preservers of genealogy who learned from their elders and had special skills or training, but all would have shared in the oral culture. To ignore these Israelites and their lives we might ask, to paraphrase Gunkel, "What have the Israelites to do with the Bible?" And yet this does not mean that no one in the villages and towns could write or read or that writing was not used in commercial transactions and letters or found upon commemorative stones or that writing was unfamiliar to people.

Once there were monarchies and royal cities, a scribal class would have developed. Kings could finance big inscriptional projects. Priests might copy down favorite compositions. Those versed in oral traditions might create oral-sounding works in writing. The use of writing in commercial contexts would escalate, its use by the military become prominent in the process of sharing tactical information, sending orders, and provisioning outposts. Nevertheless the oral culture could well dominate even a world in which an élite is able to read and write complex works of various genres and in which writing for pragmatic purposes is quite common. Literacy in ancient Israel may have been a quite different phenomenon from literacy in our world while works composed in writing may be difficult to distinguish from orally composed works. And, of course, in a courtly and urbane setting other oral traditions would have been produced and maintained: bardic tales honoring a king's victories, songs created by priests for temple ritual, oracles delivered by prophets to support or critique the leadership.

In approaching issues of oral and written, we err if we view oral and written cultures, oral and written literatures, as incompatible. It is, for example, probably wrong to suggest that the oral tradition lives in the villages from the tenth century B.C.E. on, but that at court the culture is literate in our sense. It is probably also wrong to assert that those who compose in the oral mode are necessarily illiterate, or that a work in the oral style is necessarily composed extemporaneously in the fashion described for bards in Albert B. Lord's classic *The Singer of Tales*,[9] or to suggest that once reading and writing are available the oral culture dies. All of these notions are largely passé among those who study early and oral literatures.

Rather, as John Foley, Ruth Finnegan, and others have shown, there is an interplay between the oral and the written in traditional cultures, modern or ancient, and a continuum or sliding scale of oral styles. Late in his career, Albert Lord also acknowledged, for example, that an oral culture continues in traditional societies even once literacy becomes more general and indeed that the traits typical of literature orally composed by those who do not read or write can appear in written works as well. Lord spoke of an "oral-traditional" style. John Foley, using communications language, refers to an "oral register."[10] Beowulf, Genesis 27, and a work Foley has collected from an illiterate Serbian farmer may all be somewhere in their own culture's oral registers, exhibiting, for example, the trait of fresh variation on conventionalized language and content typical of oral-style works. If one turns to the poems of e.e. cummings or a novel by Dostoyevsky, on the other hand, the oral-traditional signals will be much more faint.

One of our present interests is to explore that "oral register" or "traditional style" as it is found in the Hebrew Bible, and to uncover and describe some of the various oral styles employed by Israelite authors and preserved in the written texts of scripture.

Clearly the Hebrew Bible presents a case in which "written" and "oral" interact, for characteristics of oral-style works are exhibited in biblical literature as Gunkel saw, although we may define the traits of orality differently and more variously than did Gunkel. The Bible makes constant direct reference to the spoken words that constitute various compositions, to orally delivered messages and sung stories, and yet the Bible exists because of writing and the assumptions of people in a writing culture of some variety. How have the oral and the written met in scripture? How does the literature of the Hebrew Bible relate to actual Israelites and the cultural settings in which they lived? How do issues in Israelite orality and literacy relate to theories about the composition and preservation of biblical traditions? Several possibilities should be kept in mind as we ask about the genesis of the Hebrew Bible in terms of the relationship between oral and written composition, communication, transmission, and preservation. Some material in the Hebrew Bible may well be a transcription of an oral performance. In this case, the oracle or tale would be created orally but delivered slowly enough to be copied down. An oral performance may be written down later from memory—people's memories in traditional cultures in which people are not used to printed or written texts are sometimes extraordinary. Or a writer well versed in the oral tradition may create an idealized written text based on many performances of a narrative or hymn or epic. Orally performed works may be composed extemporaneously by people able to read or by illiterate participants in the tradition. Those who can read may use brief notes to help in their creation of an orally performed work. The one who preserves the work in writing may also, of course, take notes during an oral rendition and use these to recreate the text in writing. A writer versed in oral style may himself or herself create a work that rings true to an oral register in writing. A written work may then be reoralized, told aloud from memory, or made the thematic core of a new orally created and/or delivered work that is then written down in one of the ways described above; the earlier written work may then be lost. Even works created in writing may be meant to be delivered aloud. Very few people in the culture we are envisioning know written works because they have seen and read them; they have received the works' messages and content by word of mouth. Even if they have read the works themselves, they quote from memory.

These are the sorts of possibilities we need to keep in mind if we allow that Israelite culture reflects a traditional society in which people did not regularly rely on reading and writing as we do. A combination of the sorts of processes and relationships described above went into the composition of the Hebrew Bible: oral creation and performance; composition in writing based on specific oral works or influenced by the styles of orally produced or performed works; preservation or passing on of works, oral or written, without the aid of written texts; the importance of memory and re-oralization, with implicit possibilities for variation, transformation, and multiplicity. There were no printed books, available in multiple copies in local libraries.

But why should we assume that these images capture the process of composition in ancient Israel and that an oral culture is still reflected in what is now a set book, the Bible? How can we test this model and what are its implications for other biblicists' suggestions about the composition of the Hebrew Bible and the relationship between biblical literature and the ancient Israelites?

Our first step is to uncover a particular aesthetic grounded in the traditional cultures of ancient Israel, grounded we will argue in an oral-traditional mentality. This aesthetic produced by a range of recurring rhetorical features spans the biblical corpus and is well represented in nonbiblical Israelite evidence from paleographic finds. On the one hand, this aesthetic or poetic is common to Israelite literature of various periods and persuasions. On the other hand, within this overarching aesthetic in the oral register are a variety of differing styles that serve as markers of their authors' particular interests, messages, and settings. Oral-traditional style is never one monolithic phenomenon. Moreover, the use of orally derived styles by writers leads to all sorts of interesting possibilities of contextualization. Thus our work in chapters 1–3 is both synchronic and diachronic.

A second major objective of our work is to discover how Israelites themselves understood orality and literacy. What are Israelite attitudes to the oral and the written, to reading and writing? It is our contention that scholars have misunderstood and misrepresented Israelite literacy and thus have been inaccurate in presenting essential aspects of Israelite culture.

Chapters 3 and 4 discuss a host of contemporary studies by students in folklore, comparative literature, and early and oral literatures concerning the relationship between orality and literacy in a variety of traditional cultures ranging from ancient Greece to medieval Europe and twentieth-century Yugoslavia. The work of scholars including John Foley, Rosalind Thomas, M. T. Clanchy, Gregory Nagy, and Mary O'Brien O'Keeffe is directly relevant for the biblical case. These studies place in new light not only orality but literacy as it relates to the culture and literature of ancient Israel, raising questions (1) about the purposes of writing and the nature of literacy in ancient societies that often employ writing in commercial and pragmatic rather than creative enterprises; (2) about the ways in which archives in ancient cultures tend to serve iconic and memorial purposes rather than modern-style record-keeping functions; and (3) about the many ways in which traditional societies simply rely less on reading and writing than we do. Concentrating on examples of nonbiblical Israelite writing, I hope to show that none of the evidence often adduced for Israelite literacy is in conflict with what I mean by an essentially oral world, and that "literacy" in traditional cultures is not the sort of modern literacy with which it is confused.

Chapters 5–7 explore attitudes to writing in the Hebrew Bible with concern for the oral-literate continuum: (1) passages that convey attitudes toward writing typical of those who neither read nor write, endowing written texts with a magical, transformative capacity; (2) passages that emphasize literacy somewhat more in the modern sense (e.g., use of writing to communicate across distances; references to archives and records; specific references to what is written in the Torah that purport to quote a written text); and (3) passages that richly indicate the ways in which the oral culture and the written culture fully interact and intertwine in the implicit attitudes of Israelite authors. Even those passages that seem to be at the oral and literate ends of the continuum evidence the presence of writing in the oral culture and orality in the writing/reading culture.

The final, most difficult, perhaps most intriguing aspect of our study returns to questions about the composition, preservation, and transmission of the Hebrew Bible. If the proposed model for Israelite culture in its oral and literate aspects is a good one and if our descriptive work in chapters 1–7 is accurate, then current theories of biblical composition are seriously flawed. After reviewing some of the major theories of biblical composition that are grounded, we would argue, in outmoded notions of Israelite literacy, we offer some alternate possibilities for the complex interplays between orality and literacy that produced the collection, the Hebrew Bible. This chapter begins to take soundings, to offer hypotheses, and to lay out a framework for further speculation and work.

The heart of our study, however, is descriptive as we seek more deeply to appreciate the nature, meaning, and context of a legacy of Israelite self-expression, preserved in written form.

CHAPTER 1

Oral Register in the Biblical Libretto
Toward a Biblical Poetic

Among scholars of the Hebrew Bible, the members of the so-called Scandinavian or Uppsala School have been some of the greatest champions of the need to explore ancient Israelite literature in terms of an oral aesthetic. With interests similar to those of Gunkel in many respects, Engnell listed as evidence of the oral in biblical literature, adherence to "Olrik's laws," the existence of doublets and variants, certain recurring patterns in poetic structure, and the use of parallel terms in Israelite literary syntax. With the publication of A. B. Lord's *The Singer of Tales,* students of the ancient literatures of the Hebrew Bible, like their colleagues in Old English, Medieval French, and Old Icelandic, were intrigued with the possibility that the corpus they studied reflected the work of composers in an oral tradition. Biblicists began to think anew in terms of bards who composed their literature extemporaneously, without the aid of writing, through the fresh manipulation of traditional patterns in language and content. Continuing and refining the work of his teacher Milman Parry, Albert Lord had suggested that such an oral compositional process lay behind the elegant and complex epics in classical Greek that are attributed to Homer. Lord's and Parry's studies were comparative, grounded in the collection and analysis of numerous examples of the live oral traditions of Serbo-Croatia. Lord demonstrated that the literary creations of the Serbo-Croatian singers of tales who could neither read nor write were characterized by certain traits: (1) a specific metric scheme; (2) "disenjambement" so that the thought is complete at the end of each line; (3) a high degree of formulicity. The bard would express essential ideas and images with particular appropriate sets of words, patterns of words that could be varied to suit metric requirements and the interests of the context but that were conventionalized and traditional even in variation; and (4) an equally traditional set of themes, stretches of plot or patterns of content created by the formulaic language. Lord was then able to demonstrate that the very same traits characterized the *Iliad* and the *Odyssey*. Hence, for Lord these works too must have been orally composed. Lord believed that in the classical Greek case, as in the Serbo-Croatian, the oral mode of composition virtually required illiteracy on the part of the composer. His was a special mode of literary creativity that was somehow contaminated or transformed once the singer had access to writing and reading. For Lord, of course, this was not to say the singer was unsophisticated or simple-minded; rather it was to draw a clear demarcation between oral and literate styles and the cultures that support them.

The metric evidence analyzed by Lord tended to support, for biblicists, the notion espoused by Hermann Gunkel that an oral stage of any biblical composition would be poetic.[1] Thus John Kselman sought to recover poetic, orally based fragments in the so-called Priestly stratum of Genesis. Stanley Gevirtz, William Whallon, and Perry Yoder saw in the parallel constructions typical of Israelite poetic and nonpoetic compositions a key to Israelite oral composition[2] while I explored formula patterns used by biblical prophets, entertaining the possibility that an oracle such as Isa. 1:4–29 was orally and extemporaneously performed by the prophet.[3] He might have created and combined traditional formulas to produce blocks of content or "literary forms" that also suggest the stuff of oral composition. The most complete study of poetic formulas in the Bible is that of Robert Culley.[4] After assessing the formulicity of the poems in the Psalms according to his criteria of repeated phrase and "free substitution," Culley concluded cautiously and, I think, correctly that the amount of material available in the Hebrew Bible is too limited to draw definite conclusions about oral composition in the biblical psalms.

All of these studies of biblical material lead one to conclusions about oral composition far less sanguine than those of Lord and Parry concerning the use of formulaic language in the *Iliad* and the *Odyssey,* a corpus that evidences a very high degree of formulicity. And yet these studies begin to suggest something very special about modes of expressing content in Israelite literature, prose and poetry. Biblical authors of various periods and persuasions composing in a variety of genres share a set of traditional ways to express particular ideas or to create particular images. We cannot link these seeming formulas with systematic metric and prosodic patterns, nor with strictly poetic texts at all (see formulas in tales of the successful wise heroes in Genesis 41, Ahiqar, and Daniel[5] and in the stories of Joseph and Esther[6]), but the language of the Bible is much more stylized and conventionalized, than, for example, the writing in a modern novel or poem and involves variations on certain formulaic patterns of language.

We do well to study biblical literature on its own terms. James Kugel suggests, in fact, that scholars have superimposed their notions of poetry upon the biblical corpus, "reconstructing," to make lines more even, visually aligning the text, and drawing prosodic distinctions in the way we print manuscripts or translate them, creating a false distinction between "prose" and "poetry."[7] He suggests implicitly, as the folklorist Dan Ben-Amos does explicitly,[8] that we need to be attuned to the ethnic genres of the culture itself. Kugel's observation encourages one to reject altogether the search for poetic fragments in what now appear, in our terms, to be prose texts. More importantly, however, he implicitly urges us to explore the nuances of these ancient Israelite compositions in terms of their culture and social contexts, their authors and audiences. While biblical works cannot be proven in any instance to have been orally composed, the written works of the Hebrew Bible evidence traits typically associated with ascertainably orally composed works. They belong somewhere in an "oral register." This phrase refers not to modes of composition but to the style of compositions whether the works were created orally or in writing, whether they are performed or read to oneself.[9]

"Oral register" applies also to the patterns of content that are the plots of biblical narratives and to various recurring literary forms, employed by a range of biblical authors. Robert Alter's studies of biblical type scenes testify to this traditional style though, in some misconception about the depth and sophistication of traditional literatures, Alter himself never associates biblical modes of composition with an oral style. Many other studies of biblical patterns of content point to the Bible's oral register. These include my own work with tales of unlikely heroes and tricksters;[10] Dorothy Irvin's study of the "birth of the hero pattern" in which biblical authors craft tales of Moses;[11] Ronald Hendel's analysis of the lives of the patriarchs;[12] A. B. Lord's study of patterns of the hero in biblical narrative;[13] David Gunn's careful studies of biblical battle reports;[14] Robert Doran's and my study of Genesis 41, Ahiqar, and Daniel 7 as examples of a particular topos about the success of the wise courtier;[15] my studies of various recurring prophetic forms including the symbolic vision form,[16] the woe oracle, the cult polemic, and the lawsuit[17] and of patterns of creation in the Hebrew Bible.[18]

In the Hebrew Bible, traditional style or oral register emerges in the following features: (1) The presence of repetition in one passage, particularly in narrative but in other forms as well. The repetition serves to unify the work and to reiterate essential messages or themes that the author wishes to emphasize and that are important in the larger tradition. As A. B. Lord has noted, such repetition is not merely a mnemonic device for the illiterate performer and his listening audience who have no recourse to writing.[19] Rather, repetition has to do with matters of meaning and stylistic preferences. While this style is typical of orally composed works, it also characterizes works composed in writing that participate in the same aesthetic as do orally composed works. (2) The use of formulas and formula patterns to express similar ideas or images throughout the tradition. When a prophet describes God's power in nature or a storyteller wishes to create the image of an autocratic king, he or she has available certain phrases, vocabulary, and patterns of syntax. The composer can endow the formula with his or her own special nuance, but the phrase will nevertheless be conventionalized to mean in shorthand terms "king who is autocratic" or "God-power." (3) The use of conventionalized patterns of content that recur throughout the tradition. In the field of biblical studies, such patterns are called "literary forms." In traditional cultures there may be ways to describe the preparation for war or the birth of a hero. Each culture has its own favorite recurring literary patterns and ways of combining them into larger wholes.

All of these stylistic characteristics fall under the heading of an aesthetic that John Foley has described in detail in his work *Immanent Art*. The term that most sums up this aesthetic is "metonymy," which Foley defines as

> a mode of signification wherein the part stands for the whole and the text or version is enriched by an unspoken context that dwarfs the textual artifact, in which the experience is filled out—and made traditional—by what the conventionality attracts to itself from that context.[20]

> Submerged beneath the surface of the single tale or element lies a wealth of associations accessible only under the agreement of metonymic representation and interpretation.[21]

> Catalán's formula—and here the model could and should be extended to all phraseological and narrative metonyms—conveys its meaning by an institutionalized association, its denotative concreteness standing by prior agreement for a richer and more resonant reality.[22]

Thus for Foley, the formulaic phrase is no mere convenience for a bard who works extemporaneously, seeking to maintain a certain meter while providing a piece of content. Rather, the formula is a signifier rich in inherent cultural meanings, that draws upon the wider related literary tradition, a template of the tradition and an indicator of worldview. Formulas bring the larger tradition to bear on the passage, allowing a few words to evoke a wider and deeper range of settings, events, characters, emotions, and meanings than the immediate textual context of the phrase might suggest.[23]

In a careful discussion of one noun-epithet formula translated "the male-factor" used for the monster Grendel in Beowulf and for other malevolent figures in Anglo-Saxon literature, Foley shows how this particular phrase "adds to the atmosphere of dread that permeates this part of the poem" because "it resonates with a meaning beyond its semantic, formulaic, and literary-critical content."[24] The phraseology that combines terms for "dark," "night," and "stalking" similarly "encodes" a "terror" that "springs into the narrative."[25] "The referential meaning of this group of words is much greater than the sum of their individual denotations and connotations, and it enriches each instance with a greater than situational impact."[26]

Similarly an epithet for Achilles used in one context "promotes the interpretation of a hero's specific and present actions against his overall mythic identity, in other words his whole, extrasituational character."[27] This metonymic quality applies not only to phrases but also to larger structures that "carry with them traditional connotations that are active in the smaller situational compass of individual occurrences."[28]

Foley provides a meaning-rich context in which to understand the repetitions, formulaic language, and motif clusters that characterize works in the oral register. He shows further how this technique of "immanent referentiality"[29] is found not only in works that are orally composed such as those collected by Parry and others but also in works that we have only in libretto form whose mode of composition can never be ascertained with absolute certainty. The relevance of his work in Beowulf to biblical material is especially strong.

Foley also shows beautifully how traditional-style works vary in their adherence to this aesthetic of metonymy, the Muslim epics of Serbo-Croatia, for example, being more fully informed by the "aesthetics of traditional referentiality,"[30] "by poetically sanctioned reference to inherent meanings embodied in traditional forms,"[31] than Christian epic songs that blend oral-traditional aesthetics with "a more textual orientation" in which the phrase derives more meaning from immediate context. In such works "too metonymic" a reference may be regarded as Homer's nodding and be "corrected." This too becomes relevant to the biblical process and to our understanding of styles in ancient Israelite literature.

Foley's work encourages us to think deeply about the role of recurring language in the biblical corpus, about epithets and larger formulaic phrases of varying sorts of content, and about the literary forms that unify the corpus. This approach leads us also to question some basic scholarly text-critical and source-critical assumptions about the formation of the Bible that are grounded in the perspective of modern-style literacy and textuality.

REPETITION

Examples of purposeful repetition within individual pericopes abound in the Hebrew Bible. The repetition is sometimes of the framing variety found in the first chapter of Genesis with a "fill in the blank" quality (e.g., "And God said, 'Let there be x,'" "And God called the x y. And there was evening and there was morning, the nth day"). At other times repetition involves full sentences whereby, for example, news is delivered to someone and then is received or overheard by a second character, then repeated perhaps several times as it is passed on to other characters. Instances of this include the news that the old man Isaac plans to pass on his blessing to his eldest son Esau, and the father's instructions to his son overheard by Rebecca and repeated to her favorite son, the younger, Jacob, who then pretends he is his brother by following the instructions (Gen. 27:2–4, 7, 9–10, 31, 33). The language recurs in the uncovering of the deception. A similar passing on of news about Tiamat's plot to destroy the gods who had killed her husband is found in the Mesopotamian creation epic *Enuma elish*.

A third variety of repetition involves play on a particular *Leitwort*, or key word, a phenomenon noted by Martin Buber and more recently explored by Michael Fishbane, Joel Rosenberg, and others.[32] In Genesis 27 such key words are *'kl* "to eat" and *brk* "to bless," terms that invoke hospitality, engratiation, and fertility.

Scholars with a taste for a particular sort of literate aesthetic have sneered at repetition. One thinks, for example, of G. S. Kirk's depiction of repetitions in the Akkadian *Enuma elish* as boring and tedious.[33] Kirk is not always appreciative of the rhythms, tastes, and modes of creating meaning that are found in many traditional contexts.

Repetition is not a simple-minded stylistic device that allows an audience to follow a story that is heard rather than read or that offers a composer a quick way to create content without varying the vocabulary or the syntax. Repetition is a means of metonymically emphasizing key messages and moods in a work of literature as in a musical composition. The repeated frames in Genesis 1, for example, create the impression of a magisterial and in-charge deity whose word is all powerful, whose creations are firmly rooted, solid, and integrated. The process of creation and the overturning of chaos is inevitable and builds surely and confidently to the creation of humanity, the capstone of the process. Repetition itself is metonymic for the process of becoming.

Similarly, the refrain "it was good" emphasizes the underlying goodness of the cosmos, a world that comes to include murder and theft, violence and deception. This is a key theme to an important line of biblical thinkers in the tradition, and the repeated phrase serves simply and elegantly to weave the notion of cosmic goodness into the very fabric of creation. In a tale such as Genesis 27, repetitions in the father's words to Esau, the mother's words to Jacob, and Jacob's actions build drama and beautifully highlight complex triangles of family relationships and tensions, as the various characters stand in relation to the words that are repeated. The repetition about the father's anticipated death and about obtaining the food that he loves in exchange for blessing, in shorthand, points implicitly to parental preferences for one child over another, to causes for sibling rivalries, and to Jacob's and Rebecca's roles as tricksters as the same words become a source of deception and manipulation. The words, immanently and indirectly referential, create strong impressions of the characters' psychologies and personalities.

The single repeated word can also be a powerful source of immanent referentiality within a work, unifying and deepening the meanings of a composition in ways paradoxically more subtle than variation in language. The term "eat" in Genesis 27, for example, serves to juxtapose Isaac's and Esau's physicality, the old man's desire to eat and satisfy his appetite and the young man's willingness to hunt to obtain food, with Rebecca's and Jacob's more hidden plans, the woman's work of food preparation that allows her to influence the male (so Abigail, so Esther) and the young man's participation in the act of domesticity as deception. This word works metonymically not only in this tale, but it evokes a whole range of eating men and food-preparing women in the biblical tradition that sets up the constellation of men to be influenced, lulled, calmed, or as in this case deceived.

Repetition is thus one of the features of the Hebrew Scriptures' aesthetic of metonymy. It is important to note, however, that not every traditional-style author represented in the Bible employs the varieties of repetition within a passage described above. Such repetitions are a marker of traditional style, an important indicator of a particular traditional style, but not all traditional-style works exhibit this particular feature.

FORMULAS

Works that exhibit the aesthetic of metonymy will always employ a different sort of repetition, namely the use of certain kinds of language to convey an essential image or idea, to import into a passage of literature a particular mood or characterization or expectation of events because these terms are regularly employed in the tradition to communicate this mood or to introduce certain kinds of events. Such familiar phrases bring with them a meaning beyond the immediate content of the literary context, enriching the passage with the larger implications of the tradition and with essential denotators of a culture's worldviews.

EPITHETS

Some of the briefest and most basic recurring phrases of the Hebrew Bible are noun-epithets comparable to those John Foley explores in Serbo-Croatian, Anglo-Saxon, and classical Greek sources. An archaic epithet for Yahweh, god of the Israelites, provides an interesting case study: *'ăbîr ya'ăqōb*. The translation for this phrase in the RSV, the NRSV, and others is "the Mighty One of Jacob." This translation is itself countermetonymic, a theologically motivated attempt to invoke only one aspect of the phrase's meaning. More basically and literally the *'ăbîr* in Northwest Semitic languages means "bull," as P. D. Miller has shown in a classic study and as poetic texts such as Isa. 10:13; Ps. 22:13 (v. 12 in English); and Ps. 50:13 strongly confirm. In the latter two passages in particular, "bull" is in synchronic parallelism with "steer" (Ps. 22:13) and "he-goat" (Ps. 50:13).

The horned bull includes implications of strength (hence the translation "Mighty One"), youth, warrior skills, and fertility with a particular sort of machismo. Americans of a particular generation might speak similarly of a "young buck" or a "stud." Ancient Canaanite religion is rich in tales of the god Baal imaged as a bull. In fact, horned crowns were important symbols of god-power throughout the ancient Near East. As metonymic symbols of various deities, such crowns were set upon thrones in temples representing and ensuring divine indwelling presence.[34]

In part because of the association of the bull with Canaanite and other ancient Near Eastern deities, not all Israelites were comfortable with bull iconography or the related mythology—hence the condemnations in Exodus 32 and 1 Kings 13—and yet for many, perhaps most Yahweh worshipers the bull symbol invoked a range of positive aspects of the deity as powerful, youthful bringer of plenty, rescuer from enemies. When in Ex. 32:4 the Israelites shout toward bull icons, "These are your gods, O Israel, who brought you up out of the land of Egypt!" it is the power symbolically and metonymically represented by the bull that captures their imagination. This bull is not Baal or El or Marduk, but the God of Jacob Israel, bound to this people in a shared history of experience, in a narrative tradition that creates, preserves, and maintains the relationship. The Israelite tradition no doubt contained many additional references to the Bull of Jacob beyond the

few found in the Hebrew Bible—stories, proverbs, longer formulas in which
the Bull of Jacob appeared—but even the limited biblical references are in-
structive. Each time the epithet is used, a larger tradition of associations is
brought to bear on the context at hand, which may deal in an immediate
way with only certain aspects of the Bull of Jacob.

Thus in Gen. 49:24, the literary setting is Jacob's testament, his old-age
blessing to each son, considered in the tradition to be ancestor hero of a
particular tribe or tribes. Joseph, father of Ephraim and Manasseh, the northern Israelites, is described in a warrior context. Archers strive against him
bitterly but his bow stays firm, his arms agile. The translation at verses 23–24
is difficult, but the phrase employing the bull epithet follows these indications of fortitude in battle with a phrase meaning literally "from the hands
of the Bull of Jacob." In other words, Yahweh, Bull of Jacob, supports his
charges in battle like an Athena or a Zeus supports their favorite warriors.
The image of the bull brings this agonistic power to bear. So too at Isa. 1:24
and 49:26. The latter describes the victory over oppressors in the ghoulish
language of a cannibalistic postvictory banquet:

> I will cause those who oppress you to eat their own flesh
>> As with sweet wine they will become drunk on their blood.
> All flesh will know that I Yahweh am your savior
>> Your redeemer is the Bull of Jacob.

As we have discussed for Ezekiel 38—39,[35] the victory of Israel over her enemies takes the cosmogonic form of the victory-enthronement pattern, the
victorious banquet motif intertwining with the blood-soaked imagery of the
battlefield—in this case of the enemies' self-consumption in defeat. The
"savior" and "redeemer" who makes that possible is the Bull of Jacob. Warrior is also world-maker, establisher of cosmos after chaos, destroyer and
builder, wager of battles and peacemaker, the guarantor of fertility. All of
these nuances are contained in the bull.

Isaiah 60:16 in context emphasizes the paradise aspect of the bull, the
plenty and fertility he brings in the victory over enemies as Israel sucks the milk
of nations, the breasts of kings. Instead of a cannibalistic self-consumption,
there is an image of absorbing the enemies' strength as a baby would drink
nurturing milk at its mother's breast—an image of ultimate security and
freedom from oppression. This too is within the power of the Bull of Jacob.
And yet within this epithet emphasizing fecundity, complete security, and
peace is also metonymically reference to the warrior, the aggressive male
power.

As Foley has pointed out, the epithet brings to a passage a full range of a character's personality in the tradition, qualities beyond those emphasized in the context at hand. Psalm 132 is a pro-Davidic, pro-Jerusalem, pro-Temple hymn, in which the worldview is similar to that of 1 and 2 Chronicles. David is imagined as an ideal ruler who establishes Yahweh's holy city and prepares for God's dwelling place on earth (132:3–7). The covenant with the Davidic dynasty is emphasized (132:11, 12) as is the role of the priests (132:9, 16) and the eternal bond between God and an inviolable Zion (132:13–15). This passage deals directly neither with war (v. 8 contains only hints of the warrior enthroned, returned from battle) nor employs extensive fertility imagery (see v. 15), but Yahweh is addressed as Bull of Jacob (v. 2). David seeks a dwelling place for the Bull of Jacob (v. 5). This epithet introduces into the passage the full mythology of the bull, the special sort of male power, the fecundity, all of which contribute to the message of security under the eternal rule of David in Zion blessed by Yahweh, but the contribution is of the immanently referential or metonymic variety.

A similar sort of metonymy applies to other biblical epithets. When Yahweh is called "the God of Abraham, Isaac, and Jacob," the context does not always overtly and directly deal with covenant or genealogy, but this epithet metonymically brings these themes to bear on a context for those who share the tradition; the epithet is a template of the larger tradition.

LONGER FORMULAS

The Bible is rich also in more complex and longer formulas as studies by Culley, Whallon, myself, and others have indicated. The metonymic quality applies to these as well. For example, when a biblical figure at court has a difficult problem to solve, he "sends for" or "calls to" a formulaic chain of advisers and assistants.

The chain of wisemen can include any number of wizards, magicians, advisors, officials, and other members of the royal entourage (for example, Gen. 41:8; Ex. 7:11; Jer. 50:35; Dan. 1:20; 2:2). These terms may then be used in a variety of stylized expressions. In Jer. 50:35, for example, the prophet intones a virtual incantation over the inhabitants of Babylon, predicting that kingdom's downfall and helping to bring it about:

> A sword against the Chaldeans says the Lord
> and against the inhabitants of Babylon,
> against her officials, and against her wisemen.

In three other locations, items from this chain are used with the verb "to call" when a king facing a difficult problem calls to members of his bureaucracy to help him address the difficulty (Gen. 41:8; Ex. 7:11; Dan. 2:2). The formulaic chain appears also at Dan. 1:20 to indicate that exiled Jewish wisemen at the Babylonian court were worth ten times more than the local counterparts.

In each case, through the use of a combination of these key terms, the storyteller is able to bring into the context the aura of the foreign court and the notion of contest between those in power and those who are in a more marginal political position but who are backed by God. The longer formula "call to" + "chain of bureaucrats" is a shorthand notice that the Israelite wiseman is involved in some version of a court contest while the author of Jer. 50:35 and 51:57 is able to use the list-of-officials formula to describe the undermining of Babylon's government, her seat of power. Such a list is more than a convenience for oral-style storytelling, more than an indication of an aesthetic in which there is a marked preference for describing the same piece of content in the same language. The list is also a means of including an essential idea in a passage, of creating the proper image in the minds of members of an audience, a means of making sure everyone shares the same setting, the nuances and ranges of meaning offered by the tradition.

QUOTATION OF A SPECIFIC TEXT OR TRADITIONAL REFERENTIALITY

In Ex. 2:2 the mother of Moses is described: "The woman became pregnant and she gave birth to a son and saw he was good [*wattēre' 'ōtô kî ṭôb hû'*]." Many, including me, have suggested that the author here echoes the very language of God's creation in Genesis 1 (vv. 4, 10, 12, 18, 21, 25, 31), thereby setting in motion in the reader's mind a pattern of cosmogony that will lead to the establishment of a new and free people, the Israelites.[36]

Implicit in this suggestion is often the assumption that the tale in Genesis 1, in its written form, is being quoted. World-creation is thus a model for other creations. This, of course, assumes a relative chronology in which Genesis 1 is earlier than Exodus 2, a problem for those who would assign these passages to a sixth-century *P* source and a tenth-century *J* source respectively. Within a framework that is more attuned to an oral-traditional aesthetic, one might suggest that the creation account of Genesis 1, whatever its origins in writing or speech, was known, was popular, had become a part of the culture, and that the author of the birth story of Exodus 2 had available the words of world-creation to introduce a new creation. One does not suggest a rigid process of copying or quotation, but that Genesis 1 had become a part of the tradition, the refrain "it was good" formulaic.

And yet, perhaps even this framework does not allow adequately for the role of metonymy in assessing the relationship between the passages. In fact, the "see and was good" phrase is found in one other biblical passage, and the phrase "it was good" in numerous others.[37]

In Gen. 49:14–15 in the testament of Jacob comes the saying to Issachar:

> Issachar is a strong [bony] ass,
>   dwelling [lying down] among the encampments [cattle pens].
> He saw a resting place that it was good,
>   and the land that it was pleasant.
> And he bent his shoulder to bear,
>   and became a slaving labor band.

The various sayings in Genesis 49 provide brief overviews of the various tribes, their strengths or weaknesses, the myths or traditional stories associated with them and their geographic settings. Comparisons to animals or other natural features are common.

This piece of tradition characterizes the tribe of Issachar with a donkey metaphor: their brawny animal strength, their stubborn will and endurance, their subjugation. The metaphor works beautifully (note the double entendres and see the discussion by Westermann[38]) and is no doubt related to a perception of Issachar's status at some point in Israelite history or to an actual sociological/historical situation for one of the early Israelite groups. As we seek to understand the use of the "see and it was good" phrase in this and the other contexts, we note that once again the phrase is associated with founding or beginning, for Gen. 49:14–15 is a founding myth that addresses Issachar's settling into a particular portion of land. The resting place is beheld to be good to the one who will work and husband it, reshaping it through his labor.

Thus the phrase "to see and it was good" has to do with creation, procreation, and beginnings. Exodus 2 need not be reliant on Genesis 1 or viceversa, but all three passages may reflect the sort of metonymic or traditional referentiality that so aptly described the workings of epithets.

The smaller phrase "it was good" may also be a trigger of related cosmological themes, for it is frequently used in biblical contexts to describe God, the quintessential and eternal creator (Jer. 33:11; Ps. 34:9 [English v. 8]; 54:8 [English v. 6]; 69:17 [English v. 16]; 100:5; 109:21). The good land, the good lad, and the good earth all reflect the great goodness that is God.

This approach to recurring biblical language not only challenges the scholar to look in new ways at biblical intertextuality but also raises questions about the whole source-critical enterprise. Many scholars, for example, have seen the woman of Tekoa's description of her sons' fratricidal conflict—a tale she spins at Joab's urging to lead David to rehabilitate his fratricidal son, Absalom—as a case of a Davidic court writer's echoing the mythic tale of Cain and Abel (2 Sam. 14:6; Gen. 4:8). Both descriptions describe the killing as taking place in an open space (*śādeh*). The language, in fact, in each is quite different—different words are used for the conflict and the killing (e.g., *hrg* "to kill" [Gen. 4:8] vs. a hiphil of *mwt*: lit. "to cause to die" [2 Sam. 14:6]. Other scholars suggest that the courtly tale predates Genesis 4 and that a later writer echoes the woman of Tekoa in his telling of an early cosmogonic myth, perhaps in order to remind readers of Absalom's lack of worthiness and the rightness of the choice of Solomon as David's successor in the dynasty.

One who is attuned to the aesthetics of traditional literatures might view such questions as the wrong ones, the argument itself like the proverbial question about the chicken and the egg. Rather, the field, the open spaces, are places traditionally where subversion can take place, where social mores can be overturned. It is the world of nature: Esau's world (Gen. 25:27); the place where Jonathan assists David's escape from King Saul (1 Sam. 20:35) when the latter as political authority rules David to be a rebel, an enemy of the state; the place where a woman can be attacked with no one to hear her screams for help (Deut. 22:27). Is it not possible that the open spaces are the ideal setting for various acts of subversion including fratricide, and that references in tales of Cain and Abel and Amnon and Absalom refer to a wider field of tradition that includes not only these scenes from the tradition, these tellings of stories, but other scenes as well?

PATTERNS OF CONTENT

In the study of patterns of content, the field of folklore overlaps with the biblical subfield of form criticism. As briefly noted in the introduction to this chapter, scholars have uncovered scores of recurring topoi in the biblical corpus, constellations of motifs or clusters of content that serve authors who present their own versions of the various traditional forms. Under these traditional topoi we would include particular sorts of narratives (e.g., the tales of the hero explored by Hendel; the battle reports explored by Gunn); varieties of prophetic speech (e.g., the woe oracle and the symbolic vision that I have explored); and the various types of traditional sayings explored by Fontaine.[39]

Complex issues of genre and definition are raised by the mention of these traditional forms. How, for example, does one specify content, matters I have discussed in detail in *Underdogs and Tricksters* (chap. 2)? Is each variety of traditional narrative a separate genre or form? How can we be faithful to the Israelites' own notions of literary form without superimposing our own notions of structure and content upon the ancient material? It is, after all, an Israelite aesthetic we seek to uncover.

However one specifies the content, be it via my overlay map or via Robert Culley's Propp-influenced action sequences or via Robert Alter's type scenes, it becomes clear that the Israelite literary tradition preserved in the Hebrew Bible is characterized by what Culley has called "themes and variations."[40]

The attempt to identify Israelite ethnic genres—that is, the literary forms that Israelite authors and audiences would recognize by a specific term, context, content, and form—is important, and a topic for on-going work. For our purposes, the recognition of the use of themes and variations is essential to understanding the larger aesthetic concept behind the tradition as a whole. Culley's work, mine, and that of others prove that the Bible is rich in recurring patterns of content, and, as with the use of formulaic phrases, such clusters partake of a traditional aesthetic of metonymy.

THE VICTORY-ENTHRONEMENT PATTERN

One of the most pervasive traditional patterns in the Hebrew Bible and the ancient Near East is the victory-enthronement pattern. This narrative thread is associated with cosmogonic narratives, tales of creation and re-creation, and is related to human patterns of war. The narrative sequence at its fullest may contain (1) a challenge to a male warrior, frequently the young, powerful deity who is involved in the world-creating pattern; (2) the preparation of weapons, sometimes via magical help; (3) the battle; (4) the victory of the hero; (5) a victory shout; (6) a procession; (7) house building (which in Israelite tradition is frequently associated with the founding or rescue of Zion, the building of the Temple in Jerusalem, or the taking possession of the land of Israel); (8) a banquet/gathering in the house with (9) the young warrior's enthronement.

This pattern is found in the Canaanite tale of Baal and Anat, in the Mesopotamian creation tale *Enuma elish,* and frequently characterizes Yahweh's victories for his people Israel as well as the more universal world creation.[41] In some passages many of the motifs that belong to this cluster appear. Paul D. Hanson has shown, for example, how richly Zechariah 9 is informed by this traditional pattern. Few if any biblical texts, however, include all of the motifs listed above, a set of motifs found in the epic of Baal and Anat, which itself has been reconstructed by modern scholars from extant broken ancient texts. None of these examples of the use of the victory-enthronement pattern need in any one case exhibit all the motifs available in the tradition in order for the metonymic force of the cluster to be invoked and experienced. As Foley shows, it is our challenge as modern readers to try to identify with the ancient Israelite receiver of or participant in this material who does have an on-going connection with this essential mythic pattern and who would be sensitive to the parts as triggers of or markers of the larger whole.

A fine example of the way in which Foley's insights lead us to read the ancient traditional material with new eyes is offered by an exegesis of the opening verses of Isaiah 55, one of the works in the sixth-century B.C.E. corpus attributed to the pseudonymous prophet called by modern scholars Deutero-Isaiah. The first two verses are an invitation to all to drink and eat. Reference is then made to the covenant with David (3–5), the call to repent (6–7), the uniqueness of God (8–9), and the inevitability of God's word (10–11). The passage concludes with the imagery of fertility and peace that betoken a sort of reversal of the loss of paradise (12–13). In terms of context, the welcome to eat and drink rich foods, wine, and milk, can be seen as an inclusio with paradise imagery at the end of the pericope. God's salvation brings fullness and plenty. But if one reads more widely in the Deutero-Isaiah tradition and in the Israelite tradition as a whole, 55:1–2 can be perceived to invoke the banquet motif of the victory-enthronement pattern.[42] A similar invitation to eat and drink is offered by Woman Wisdom in Prov. 9:5. A figure closely associated with creation in Proverbs 8, God's "master-builder," a virtual divine consort, Woman Wisdom existed before there were depths, before mountains were dug out. She builds her house (9:1) and prepares a feast in another biblical example of the victory-enthronement pattern.

Pieces and parts of this pattern lace through the fifteen chapters attributed to Deutero-Isaiah. In this way salvation becomes liberated from one specific historical event, hoped for and contextualized, but becomes part and parcel of the re-creation of the world, Israel's rescue a new beginning of the cosmos. The warrior, the battle/victory, and procession are found in 42:10–17, battle-victory/procession in 51:9–10, procession in 49:8–11, city or world building and ordering in 45:11–13 and 45:18–19. As Foley notes for Christian Yugoslav epic, the metonymic referentiality of traditional-style immanent art combines with the more immediately contextualized referentiality of nontraditional literatures.

The skilled biblical author, at home in the oral world and aware of the audience's expectations within the tradition, can quite consciously invoke traditional patterns to manipulate them in recognizably less than traditional ways in order to shock and to make those who receive the message take notice.[43] Amos, for example, invokes the motifs of light and brightness by mentioning "the day of the Lord," usually associated with God's liberating acts on Israel's behalf. Instead, with dramatic irony, Amos declares that for a sinful Israel the day of the Lord means punishment and devastation, darkness and not light (Amos 5:18–20).[44] The power of the traditional pattern thus operates in a transformed capacity. The pattern also plays a role in the biblical tradition in the redaction process itself.

The victory-enthronement pattern, for example, holds together important portions of the Hebrew Bible that probably originally circulated quite separately or that at least admit of different sorts of style, content, and concern. The last ten chapters of Ezekiel include at least two collections: (1) the apocalyptic battle with Gog of Magog in chapters 38—39, probably the work of a postexilic writer who expects an overturning of Israel's current situation with a final world-shaking battle, and (2) Ezekiel's plans for the rebuilt temple in chapters 40—48, a visionary excursus that I have compared to the mandala visions of the Hindu and Buddhist traditions, as the holy man reports in great architectural detail his vision of God's temple on earth.[45] The temple is a new center of the cosmos that mirrors the heavenly realm but that is of this earth, peopled by priests, princes, and people who now participate in a reinvigorated covenant with God.

Holding this disparate material together is the pattern of victory-enthronement. Within chapters 38—39 comes the battle (38:1–16), the victory (38:17–39:16), the banquet (39:17–20), and in chapters 40—48 the housebuilding, the building of the dwelling place of the victorious deity that is a cleansed Edensque cosmos, where all is ordered according to God's plan, peaceful and plentiful in accordance with God's peace.

Similarly, Exodus 1–15 includes the epic of Israel's escape from slavery in Egypt into the wilderness. In chapters 20—40 come legal and ritual material, albeit presented within the narrative context of the exodus. Exodus 15 includes motifs of challenge (15:9); battle/victory (15:1, 4–8; 10–12); procession (15:13; 16), and enthronement (15:17–18). Then comes the world-ordering via law, culminating with directions for the building of the tabernacle, the moveable tent shrine that, like the later temple, is the locus for God's indwelling presence on earth. Thus as in Ezekiel 38—48 the cosmogonic victory-enthronement pattern serves as a connecting web in Exodus.

The traditional victory-enthronement is extremely important in shaping the slice of the Israelite tradition we call the Hebrew Bible. Its force is not superorganic without reference to actual people set in cultures but rather is testimony to the power of "immanent art" in the minds and work of redactors, for people at home in an oral culture have determined the form of what ultimately became the written words of scripture. In the final formation of the biblical tradition, redactors compile materials that were by then perhaps quite fixed, either orally or in writing, influenced by an orally derived sense of what sorts of themes or motifs belong together.

The important message from our study of formulaic patterns of language and content in the literature of the Hebrew Bible is not that the Bible is derived from orally composed literature in some simple evolutionary process. Certainly some works may have been composed extemporaneously, an issue we will discuss in chapter 8. The important message from our study of Israelite literature, however, is that an oral aesthetic infuses Hebrew Scripture as it now stands. Without an understanding of this aesthetic and the world that provided its context, we cannot fully appreciate the literature of ancient Israel preserved in the Bible.

Variations in the
Oral Register

Comparisons between the creation accounts in Genesis 1 and Genesis 2—3 have helped to lay the groundwork for biblicists' efforts to distinguish between some of the various contributors to the larger tradition. Scholars have long pointed to differences in style, structure, content, and theme between the narratives. Too often the comparison becomes a mechanical homage to Julius Wellhausen's theory of biblical sources, the so-called documentary hypothesis.[1] We will have much to write about source theories, the history of scholarship on the genesis of the Bible, and about the relevance of our studies in orality and literacy to these matters. In this chapter, however, we take a fresh look not only at Genesis 1 and Genesis 2—3 but also at an additional creation narrative in the work of the sixth-century B.C.E. prophet Ezekiel in order to explore variations in the Israelite oral register.

While work in chapter 1 tends to be synchronic, pointing to certain aspects of Israelite aesthetics rooted in the oral mode that seem to be found across the tradition, the present analysis explores how specific varieties of traditional style characterize these biblical authors and distinguish them. We show, moreover, in each case how the particular medium suits the work's particular setting and message.

GENESIS 1

Genesis 1 exhibits many of the characteristics explored in chapter 1 as typical of the Israelites' traditional literature preserved and presented in the Hebrew Bible.

The overall pattern of Genesis 1, like that of countless creation stories worldwide, traces the movement from the nondifferentiation and sterility of watery chaos to a defined and productive cosmos with its forms of life and geographic markers. The actual order of what is created parallels in a general fashion the order of creation in the Mesopotamian creation epic *Enuma elish* as the light is followed by creation of the firmament and the creation of the firmament by dry land, the luminaries, and humanity.[2] The account in Genesis 1 does not include the battle motif and the larger victory-enthronement pattern that is essential not only to *Enuma elish* and other ancient Near Eastern creation tales but to a central slice of Israelite tradition as well. This version of creation, like that of Genesis 2, thus involves particular authorial choices that will help to identify the particular religious worldview it reflects and shapes. Like much of the biblical literary tradition, some of the language in Genesis 1 reveals content in brief lines that are frequently self-contained and that parallel with nuances the content of one or more lines linked to it:

> The world was empty and void
> Darkness was on the face of the deep
> And the wind of God hovered on the face of the water.
> >   (Gen. 1:2)

In Genesis 1, some of the thought segments are rather more complicated with subordinate clauses (e.g., vv. 11, 12). Also very brief segments of content will follow quite lengthy ones:

> And the earth brought forth fresh shoots of herbage
> Putting forth seeds each according to its species
> And each tree made fruit that was according to the species of the seed in it
> And God saw that it was good.
> >   (Gen. 1:12)

The dominant and most marked feature of the language of Genesis 1 is the high degree of repetition, the recurring frames into which are inserted the particulars of each day's work in creation:

> And God said [creation by word]
> And it was so
> And God saw the [created thing] that it was good
> And God called [the created thing] [a name]
> And it was evening and it was morning [number of day]

Language of division, distinction, and definition recurs as well, emphasizing the theme of creation as a process of differentiation.

Certain phrases and longer pieces found in Genesis also recur in the tradition. We discussed the phrase "it was good," for example, in chapter 1. Another interesting combination of words encapsulates God's creation of living things by listing those animals that live in sky, walk upon earth (usually mammals), and crawl upon the ground. Israelite taxonomy might be described as flyers, walkers, creepers. Sometimes the formulaic list is expanded by fish (swimmers) or other living beings. For the "wild animals" or "beasts of the earth" (*ḥāyyāt hā'āreṣ*) may be substituted another term *běhēmāh*. This list of terms for groups of animals with its traditional variations means the created living world and is a fine summary of an important slice of Israelite cosmology. The phrase betokens a process of world ordering that can be brought to any context.

Thus Gen. 1:28 refers to the world that humans will control, Gen. 1:30 to the living beings' diet—the way in which the vegetative and animal worlds join in the life cycle. Genesis 7:8, 14 refers to the minicosmos of life forms that survive on Noah's ark while Gen. 7:23 refers to the larger cosmos that is destroyed in the new chaos of the flood. Gen. 8:17, 19 following the flood refers to letting loose the life-forms to recreate the world, and 9:2 refers, like 1:28, to human dominion over a cosmos teeming with animal life. Leviticus 11:46 makes use of the chain signifying living creation to emphasize the ongoing process of world ordering that is part of an Israelite priestly worldview, namely the further division of the living beings into clean and unclean animals (so too Lev. 20:25). Deuteronomy 4:16–18 forbids the iconizing of elements of animal nature in religious symbolism. The creation is not to be concretized in this way in the view of the writer, though Israelites who are more sympathetic to iconic representations no doubt would have regarded such religious objects, like the word phrase itself, as an expression in brief of God's creation. In Ezek. 38:20 the formulaic chain of beings refers to the cosmos that will be disrupted in an apocalyptic battle with forces of chaos.

The presence of its pattern of content elsewhere in the tradition, its inner repetition, and its use of formulaic language all testify to the place of Genesis 1 in the category of traditional-style literature of ancient Israel. Its particular variety of traditional-style, however, helps to convey or create a particular sort of message appropriate to its context in the Hebrew Bible and to the worldview of its author.

Genesis 1 has an imposing, architectonic, extremely solid style. The framing repetition serves to suggest that creation by God's word is inevitable, the process unstoppable. The world, repeatedly declared to be good, is moreover orderly as smaller, less-developed creatures lead finally to humankind in its genders, male and female. The weekly calendar with its daily divisions is part and parcel of the creation process as each week framed by the seventh holy day becomes a walk through the pattern of the world's becoming. Nothing is left to chance. This creation account does not rest upon a conflict as does *Enuma elish* or biblical versions of the victory-enthronement pattern. No villain Rahab or Leviathan or Pharaoh offers challenge. The elegant, flowing style beautifully suits the smooth passage from chaos to order.

Why tell such a creation account? To whom would it appeal and when? Whose interests does it reflect? The style of Genesis 1 is scholastic and suits the orderly, detailed outline of the content. The content builds to emphasize the power of the one God as creator over all nature. There are no competitors or doubts.

Such a theme and such a style could theoretically be found during any period of the monarchy or after. The elegance and scholasticism imply an aristocratic, urbane writer. The implicit insistence on absolute divine power may well be from a staunchly Yahwistic writer who confronts those who suggest that Yahweh is weak in the wake of the Babylonian conquest of Judah in 587/6 B.C.E. The writer is confident in God's power as the marching, repeating language insists. Genesis 1 is also from a writer who chooses purposefully not to begin the story of God with the victory-enthronement pattern so popular in Canaanite and Mesopotamian myth. There is never any doubt about victory or defeat. The writer's God is unique, unitary, and omnipotent.

This author ends the account with an explanation of the Sabbath, the seventh holy rest-day upon which God himself rested from the work of creation, the keeping of which becomes a quintessential defining feature of early Judaism near the end of the biblical period. The author of Genesis 1 imagines creation, not during the heyday of the monarchy, but when the people face the economically and politically disruptive experience of the Babylonian exile, a time when many suggested that the Israelite God was weak. Had God's temple not been razed, the king of God's city exiled? The response of the author of Genesis 1, like that of a contemporary, the author of Isaiah 40—55, is a strong affirmation of God's power manifested in the very creation. The medium of Genesis 1 thus beautifully suits its message.

GENESIS 2—3

The author of Genesis 2—3 allows for a less absolutely controlled tale of creation, one that includes a story of paradise. In Genesis 2 the cosmos emerges from a misty bog. An ancient mist or stream waters the ground but the normal rains have not yet come. The definition of the sterile time of chaos is that there is yet no one to work the earth. Cosmos is thus defined in farmer's terms. In this account, a man is created first. God plants a garden and places the man in the garden so circumscribed and microcosmic. Then vegetation is provided while four rivers course through the land, creating borders and geographic definition. Even though the composer of Genesis

2—3 shares the outlying pattern that traces the passage from chaos to cosmos and like the author of Genesis 1 does so without the use of the victory-enthronement theme with its battle motifs, this author is less taxonomic or phylogenic than the author of Genesis 1, who describes this world in terms of species, man and woman being the two varieties of God's most complex living creation. The author of Genesis 2—3 is much more interested in creating characters and in telling a story. We picture a sculptor God who forms the man from the dust of the ground and blows life into him, a farmer God who plants a garden and places his live art in it, a God who presents the man his food with a prohibition—"from every tree of the garden you may eat, but from the tree of knowledge of good and evil you will not eat, for upon the day that you eat from it you will surely die!" (2:16–17).

The existence of such a prohibition guarantees a story, but first follow other enveloping, reader-catching details as creation continues to unfold. God, now the parent, says, "It is not good for man to be alone. I will make him a helpmate, his counterpart." The term translated "helpmate" literally comes from *'ēzer*, the root meaning "to help, aid" combined with a preposition *neged*, literally meaning "opposite" or "against." Phyllis Trible translates "helper fit for him"[3] and "a companion corresponding to it."[4] The Rabbis in a misogynistic tongue-in-cheek suggest that if a wife is good she is an *'ēzer*, "a help," if not, she is *negdô*, "against him"! In any event, the search for the man's alter ego or mirror image in Genesis 2 emphasizes man's and woman's shared humanness and initial equality at creation as much as the phrase about the human species in Gen. 1:27, "male and female created he them." Is the deity of Genesis 2 less intelligent than the god of Genesis 1, for he proceeds to look for man's helpmate and counterpart among the wild animals and the birds that he has created and allowed the human to name, and of course among these "for the human he could not find a helpmate, his counterpart (2:20)." Or are all mammals and birds pretty much alike at first glance if you are god? Finally God creates woman out of man's rib and elatedly the man speaks in a good folksaying, providing an etymology that comments on their biological closeness:

> bone of my bones,
> > flesh of my flesh;
> this one will be called *'iššāh* [woman]
> > for from *'îš* [man] this one was taken.
> > > (Gen. 1:23)

The narrator also provides a saying about the passage of generations and the related marriage bond (2:24).

Paradise is described most essentially in 2:25: "The two of them, the man and his wife, were naked and not ashamed." Many have perceived in this verse a description of innocence and youth, a time before fully awakened sexuality. The notion of nakedness without shame implies a time before full social responsibility, a period before self-definition and the differentiation of roles and statuses implicit in adult social structures. Food is provided. Animals are not used for clothing or food. Life is safely fenced about in the garden, and the man and woman have no explicit work roles, no knowledge of good and evil. There are no children in the garden except the children of God who will do what all children do, shake things up and break out of the orderly boundaries set by the parent, thereby fully becoming themselves. To do so they must give up the all-provided ease of paradise.

The way in which the emergence from initial cosmos to reality is achieved, the roles of the snake, woman, man, and God, and the symbolic function of the eating motif have been discussed elsewhere in detail.[5] Ideal and reality are linked by a joining of God's and the humans' realms—in this case by the eating from God's tree. The tree, as the trickster snake knows, endows one with the ability of discrimination that is a quality of the divine (3:5, 22), a knowledge jealously but unsuccessfully guarded by God. Thus, paradoxically, to become human and lose paradise is also on some level to become partially divine, a member of that troubled, mixed breed who like Achilles and other heroes leads a complex, difficult, and rich life that is filled with adventure but ends in death.

Life in paradise involves no work roles, no birth, no hierarchy, no knowledge, and perhaps a chance for immortality, taken away for certain with the expulsion from the garden. Reality and paradise lost in God's words of punishment mean work roles, hard work on the land that too often yields little, birth with pain, hierarchy—man, woman, snake—clothing, knowledge, and death. Such is life outside the garden. And yet the account in Genesis 3 does not leave humanity weighed down by sin, corrupted, and utterly lost. The word "sin" is not found in this tale, in contrast to the story of the first murder in Genesis 4. The quality of life has changed for human beings forever, but this tale of origins implies an acceptance of the way things must be, an explanation for it all. In the realization that we have inherited a long-standing situation, guilt, in fact, is lessened.

The pattern that leads to reality—ideal/implicit or explicit breaking of prohibition/reality—is a common one throughout the world and is found three times in the creation myths of Genesis 1—11. In these Israelite versions, the transgressed prohibition involves an attempted meeting or mixing of divine and earthly categories: humans eating from God's tree (Gen-

esis 3), the sons of god marrying human women (Gen. 6:1–4), human beings' building a tower to the heavens (Gen. 11:1–9).

Thus, like Genesis 1, Genesis 2—3 includes traditional and recurring patterns of content. But imagery and style in Genesis 2—3 differ from the recurring frame style of Genesis 1. This account describes the precreated
world and the process of creation in the parallelistic couplets or triplets typical of Israelite prose and poetry. The opening verses of the account might
be laid out as follows:

> On the day that Yahweh God made earth and heaven
> All vegetation of the open space, before it was on earth
> All grass of the open space before it grew
> For Yahweh God had not made rain upon the earth
> And there was no human to work the ground
> A mist would rise from the earth
> It watered all the face of the ground.
>
> (Gen. 2:4b–6)

Similarly at verses 15–18:

> And Yahweh God took the human
> And he set him the garden of Eden
> To work it
> And to guard it
> And Yahweh God commanded the human saying
> From every tree of the garden you may surely eat
> But from the tree of the knowledge of good and evil do not eat
> For on the day you eat from it you will surely die

Touches of this style are found in Genesis 1, but it dominates more fully
and consistently in Genesis 2—3. Vocabulary is somewhat limited, syntax
recurring. There is no grand repeating frame, but in a style frequently represented in the Hebrew Bible the picture is created by brief phrases, each
of which adds a bit more color or tone, a bit more information.

The style of Genesis 2—3 is both playful and aural. In addition to the
proverbial sayings in 2:23, 24, Genesis 2—3 contains some excellent examples of wordplay. The word *'ărûmmîm*, "naked," found in the symbolic description of man's and woman's condition in the garden in the last line of
chapter 2 is played upon in the first line of chapter 3. The snake, the trickster whose clever speech leads to the breaching of God's territoriality (like
a Loki or a Prometheus) is described as the most *'ārûm*, meaning "the most
clever" of all the living creatures that the Lord had made. Thus "naked of
knowledge" plays on "clever" or clothed in knowledge. The woman sees
that the tree is pleasurable *lĕhaśkîl*, a double entendre meaning "to look

upon" (a parallel phrase to the previous two cola) and "to make one wise" (3:6). The tree was pleasing for perception. We have also mentioned the author's skill as a storyteller, the prohibition tucked into the cosmogony of chapter 2 that leads to the breaking of the prohibition and the plot of chapter 3, and the use of a traditional narrative pattern found in the tales of origin all over the world. Like all good traditional narrators, the author suits the tale to his or her own audience, those for whom agriculture means a daily way of life and for whom the vagaries of nature pose constant threats, a culture in which men on some level rule over women as is true in virtually any traditional agricultural culture. The narrator and the presumed audience are capable of imagining God as less absolutist and more humanlike than in the account of Genesis 1.

The deity of Genesis 2—3 creates in a tactile fashion. God shows concern about the human creation's social isolation. The prohibition betrays a desire jealously to guard the divine prerogative to be wise. Divine warnings to kill if the humans eat from the tree turn out to be an exaggeration as the trickster snake suggested (3:4). God's human children, like all children, turn out to be less than predictable and must be thrust out into the world on their own lest they cause more mischief and eat from the tree of life and truly become gods. There is no divine plan. Rather like all the great gods such as Zeus or El, Yahweh reacts and operates on an ad hoc basis.

Events and characters are treated with humor in understated dialogues. God says to Adam, "Who told you you were naked?" A pathetic Adam says, "The woman that you gave to be with me, she gave me from the tree and I ate" (3:12). The deity is not assumed to be omniscient while the first man is not assumed to be noble.

And so Genesis 2 reveals a skilled narrator, employing humorous tone and traditional style to tell a story about the coming of reality, distinguished from paradise by its work, structures, life cycles, and statuses. There is no revolving door, no way to return to the harmonious community of paradise. On the other hand, no guilt burdens future generations. The deity is not fully transcendent. God is more powerful than anyone else but not allknowing. Scholars have suggested various sorts of authors for Genesis 2—3: for example, a theologian working at the court of King David, or an aristocratic literateur of the period of the monarchy. Each of these suggestions seems unlikely. Genesis 2—3 is a traditional, very old tale, and this telling so little tied to a specific Yahwistic or monarchic agenda that it is extremely difficult to situate within a particular known group or setting. The author is an excellent popular storyteller engaged in conveying essential Israelite myth. This author seems to be fully at home in the sort of oral register described in chapter 1, perhaps providing a written version of a popular myth, one that finds its setting in the agrarian consciousness of all Israelites for whom Yahweh was Creator, the primal parent. Such a narrative would have held appeal throughout Israel's history. It is therefore virtually impossible to set a date for this version of creation and its author. The distinctive characteristics of Genesis 2—3 emerge in contrast to another story of Eden drawn by the sixth-century B.C.E. exilic prophet Ezekiel. Ezekiel's tale is not anonymous though Ezekiel too draws upon tradition, but the Eden tale with which he describes and shapes paradise betrays a worldview and a voice quite different in orientation from those behind Genesis 2—3.

EZEKIEL 28

Ezekiel also employs the term "Eden," which some trace etymologically to a root meaning "pleasurable," and as its appositive or gloss, applies the phrase "the garden of God." Like the garden of Genesis 2, this Eden-garden is also an ideal microcosm or paradise. In this case a tale of paradise is employed dramatically to describe the rise and fall of the king of Tyre, Tyre being one of the Phoenician coastal city-states with whom Israel had had both cooperative and competitive relationships, depending upon the era. In this section of Ezekiel, the prophet condemns all of the Israelites' economic and political rivals, paving the way for predictions about Israel's eventual resuscitation as a people. Ezekiel, like the author we hypothesize for Genesis 1, works during the period of the sixth-century B.C.E. exile, when Israel has been conquered by the Babylonians, her ruling élite exiled, her social structure in disarray.

In Ezekiel 28 the description of Eden is set within the framework of a theme of hubris, frequently found in ancient Near Eastern texts as a tale about rebellion of the gods. A version of this traditional theme is employed to condemn the king of Babylon, another of Israel's enemies at Isa. 14:12–20.[6] For Ezekiel this tale of Eden is a "fall," a term we avoided, I think correctly, in assessing the worldview and paradise view of Genesis 2—3. The prince of Tyre was wiser than Daniel, the archetypal ancient Near Eastern wiseman, and no secret was hidden from him. He was greatly wealthy (28:3, 4), but because he dared to say "I am a god. In the dwelling of gods I dwell, in the heart of the seas" (28:2), he will be thrust down into the Pit, the underworld (28:8). Is Adam and Eve's punishment caused by hubris, by their pretending to be God? By eating of the tree they acquire the godlike capacity to discriminate, and they have breached God's territory by eating from the forbidden tree, as do the builders of the tower in Gen. 11:1–9, but

Eve's intention appears more modest, to acquire wisdom, while God's accusation is more specific to the story: "Because you have eaten from the tree" (Gen. 3:17). It is only after the event that God reflects on the implications of the humans' actions: "Humankind has become like one of us knowing good and evil" (3:22). The humans are driven out lest they eat from the tree of life and "live forever." The cherubim and the flaming sword are placed to guard the way to the tree of life (3:24). In Ezekiel 28, however, there are direct accusations. The Hebrew text is very difficult but with Greek manuscript traditions we can reconstruct the meaning to be something like this: "Your midst was full of violence and you sinned and you became a profane thing and I banished you [lit. destroyed you; blotted you out] from the mountain of God" (28:16).

Terms for "sin" (*ḥṭ'*), "violence" (*ḥms*), and "profane" (*ḥll*) are clear in both manuscript traditions, strong language completely absent in Genesis 2—3. See also *šiḥattā* (you "ruined, corrupted" [28:17]), and "by the multitude of your iniquities [*'wn*] . . . you profaned" (28:18), and a third term for "wrongdoing" (*'wl*) in 28:15. The punishment is to be banished from God's mountain (28:16), to be cast to the ground, and to be presented before other kings (28:17) that they might gawk. The king is to be consumed by fire and become ashes (28:18).

If the fall is destruction, fire, conquest, a total loss of status, a banishment from the seat of God, his mountain throne, the prefall state is described as the king's being "full of wisdom and complete in beauty" (28:12):

> In Eden, the garden of God you were
> Every precious gem was your covering.
> (28:13)

A list of precious stones is found in verse 13, a veritable jeweler's inventory. The king was in the holy mountain; he walked in the midst of stones of fire— all of this is addressed to the king in the second person: "You walked . . . ," etc. (28:14). In the garden "you were pure in your ways from the day of your creation, until sin was found in you" (28:15). So paradise is synonymous with God's holy mountain. One's state of purity allows one like an Indian ascetic essentially to walk on hot coals. Paradise is not a lack of knowledge but possession of wisdom and beauty. It is, moreover, not a naturalistic world, but one filled with gems and riches, reminiscent of views of the heavenly realm found in Exodus 24 (the sapphire richness of God's realm) and later Rabbinic imaginings of heaven (see also Rev. 21:18–21). Carol Newsom finds a priestly metaphor in the gem-encrusted covering of the king, reminiscent of the priestly breastplate of Ex. 28:17–21 (note the gems listed in Ezek. 28:13 and Ex. 28:17).[7] Paradise appears to be synonymous with heaven, God's holy mountain, the top of the world, and the king is on a virtual par with the deity as long as he does not claim to be more than mortal. This is a very worldly vision of Eden that jars with the description of a garden in Genesis 2. What sort of garden offers gems? This garden is a heavenly palace—Newsom suggests a further parallel with the Jerusalem temple[8]—its king a most wise and beautiful man able to perform superhuman feats, surrounded by worldly riches until he dares to claim god status himself. Then he loses his status, his wealth, his place on the mountain—all. This is a citified, hierarchically conscious, worldly, and sophisticated view of paradise, one either beyond the ken of the writer of Genesis 2—3 or one rejected in the search for harmony and the evenness of unworldly, innocent, and nonhierarchical existence.

Style in Ezekiel 28

Style depends on language chosen, arranged, and juxtaposed—word length, line length, metrics, alliteration. The language of Ezekiel 28, however, is devilishly difficult to decode. Are combinations of words that seem quite awkward or words whose form is unusual "mistakes" because of errors in scribal transmission? Do these awkward phrases reflect "errors" in an original writing down of an oracle that was orally delivered? Is the awkwardness meant to be part of the style? Which words have been left out or miswritten or added? Do we have permission to emend the text so that it makes more sense to us? What if our choices as exegetes are wrong? Do we not risk then discussing the style of an artificial creation of our own making? These are essential questions in the field of biblical studies that cannot be easily resolved and are ones increasingly argued by colleagues in other fields. In discussing manuscripts of Old English verse, John D. Niles writes, "We look for a flawless text arranged in lines and half-lines on the page. What we find at times is metrically unkempt in the manuscript version that underlies our critical editions."[9] Though by no means a hard-liner in this respect, Niles makes the case for nonemendation in certain circumstances, suggesting that the particular orally grounded aesthetic of the literature may not be in accordance with our particular aesthetic expectations.[10] Ellen Davis suggests in fact that the awkwardness of Ezekiel's language may be because of its place on a boundary between oral and literate aesthetics. Davis sees Ezekiel as an innovator in the Israelite literary tradition.[11] In dealing with Ezekiel 28, we therefore hesitate to make major reconstructions. Even so, we can learn certain things about the style of this paradise cameo that suggest interesting contrasts and comparisons with Genesis 2—3 and Genesis 1.

Like Genesis 1 and Genesis 2—3, Ezekiel does employ some of the brief-line constructions typical of the Israelite tradition (and of much traditional literature according to Dell Hymes):[12]

> Mortal, say to the Prince of Tyre
> Thus says the Lord Yahweh
> Because your heart is haughty
> You said I am a god
> In the dwelling of the gods I dwell
> In the heart of the seas
> But you are mortal and not a god
> You take on airs as the airs of a god
> Behold you are wiser than Daniel
> Everything that is locked up they could not keep in the dark from you
> In your wisdom and understanding, you achieved wealth for yourself
> And have amassed gold and silver in your treasuries.

> (28:2–3)

In contrast with classical forms of Israelite poetry, the lines are metrically leggy, with synonyms and modifiers piling up in each segment, but the process of revealing information via a sort of versification is present.

Ezekiel is commanded by God to place a dirge or lament upon the king of Tyre. The dirge is a mourning song. In the prophetic medium, often such a song recited before the death of its object helps to bring about the object's downfall in a magical transformative way. The classic Israelite dirge song is characterized by a limping meter, so that one line of parallel poetry set up in pairs of lines or bicolons is longer than its mate. A quality of parallel thoughts is conveyed by the words of Ezek. 28:11–19 and sometimes by the uneven beat. Modern scholars face difficulties in scanning ancient Israelite poetry, some preferring to count stresses, other syllables. There is some question as well concerning the pronunciation of the ancient language of the Hebrew Bible that has been vocalized by medieval Rabbis. The following syllable count, approximate though it may be, nevertheless conveys a sense of the Hebrew's limping meter in verse 17:

> your heart grew haughty in your beauty [8 syllables]
> you ruined your wisdom because of your splendor [11 syllables]
> on the ground I threw you [6 syllables]
> before kings I gave you to gawk at you [14 syllables].

Some parallel lines are quite even. See verse 13, for example:

> in Eden the garden of God you were [10 syllables]
> every precious stone was your covering [10 syllables].

This text, which teeters on the border between what we would call prose and poetry, is punctuated by a long list of gem stones that has a scholastic quality. While the very use of the dirge form, the parallelism, and the occasional adherence to the limping style of the dirge are much expected in the oral register, an adherence to a style inherited in the tradition, such a long list and the use of so many varied terms for sin and corruption not only indicate a certain thematic fixation, absent in Genesis 2—3, but a sophisticated and scholarly orientation. Of course, sophistication and scholasticism do not preclude orality. Oral cultures are of various types.

The urbane, hierarchically oriented paradise thus suits the style of the work, as the paradise of Genesis 2—3 content suits its style, simple, harmonious, and earthy. Both passages evidence adherence to certain traditional forms or patterns, but Ezekiel, a priest and an aristocrat writing at a crisis period in the history of Israel, endows the tradition with qualities one expects in literate cultures. In exploring the place of Ezekiel 28 on the oral-literate continuum, it is also of note that Ezekiel incorporates and contextualizes his Eden story, a creation tale of paradise lost through a mortal's challenge to the gods, within a condemnation of Israel's political and military enemies. The story serves quite specifically as a condemnation of Tyre. While we can posit the independent existence of a story in which the main character is the first human and the context more cosmogonic, this version is fully intertwined with Ezekiel's message about his people's overcoming their enemies with divine help. The story serves to characterize one of these enemies, Tyre. This quality of the contextual is, as John Foley has shown in a contrast between Christian and Muslim epics of Serbo-Croatia, at the more literate end of the continuum.

Genesis 1 and Genesis 2—3, of course, are currently contextualized in the primeval history of Genesis 1—11 or in the larger book of Genesis or in the Hebrew Bible as it now stands. Indeed it might be suggested that an author consciously creating an account to open the sacred history of Yahweh and Israel chooses to tell of creation without battles and to emphasize God's singularity and omnipotence. And yet Genesis 1 and Genesis 2—3 can each stand on their own. Each is a whole that signifies world-creation and is in this sense less contextualized than the account in Ezekiel 28.

The style of Ezekiel 28 is characterized by baroque and scholastic use of language and terminologically rich emphasis on sin and loss of paradise. Its particular view of the ideal existence strongly identifies heaven, Paradise, and kingly courts and accepts hierarchy as a feature of paradise. To be in paradise is to be a wisest and most beautiful king. Such is the worldview of the priestly aristocrat Ezekiel. Aspects of this worldview are shared by others represented in the Israelite tradition, for example by the author of Genesis 1, whose world is created on hierarchical principles. This view of paradise in Ezekiel 28 is, however, at odds with the naturalistic, nonhierarchical paradise of Genesis 2—3. In Genesis 2—3, moreover, the loss of paradise involves the inevitable unfolding of reality, the work of a trickster, the culture-bringing snake, and the result of humans' desire for knowledge. It is not the result of human sin or hubris.

Ezekiel bears further witness to the oral-literate boundary, to the way in which traditional material is incorporated in a specific literary setting that individualizes it apart from the tradition. That is, Ezekiel's story of paradise lost is no longer primarily about creation and the loss of paradise but is about the king of Tyre.

CONCLUSIONS

This study of three biblical acts of narration having to do with world-creation is a comment on variations that are possible within the contours of traditional Israelite aesthetics. All three accounts use motifs and patterns of motifs found in the lore of other cultures but more specifically that are popular within ancient Near Eastern and Israelite tradition. Each employs forms associated with the oral register: the repetitive frames of Genesis 1, the wordplays and proverbs of Genesis 2, the dirge of Ezekiel 28, and the tendency to employ verses or lines to present full thoughts in fairly brief, self-contained segments. Genesis 2—3 adheres to the brief-line styles most closely while Genesis 1 offers somewhat greater complexity in sentence structure. Ezekiel 28 is the most complex and inconsistent in this regard. The simplicity of style and story in Genesis 2—3 contrasts with the architectonic elegance of Genesis 1, both of which contrast with the particular baroque eclecticism of Ezekiel 28 with its erudite use of synonyms for sin and its list of gem-quality minerals. Each account in style and content serves to identify the worldview of its author while all three find their place on the oral-literate continuum, Ezekiel 28 being closer than the others to the literate end.

The first two chapters of our study have much to say about the oral aesthetic that lies behind the written texts of the Hebrew Bible. In seeking to understand the people behind the texts and the nature of their intellectual and social world, we now turn the question around. How did the Israelites whose surviving written literature is so informed by the oral register understand literacy? Were the Israelites literate?

CHAPTER 3

New Ways of Thinking about Orality and Literacy

Israelite Evidence

WHAT IS LITERACY?

It is axiomatic among some students of ancient Israelite culture that in general the Israelites were literate:

> The ostraca and simple inscriptions on potsherds and pottery jars as well as the abundance of seals are evidence that, at least during the last two centuries of the Monarchy, the knowledge of writing was widespread.[1]

> Literacy was at first confined to the professional scribes. But with the development of the alphabet and the consequent reduction in the number of signs, reading and writing could be mastered with greater ease, and literacy spread to ever wider segments of the population. The process was gradual. At the beginning of the Iron Age II inscriptions are rare and are mostly written in Phoenician characters. With time writing spread. The increasing number of inscriptions uncovered in excavations at Iron Age II-III sites in the Land of Israel, as well as the content of the inscriptions, testify that by the end of the eighth century Israelite society as a whole was literate.[2]

Recent studies of literacy in ancient cultures suggest that fewer than 10 percent of the population were literate in ancient Greece,[3] perhaps only 1 percent in Mesopotamia[4] and Egypt.[5] One might well ask why Israelite society should have been so much more literate than all other ancient societies or than many modern traditional societies in today's Third World.

Carol Meyers, after W. F. Albright, points to the accessibility of an alphabetic script in Israel versus more difficult and élitist systems of writing in Egypt and Mesopotamia.[6] Yet ancient Greece had an alphabetic script, and Harris suggests the vast majority of the population was illiterate. Of course, such estimates as Harris notes are only a guess, and as Baines and Eyre write, matters might differ in various locales and periods. Harris's and others' more important question for us is: What does "literate" mean?

To modern Americans, the term "literacy" evokes particular notions: the capacity to read any combination of words that makes sense in his or her language—at least at the level of the daily newspaper; the ability to write a letter for oneself that expresses one's feelings or conveys information in one's own chosen words. We think of the availability of books, libraries equipped with catalogues and a reference system, the doing of research, the keeping of written records for purposes of future consultation.

Students of ancient and traditional cultures suggest that literacy in the cultures they study is a quite different phenomenon. As Meyers notes, "pragmatic" literacy in the premonarchic period probably meant "learning enough to read a list, a name, some numbers."[7] Joseph Naveh suggests, in fact, that the quality of the script reflects the class and training of the writer, be the writer a professional scribe of the first grade or second grade or a nonprofessional exhibiting a "vulgar" style.[8] Mazar, writing of the monarchic period, appears to be less cautious and seems to juxtapose the literary creations of the Bible with inscriptions, seals, and other sorts of material as evidence of Israelite literacy, especially in the late monarchic period.[9] So too G. Barkay: "The eighth century was a period of extensive literary activity, the days of the prophets Isaiah, Micah, and Amos and when the biblical canon began to crystallize."[10] It does seem that at least Mazar and Barkay do mean something like the modern phenomenon when they write of Israelite literacy.[11]

A number of scholars in fields ranging from the literature of classical Greece to the works of various medieval European cultures to the traditional cultures of Africa and Oceania have much to contribute as we seek to understand the nature of literacy in traditional or premodern societies. Students of classical Greek and Anglo-Saxon literatures, like biblicists, work with rich and complex traditional-style material that resonates with the aesthetics of oral composition but that has been handed down, preserved, possibly even composed in written form, and that has existed in written forms for centuries. What are the boundaries on the oral-literate continuum that allow this literature to exist in writing while seeming to breathe with the aesthetics of an oral culture? To begin with a most basic question, what does literacy mean in such cultures?

Rosalind Thomas, exploring the ancient Greek case, cautions that "literacy" is not necessarily as we would define it. For example, while people may be able to read, they may not be able to write. Moreover, "ability to read or write very simple messages was probably not rare in a city like Athens, but the written texts of poetry and literary prose had a reading audience confined to the highly educated and wealthy elite, and their secretaries."[12] The inability to read, or especially to read and write, however, were not necessarily social drawbacks, depriving the nonreader of status or respect.[13]

> Ancient Greece was in many ways an oral society in which the written work took second place to the spoken. Far more was heard or spoken, rather than written and read, than we can easily envisage.
>
> The extent of oral communication needs particular emphasis for classical students who are so familiar with the ancient world through reading written texts that an effort of imagination is required to appreciate the sheer extent to which written texts were simply not created or used. . . . Most Greek literature was meant to be heard or sung—thus transmitted orally—and there was a strong current of distaste for the written work even among the highly literate.[14]

Scholars suggest further that the appearance of a work in manuscript provides no assurance that the work was conceived of as a "text" in the modern sense or even originally written, as opposed to composed orally.[15] The oral register is often still very apparent in the manuscript as well—just how apparent has recently been demonstrated by Katherine O'Brien O'Keeffe's studies in Anglo-Saxon traditions. She suggests that the more literate a work is in manuscript, the more readers' cues such as periods, capital letters, and chapters there are, the less varied the orthography.[16] "Numerous appropriate variants" (in orthography) and "minimal graphic aids for decoding" call forth "formulaic guesses as an essential part of reading activity."[17] That is, one needs essentially to know on some level what one is reading in order to read. The written text gives evidence of the oral world behind it and is, as O'Keeffe has termed it, a "visible song."

In traditional cultures, manuscripts, moreover, would have frequently been unwieldy, lengthy rolls of leather, in which simply finding "the right place" would have been difficult, a certain impediment to reading.[18] As Doyne Dawson notes, "The form of an ancient book made it so difficult to look up exact references that authors usually relied on their excerpts, notes, and memories; and the notion of a 'book' implied not so much a fixed text as an oral presentation, sometimes with commentary."[19]

In addition to questions concerning the nature of literacy in traditional and/or ancient cultures, the status of the illiterate, and respect for oral communication among the literate, there are questions about the preservation of written documents, and the possibility of consulting written works even by the literate. The latter weigh heavily, not only in our effort to understand what literacy meant in ancient Israel and how the Israelites' attitudes to written works compare with our own, but also in evaluating theories about the genesis of the Hebrew Bible and the kind of social world in which the composition and transmission of its literature took place.

Thomas suggests quite convincingly that record keeping in the ancient world was not like modern record keeping.[20] Often what we call "archives" in the ancient world are simply collections of documents.[21] Families might keep documents, the state may do so, but moderns tend to "overestimate both the amount of documents and particularly their easy accessibility in the state archive."[22] Thus one issue involves the degree to which written records were kept, another the degree to which they could be consulted. The record keeping that is a part of modern literacy involves a degree of user-friendliness absent, Jacoby and Thomas suggest, in ancient Greece. Equally important in assessing how and whether written records serve as indicators of literacy is the matter of function. As M. T. Clanchy notes, "making documents for administrative use, keeping them as records and using them again for references were three distinct stages of development which did not follow one another automatically and immediately."[23] Each is closer and closer to the literate end of the continuum but not equally so. These are important distinctions to keep in mind when assessing the sources and nature of Israelite historiography.

Clanchy writes of medieval England, "Records had not originally been made for utilitarian purposes measurable in cost-benefit terms. Rather they had been pledges to posterity and an assurance of the continuity of institutions under God's providence . . . a monument for posterity."[24] What Clanchy again implicitly questions is the function of record keeping in traditional cultures. There is no question that the keeping of written records in one location is more like literacy than not having any written records. What, however, if the records or documents are not easily accessible, not public, nor kept for purposes of archival consultation? What if, rather, they are understood as a family's or society's legacy, proof of their status and history in a more wholesale and symbolic fashion? Such instances of literacy are bounded by the old-world assumptions of those for whom the record keeping features of modern-style literacy are not at play. It is in this sense that Clanchy uses the phrase "monument for posterity." And what of writing on actual monuments, inscriptions on plaques, steles, or walls, and other public inscriptional material such as graffiti? How does one assess the variety of literacy implied by these examples of writing, often cited in making the case for Israelite literacy?

Thomas asks about monument inscriptions, "But how far did Athenians read them? Were they used as a source of reference?"[25] "In ancient Greece, inscriptions were often thought of primarily as symbolic memorials of a decision rather than simply documents intended to record important details for administrative purposes."[26] Thomas emphasizes the monumental and symbolic roles of such inscriptions.[27] The term "iconic" comes to mind.

Peter Machinist provides insightful comments on the sort of literate mentality that lies behind Assyrian royal inscriptions, material from a culture geographically and culturally closer to that of ancient Israel:

> The probability, as we have seen, that even the Assyrian kings were not or barely cuneiformly literate is indicative of the general situation in the Assyrian core triangle and certainly in the provinces and vassal states, where cuneiform literacy must be understood as largely a professional attainment of a small network of scribal officials. Moreover, even for those who could claim such literacy, Assyrian kings or otherwise, we must distinguish sharply levels of competence. Various officials might have been able to read, say, an administrative order or list in Akkadian, but one cannot assume from this that they could handle the much more difficult Standard Babylonian dialect and cuneiform script usage exhibited by the royal inscriptions.
>
> What all this means is that we have to become sensitive to the range of ways in which a written text and even speech can and could communicate. Of course, only the fully literate in cuneiform got all the message of the Assyrian royal inscriptions, and the inscriptions, thus, must have been intended primarily for them and their circle—i.e., the ruling "insiders"—to reinforce their royalty and commitments. But we should not forget about others as well. Thus, even if an onlooker could not read the Akkadian cuneiform on an Assyrian stela in the public square of his city, and even if there were no one around to interpret it for him, he would still have been guided to its sense by the adjacent relief, on that stela, of the Assyrian king and his insignia. In this manner, the cuneiform would have become part of the relief, part, specifically, of the royal insignia; and the very alienness of this script—the recognition by the onlooker that while it constituted a communicative system it was one beyond his control—would have collaborated with the rest of the relief to convey the message of power, fear, and obedience. Put another way, the helplessness of our onlooker when faced with the cuneiform had the purpose of confirming him in his place in the Assyrian hierarchy of power, over against the place of the fully literate and his circle.[28]

Such insights also capture the iconic and symbolic quality of monumental inscriptions that convey meaning whether or not specific texts can be read fully and decoded.[29]

As Ruth Finnegan notes, once writing is available in a culture, it inevitably finds its way into everyone's life, even the lives of the illiterate. The folklorist Bengt Holbek has noted that people at home in oral cultures sometimes treat writing with a respect accorded the numinous. Writing comes to be regarded as capable of transformation and magic, the letters and words shimmering with the very power of the gods.[30] Writing, which is always symbolic in a sense, involved in a process of communication by signification, holds a more overt kind of symbolism in such cultures. God is in the name; a curse is in the words; a person leaves traces of himself in his writing.

Finally some comments on the interrelationship between orality and literacy in traditional cultures. Ruth Finnegan has been especially insistent on the interplay between the oral and the written. Oral literature does not cease to exist once people read or write, and the oral aesthetic continues to be manifest even in written works. At the same time, even those who do not have a full range of skills in literacy find themselves around writing. In the commercial realm writing may be found on merchants' weights, in a city context writing appears upon a monument. The oral and the written exist on a continuum or a sliding scale. Writing and reading may become more popular over time in a certain community. Orality or literacy may dominate certain segments of a society or aspects of a culture at any time. Another aspect of the continuum is the way in which each modality overlaps with the other in the form, orientation, and context of a work, in its composition and transmission. In a particular case, the oral or the literate end of the continuum may be more apparent.

There is no gainsaying the importance of writing for essential aspects of Israelite life—the commercial sphere, for example—nor archaeological evidence that the use of writing increased in Israel over time. Artisans, traders, a variety of government employees, and others were familiar with a set of skills for reading and, to a lesser degree, for writing certain kinds of messages. The relevance of this sort of literacy to the formation of the rich and complex biblical tradition and the creation of its various compositions is another matter. None of these observations about literacy in ancient Israel, moreover, contradicts the assertion that Israelites lived in an essentially oral world. Indeed, the very nature of the epigraphic evidence even in the second half of the monarchy testifies to how fully Israelite society was informed by an oral mentality. We recall that our list of traits of such a mentality includes (1) writing frequently used for short, pragmatic messages; (2) magical, transformative qualities attributed to writing; (3) preserved writings perceived as monumental or iconic rather than a means of keeping records for administrative purposes or for scholarly consultation; (4) the possibility of managing well in life without skills of modern literacy; (5) great reliance on oral communication and hints of orality even in written texts, so that the written text is not fully appreciated or understood without knowledge of the oral world.

When writing of a dominant oral culture in ancient Israel, of course, we do so always aware that the oral and the written/read are part of a continuum. As we saw in chapter 1, oral style informs the written works of the Hebrew Bible, and the contextual "writing world" concerns of writers in turn influence the forms of traditional-style works preserved in the Bible. As we hope to show in this chapter, literacy in a traditional culture is very much informed by the worldviews and aesthetics of orality, even while writing increasingly becomes a useful tool in many facets of Israelite life.

We explore evidence in ancient Israel under three essential headings: (1) short message texts, (2) letters, (3) monumental or iconic texts.

SHORT TEXTS

One basic variety of "short text" found by archaeologists is the so-called abecedary, a string or list of Hebrew letters of the alphabet, an early example of which from Iron Age I (1200–1000 B.C.E.) was discovered on an incised ostracon (a broken piece of pottery used for messages) at 'Izbet Ṣarṭah. Later examples of abecedaries have been found as well.[31] A. Mazar notes[32] that several letters are omitted or changed from the canonical order in the 'Izbet Ṣarṭah inscription, and letters are written from left to right, which may be evidence of the fluid "oral-in-writing" phenomenon to which O'Keeffe points; the alphabet will be written in a regularized and uniform right-to-left way later. Scholars have frequently treated abecedary texts as evidence of school book exercises, but Gabriel Barkay offers the suggestion that some may have been of "magic or religious significance."[33] In light of comparable use of the alphabet or portions of it on Aramaic incantation bowls or in the Greek magical papyri, this suggestion seems quite feasible. The abecedaries thus may provide further evidence of the use of writing in an oral culture.

Another early brief text frequently cited as evidence of a school exercise is the Gezer Calendar (late tenth century B.C.E.).[34] This little incised text on limestone refers to the seasons of the year according to the agricultural activity usual in them (e.g., two months: ingathering; two months: sowing, etc.). No sigla separate words or mark sentences, though the thought is complete in the last five out of seven lines. Again O'Keeffe's "visible song" comes to mind. In the margin, drawn perpendicular to the main text, are three letters, perhaps a word, perhaps the beginning of another abecedary. The text employs a repetitive style (Two months x/ Two months y/ Two months z/ etc.) and is songlike in the style of folk wisdom on the environment and the tradesman's activity (similar to "red sky in the morning, sailor take warning"). Rather than use this text to speculate on the existence of scribal schools or home education,[35] we do well to notice in its format, style, and theme the stuff of an oral culture. Another fascinating set of brief texts that Lemaire and others view as evidence of school exercise come from Kadesh-Barnea at the border of the Negev and the Sinai, texts dated by Lemaire to the seventh or end of the eighth century B.C.E.[36] Three of the texts present sequences of numbers including one large ostracon containing a series of numbers and units of weight[37]—exercises or an aid to commercial activity of some sort?

From Kuntillet 'Ajrud in the Sinai come other early brief text inscriptions on decorated large storage jars and a stone vat. These texts, perhaps from the beginning of the eighth century B.C.E., include brief formulaic dedications and blessings. The 'Ajrud blessings consistently include an epithet of Yahweh apparently popular in the northern kingdom, which McCarter suggests controlled this area west of Edom in the early eighth century B.C.E.[38] and a fascinating reference to Yahweh's consort: "To Yahweh of Samaria and his Ashera."[39] The style and content of these messages are at home in the world of oral traditions, such brief dedicatory formulas being metonymic markers of intriguing aspects of a worldview to which we are no longer privy. The act of writing down the above dedication or the blessing on the stone trough "Obadyau, son of Adnah, may he be blessed by God"[40] brings the God-presence into a sort of material reality, and the materialization lasts—such are the undoubted benefits of writing—but such metonymic messages accompanied by drawings are more in O'Keeffe's category of visible song than indication of a modern-style literacy.

In a similar "brief message" category are the two preexilic (Iron Age II–III) silver talismans found in a burial cave at Ketef Hinnom (Jerusalem).[41] Barkay describes them as "two rolled-up silver plaques, amulets of some kind, inscribed with blessings resembling the priestly blessing recorded in the book of Numbers" (6:24–26).[42] The blessings are inscribed in tiny letters; one version is almost identical to the biblical text, the other a shorter variant. Such finds again testify to the use of writing and to the power ascribed to words that are written down and able to be preserved for more than 2,000 years. Understood in context, however, they are testimony to the oral-literate continuum and to the on-going mentality of an oral world once writing is available. The blessing is not a set, fixed text but found in two versions, even in written form. Shorter versions, like partial strands of DNA, have efficacious metonymic power. The text, moreover, brings God-power to the realm of the dead, abiding with the departed to protect them. So too the wall inscriptions designed to protect the burial place from intruders. The words of the curse have a live visceral power to ward off or destroy enemies as in the Royal Steward Inscription (c. 700 B.C.E.).[43]

Three other intriguing examples of inscriptional evidence in the brief message category have been presented by scholars at least implicitly as examples of writing in a literate mode and seem especially appropriate to mention in this context. Again what emerges is evidence of the oral-literate continuum.

The earliest example is from the preexilic period, perhaps late eighth or early seventh century B.C.E. Written elegantly in black ink by a "trained hand,"[44] on "a huge column-shaped stalactite" within a natural cave near En Gedi in the Judean Desert, the passage appears to include a curse against anyone who would efface the inscription, followed by a series of blessings that say "Blessed be + name." Some would read *yhw* in one of the lines as Yahweh, others as the beginning of a name beginning with the theophoric, for example, Yehonatan.[45] Bar-Adon asks who the writer of this ink inscription could be:

> He may have been a refugee seeking shelter in the cave from the wars and invasions so frequent in this period, as has been suggested in the case of other cave inscriptions. However, the fact that he brought with him writing materials—ink and pen or brush—shows in my opinion that his motives were of a more personal nature. He may have been an inhabitant of En Gedi—perhaps a scribe in view of the elegant handwriting—who sought solitude and peace of mind in the cave. While contemplating the primeval landscape spread out before him, he may have been inspired to write words of praise and thanksgiving to the Lord.[46]

Clearly, here is someone who has writing materials with him or her, who composes in ink with no audience present—this seems the very image of the modern intellectual. And yet, what the person writes is formulaic in form, includes the power of blessings and curses reinforced by writing typical of traditional cultures. The words, set down and preserved, give the blessing a capacity to emanate protection from the location while preserving in words those who are mentioned by name.

The same might be said of the exilic-period graffiti accompanied by nonprofessional line drawings in the burial cave near Khirbet Beit Lei. The engraved inscriptions on limestone walls include, in Cross's view, an inscription for deliverance, "Deliver [us], O Lord"; a request for absolution, "Absolve [us], O merciful God! Absolve [us], O Yahweh"; and a "prophetic oracle in which Yahweh speaks in the first person, and in poetic form."[47]

> I am Yahweh thy God
> I will accept the cities of Judah,
> And will redeem Jerusalem.[48]

Cross[49] suggests these prayers and the oracle were left behind by a prophet and his followers fleeing the troubles in Jerusalem. This is entirely possible, but again our appreciation for these written words is greatly deepened by attention to the role of written words in traditional cultures. The cave has been made a beacon to Yahweh, an on-going request. The oracle is not written merely to preserve a precious thought or composition on a cave wall in lieu of papyrus or skin. The very writing serves a more transitive religious and ritual function, as a powerful message that helps to bring about divinely ordained events: absolution, salvation, deliverance. This is one of the major contributions made by writing in the oral world.

Itzhaq Beit-Arieh recently published a thirteen-line text from Ḥorvat ʿUza in the eastern Negev. Dated to the second half of the seventh century B.C.E., the message is inked onto an ostracon and is indeed a somewhat longer "brief message." Beit-Arieh suggests it is of "special significance due to its apparent literary character. . . . The content is neither economic nor administrative (like most eighth- to sixth-century B.C.E. ostraca from Israel and Judah), but rather of a literary character couched in elevated biblical language."[50] The text is broken and unreadable in many places, but the apparent thrust of readable portions is a curse against the receiver of the text who will suffer destruction if he does not do something required of him. The last line and one of the most clearly readable states "and your grave will be destroyed," the ultimate curse in a culture that highly valued proper and peaceful burial as a means of procuring eternal rest after death. While the reconstruction of F. M. Cross in an appendix to Beit-Arieh's publication implicitly indicates how the language of curse and incantation can be seen to overlap with the language of the biblical prophets, it is clear that this text (like the prophetic texts of the Bible) is rich in traits of writing as employed in oral cultures. The text makes more permanent the curse and ensures its execution. Portable, the sherd could have been delivered to the curses' object, again pointing to the way in which the technology of writing can serve members of a traditional society.

Perhaps the largest corpus of brief message texts is sealings. A large portion of these texts were involved in ancient Israelite commercial life. Seals are carved and smoothed pieces of hard stone that contain the sender's symbol and/or name and other brief identifying information, carved as a mirror image. The seal could then be impressed on clay jars before firing, the jars later sent off with contents of wine or oil or some other product. More than 1,200 sealings of a particular variety from late-eighth-century B.C.E. Judah have been found impressed on the handles of such jars marked with one of two symbols and *lmlk* "belonging to the king" inscribed above the design. The name of one of four towns appears below the design.[51] It is suggested that these sealings may have had to do with the food supply of Hezekiah's army.[52] Additional notations in ink concerning contents of the jars have been found on some jar finds.[53] Thus writing has the pragmatic value of indicating ownership, place of origin, and contents. We should add that some of the "lamelech" sealings lack city reference or the term "lamelech" and some lack inscriptions altogether, thus relying on the pictorial symbol alone to provide commercial information.[54] Again, one is reminded of the oral-written continuum.

In a similar commercial small-message category are the 102 "ostraca" or sherds found in the ruins of an administrative complex in Samaria, the great capital of the northern kingdom. This find has been dated to the time of King Jeroboam II (785–749 B.C.E.)[55] and predates the fall of Samaria in 720 B.C.E.[56] Ostraca, as noted earlier, are brief inscriptions, often written in ink as in the case of the Samaria finds, on flat pieces of broken pottery, an inexpensive and readily available writing surface. The Samaria ostraca are essentially dockets recording information about oil and wine deliveries, including notations of date, personal name, and quantity of goods.[57] The format in which information is provided is quite stylized, for example, "In the tenth year, vineyard of Yehaweli, a jar of oil for washing" (no. 55), or "In the ninth year from Quseh, to Gaddiyaw, a jar of old wine" (no. 6).[58] Writing has also been found on weights used in commercial activity.[59]

All of these shorthand identifying markers must have been accessible to those involved in the discourse of commerce, but one should not leap to equate this sort of literacy with the writing and reading of the Hebrew Bible in accordance with notions of modern literacy. One thinks in this context of Italian or Jewish immigrants of early twentieth-century America who established businesses, ordered stock, prepared receipts, and communicated as necessary with the English-speaking world without being able either to write a letter in English or to read an English newspaper.

Another use for seals impressed in clay involves the utilization of another writing material, papyrus. A written document would be rolled, a string wound around it, and a lump of clay pressed on the document and string;

a seal was then impressed upon the clay. Such seals would include a name and patronym of the owner and in some cases his or her title as well.[60] The impression is called a "bulla." All of the documents so sealed have disintegrated over the years—only one paleo-Hebrew papyrus document has survived, a seventh-century B.C.E. text found in a cave in Wadi Murabba'at. It had been used twice, once as a letter that had been partially erased, a second time for a list of names. Many of these bullae have survived, however, the tracings of papyrus still visible on the back of some, such as the one that reads "Baruch, son of Neriah the Scribe."[61] A cache of bullae of the sixth century B.C.E. was found in the remains of a residential quarter of the City of David, a portion of Jerusalem. Bullae were found at Lachish and elsewhere as well.[62] G. Barkay notes that in a collection of eighth-century bullae from Samaria only one has a bit of Hebrew lettering, the others being pictorial symbols of the sender, a person's sign, whereas most bullae from the seventh and sixth centuries found in Jerusalem and Lachish have only writing and no symbols.[63] The bullae testify to the increasing popularity of the use of certain types of writing and to a nudge toward the writing end of the oral-literate continuum. To conclude from these large quantities of bullae that many people were writing their own letters and preparing documents and that literacy—again in our modern sense—was therefore widespread by the seventh and sixth centuries in Judah is, however, to draw the wrong conclusion. Indeed, the seal, which no one had to write by hand himself or herself, but which was quite often an artistically and professionally prepared object, may indicate just how few people wrote. The document itself prepared by a scribe, a writing professional, was essentially personalized by the seal in a world in which writing lengthy documents was more often than not the purview of the professional. Certainly some who were not scribes had been trained to write like a scribe and the writing of a country scribe was not equal to the productions of those in the employ of the king, but the presence of many documents, while it assures the existence of scribal classes of various sorts, does not offer evidence of general literacy in the modern sense.

One other interesting brief find is a list of four names that follow an opening term, *mipqad,* possibly the list's heading. In Hebrew Scriptures this term indicates a roster or census in military (2 Sam. 24:1–9) or other administrative contexts (Num. 3:15, 40). The list is inscribed in black ink on an ostracon and was found in an excavated house in Tel 'Ira in the Beer Sheva Valley in an archaeological stratum dating to the second half of the monarchy, an eighth/seventh-century B.C.E. date being confirmed by the paleography. Itzhaq Beit-Arieh[64] notes that the list is complete and not a fragment and suggests that it is either a local list serving some administrative function or a military or other administrative roster used for wider regional administrative purposes. Beit-Arieh suggests that the first name "Berekyahu" may be that of the scribe or local administrator. If this list is an administrative or military roster indicating who is in service at a particular time or who is available for some sort of draft, then it would be another example of writing at the literate end of the oral-literate continuum. Writing is used to preserve or convey information, the military or political leadership making, as we have seen, increasing use of the technology of writing to assist in its functioning over large geographic areas. One wonders what such a list is doing in an apparent house and if the list of only four names may have to do with more immediate household matters.

LETTERS

The letter is another important indicator of activity more toward the literate end of the oral-literate continuum. Writing is used to communicate across distances, accurately to convey thoughts in words over physical distances without the sort of changes that might occur in a strictly oral conveyance by messenger or the like. The literary texts of the Bible portray letters being dictated to scribes and read aloud at the receiving end by someone other than the addressee, matters to which we will return in chapter 6. Again writing finds itself in an oral context. It should be added that in contrast to the numerous brief messages in the commercial category, only forty-eight Hebrew letters have been discovered for a period from 700 B.C.E.–135 C.E.[65] Perhaps numerous letters on papyrus have disintegrated, but surely more ostraca might have survived had letter writing been a usual and frequent activity by most Israelites. As Pardee notes, the letters are brief[66] and "virtually all of the letters come from military contexts and show a disconcerting sameness of interests and allusions."[67] Pardee suggests via comparison with the corpus of letters in Aramaic that "if we had Hebrew letters on papyrus from ca. 600 B.C.E.," we might have longer and more varied examples.[68] This may be so, but forty-eight finds (about one fourth of which are from the postbiblical period of Bar-Kochba) is an impressively small number. Nevertheless the finding of letters by archaeologists, the oldest dating back to the early or middle seventh century (the palimpsest from Wadi Murabba'at mentioned above) is evidence of a growing literacy of some kind, but again a literacy typical of an essentially oral world. Pardee has nicely outlined "the formulaic features of the Hebrew letters": the use of various address formulae, the identification of the sender and recipient, the greeting formulae, the body, and closing formulae.[69] Even in our own Western literate culture, letters remain some of the most stylized literary forms we use, especially business or official letters, categories into which most of the ancient Hebrew letters fall. Its formulaic and typological quality should make this particular written form one of the more accessible ones in an oral culture as in our own, a form that a scribe (like a modern secretary or a computer program, for that matter) could use to fill in the blanks for his or her client.

In addition to the partially erased palimpsest, the corpus of archaeological finds that are letters is as follows: (1) a fourteen-line letter found at Metsad Hashavyahu about a mile south of Yavneh-Yam, generally interpreted to be a plea from an agricultural worker to an official concerning the worker's garment taken in pledge by a man named Hoshayahu ben Shabay and never returned, contrary to customary law (expressed in Ex. 22:25–26; Deut. 24:12–15, 17). The letter is an ostracon, ink on a sherd, and probably dates to the time of Josiah.[70] (2) A collection of twenty-one letters on ostraca from Arad in the northern Negev; all except for one have been dated to the period immediately preceding the area's conquest by Babylonian and Edomite armies in 597 B.C.E.[71] Text 40 is somewhat earlier though scholars disagree about the date. Most of the Arad letters deal with the sending of supplies in a military context, again a circumscribed variety of commercial writing with references to amounts of wine, donkey-loads, loaves of bread (e.g., Arad 3 [Catalogue no. 4] ll. 2, 5, 8) and expected delivery times (e.g., Arad 2 [Catalogue no. 3] ll. 5, 6; Arad 5 [Catalogue no. 6] ll. 12, 13). One letter appears to make reference to previous correspondence (Arad 40 [Catalogue no. 22] ll. 5, 10, 12) but the subject under discussion is not clear. Yet that very lack of clarity indicates that the writers know what they are "talking about." (3) The Lachish letters are ostraca dated to the period before the destruction of 587/6 B.C.E. and deal primarily with military matters. There are, for example, a reference to the movement of a general (Lachish 3 [Catalogue no. 25] ll. 14, 15), the mention of an apparent military arrest (Lachish 4 [Catalogue no. 26] ll. 6–7[72]), and references to the distribution of food and other supplies (Lachish 5 [Catalogue no. 26] ll. 8–10; Lachish 9 [30] ll. 3–4).

These three sets of ostraca are further witness to the oral-literate continuum. On the one hand, especially the Lachish letters evidence a lively correspondence in the military; letters frequently refer to previous communiqués and future requests or intentions to write (Lachish 3 [25] ll. 8–13; 4 [26] ll. 3–4; 6 [20] ll. 3, 4, 8; 9 [30] ll. 4–5; 18 [35] ll. 1, 2). So too the Arad letters (40 [22] 5, 10, 23). In the case of the inscription from Metsad Hashavyahu, even a poor corvée worker has access to communication by letter in an emergency situation.

On the other hand, letters such as that of the corvée worker were probably written down by a scribe, perhaps a scribe who worked "at the entrance to the local governor's residence."[73] The worker himself does not write. The style is repetitive and conversational:

> Your servant is working at the harvest. Your servant was in Hasar-Asam. Your servant did his reaping [3–4]. . . . When your (se)rvant had finished his reaping . . . Hoshayahu ben Shabay came and took your servant's garment. . . . When I had finished my reaping . . . he took your servant's garment [6–9].[74]

This style betokens an oral delivery set down on a writing surface as dictated and spoken.[75]

Lachish letter 3 is frequently cited as proof of how widespread literacy had become in Israel by the sixth century B.C.E. The military man who sends the letter to a superior is responding to some sort of accusation by the superior that he had misunderstood a previous communiqué because of inability to read or that he had allowed secret or delicate information to be read by others, a professional reader or secretary perhaps. He insists to the contrary that he himself knows how to read and that no one had to read the letter to him.[76]

His protestations of competence as a reader may well imply not that everyone of his class and status read, but to the contrary that the ability to read was not the norm even among military officials. The receiver of the letter is proud of his skills as the tone and content of the letter imply:

> For your servant has been sick at heart ever since you sent (that letter) to your servant. In it my lord said: "Don't you know how to read a letter?" As <Y>HWH lives, no one has ever tried to read *me* a letter! Moreover, when any letter comes to me and I have read it [,] I can repeat it [down] to the smallest det[ail].

(11.6–13)[77]

Notice too his pride in his oral-world ability to repeat the letter verbatim after having read it only once, a skill typical of those who rely on reading less than we do. Finally, in regard to evidence from the Lachish and Arad ostraca, a reminder is necessary that the ability to read letters does not necessarily mean ability to write them. When a person says he will write, he may well mean the use of a scribe in the process.

Thus literacy in this ancient world is again seen to be somewhere on the continuum between orality and literacy, the context of writing and reading still being that of a traditional oral-style society.

MONUMENTAL EVIDENCE

The third category of epigraphic evidence for reading and writing contains longer inscriptions hewn on walls, drawn on plaster, or inscribed upon free-standing stone monuments. In the late eighth century B.C.E. a fascinating Hebrew inscription was inscribed on the wall of a water tunnel built from the Gihon spring to the pool of Shiloah (= Siloam). This tunnel linked the oldest part of Jerusalem, the City of David, with the water spring east of the city and was an incredible engineering achievement in its day. Two crews dug toward one another, one working from the north and the other from the south. The inscription commemorates the momentous event when the two crews met.[78]

The style of the inscription is narrative and nicely descriptive, creating a cameo scene of the moments before the crews met, as the workmen heard one another's voices and the sound of digging on the stone without yet having broken through to see one another. The length and height of the tunnel are given. No kings or officials are mentioned as protagonists, only the stonemasons.[79] The inscription conveys the tone of excitement and tension appropriate for such a moment. The text uses repetition "strike and each toward his comrade," conveying a bit of the rhythm of the work. Writing is employed to describe a specific occasion in a historical mode. Where does such a text rest on the oral-literate continuum?

Smelik suggests that the text was transcribed from a Judaean Chronicle, suggesting that a passage concerning this tunnel is alluded to at 2 Kings 20:20, a fuller text having existed in the "Book of the Chronicles of the King of Judah": "The rest of the deeds of Hezekiah, and all his might, and how he made the pool and the conduit and brought water into the city, are they not written in the Book of the Annals of the Kings of Judah?" Whether or not it is this project to which 2 Kings 20 alludes or whether such Annals were being consulted by the author of 2 Kings 20, one cannot say. Copying a copy of a written annal would certainly point in the direction of a modern sort of literacy.

Barkay notes that the inscription "was carved on the rock wall of a dark water-supply tunnel. It was not a monumental inscription intended to impress the populace." He suggests the chief engineers and builders of the project "immortalized their work" and that since the inscription does not fill the space prepared for it "its carvers were not professionally trained, despite the fine execution of the letters."[80]

While such an inscription does point to Israelites' use of writing to preserve information, clearly a use of writing in the direction of a literate mode,

Smelik's suggestion seems to go quite a bit further than the information allows. The inscription, as Barkay notes, was not readily available to passersby and may not have been read by anyone for hundreds or thousands of years, but in a monumental fashion the inscription freezes and iconizes an event, making the builders of the tunnel immortal, a part of their project. It is a classy graffito or perhaps the graffito is the poor man's monument. This is writing in the oral mode.

Indeed, if R. Thomas is correct, monuments—even those in plain view—are not so much meant to be read word for word to obtain information or to verify a date as to point to, verify, and eternalize an event in a more holistic and symbolic fashion. One might draw comparisons in our own culture with the Vietnam War Memorial. Certainly people can find upon it the names of individual loved ones and acquaintances, but no one comes to the wall to read every word. Rather the wall makes a cumulative statement to passersby and to those who stop, a statement about loss and memory and about the acceptance of pieces of one's history and the history of one's people. Monuments are man-made features of landscape and a perfect example of the oral-literate continuum even in our own times.

We should note, however, that with the Siloam Inscription we are able to see parallels to some of the varieties of narration found in Hebrew Scriptures. Like creative writing, the inscription lacks the immediate pragmatic purpose of a letter, but like a letter includes details pertaining to an actual event. And yet the context of this writing is monumental and iconic, not necessarily proof that this sort of writing was usual on papyrus in Hezekiah's time, held in archives for record-keeping purposes, or the product of a literate culture in our sense.

No stone stelae have been found in ancient Hebrew script—independent, publically displayed monuments with writing upon them to indicate what is being monumentalized. As A. Mazar notes, however, "Two fragments have been found in Jerusalem and one at Samaria (the latter includes only one word). These fragments may have been from royal stelae erected in the capitals, like that of King Mesha of Moab" and were prepared in a "formal script most probably by royal scribes."[81]

There must have been such monuments in the capitals, northern and southern, in praise of kings' accomplishments, the shared victories of their people. Evidence from Israel's immediate neighbors helps us to visualize the sort of monumental inscriptions that may have been found in Israel. The inscriptions in Aramaic discovered in Tel Dan of the Galilee appear to have belonged to a victory stela of an Aramaean king who commemorates his defeat of kings of Judah and Israel in the ninth century B.C.E.[82] The Mesha

Inscription, written in Moabite, a language related to ancient Hebrew, provides a fuller example of such a monumental inscription from Israel's southeast neighbor. The stone, made of basalt, was described by an early archaeologist, F. A. Klein, as "rou..ded at both the top and the bottom, measuring 113 cm in height, 70 cm in width, and 35 cm in thickness,"[83] though these measurements were disputed. Unfortunately the stone itself was destroyed before its decipherment, and the inscription has been reconstructed from retrieved fragments and squeezes. Clermont-Ganneau estimated its original size to have been 100 × 60 × 60 cm and the base flat. In any event it would have been an imposing piece, inscribed with writing in thirty-four lines, the words "divided by dots and the "verses" or sentences by bars."[84] Notice that this ninth-century piece, in contrast to the Gezer Calendar, does have some of the markers that assist the reader who does not "know the song"[85]—a move in the direction of the world of writing at an early date.

Moreover, the text provides its author's version of the history of the relationship between Moab and Israel in which the latter appears as the oppressor (ll. 4–7). Mesha, king of Moab, declares that he has successfully liberated his people with the help of Kemosh, his god (7–9), restoring his rightful control of certain lands (8). He describes in particular the seizure of Nebo (14) and the imposition of the ban upon its inhabitants (14–17). Other annexations are mentioned (20), building projects (21–27), successful pacification of conquests (28–30), and further battles and victories (31–34).

The style of the Mesha Inscription is narrative but straightforward and unadorned. There is a cameo description of the imposition of the ban, similar to descriptions in Numbers 21:2–3, Deuteronomy, and Joshua. The historical background section is similar to the prologue in the ancient Near Eastern treaty form and to the brief background accounts accompanying war references in Numbers (e.g., Num. 21:1–2; 21–23) or Deuteronomy (Deut. 2:26–30). It is also typical of what J. Maxwell Miller and Joel Drinkard call "memorial inscriptions," as is the use of the first person.[86]

For some scholars, as Graham notes,[87] "the very existence of the MI [Mesha Inscription] argued for the antiquity of writing and so allowed one to propose an earlier date for the composition of the Pentateuch and historical books of the Old Testament." And yet as Drinkard notes, the "stela was not an annal, nor a diary of the campaigns, it was a memorial." The inscription is "religious" and "cultic in nature."[88] He notes that the stone was to stand on a holy high place built for the god Kemosh, deliverer of Moab. Context is extremely important in understanding the place of such a monument on the oral-literate continuum. The stela is not an archival record, a full historical account of events for scholarly consultation, but a religious object and iconic. Writing on stone is different from writing on a scroll, though even the scroll can be an iconic object depending upon how it is regarded and used, as we will see in discussing Torah below.[89] The stela exhibits writing as part of the memorial; writing is permanently etched into it and one with it as in the case of Hezekiah's tunnel wall. Writing serves a sacred function and invests the stone with identity and referentiality for all time. It has such meaning whether or not passersby can read the words. The relationship between such a monument and literacy is thus complex. Without literacy and respect for writing there would be no such monument, and yet the writing itself is endowed with a symbolic, religious quality that typifies the oral end of the continuum.

One other inscription that may provide a parallel to the sorts of monumental writing used by Israelites is the seventh-century Deir 'Alla Inscription. This text is in a language related to Hebrew that Jo Ann Hackett suggests is a first-millennium B.C.E. South Canaanite dialect.[90] The text was written in black and red ink on plaster applied to a stela that was possibly attached to the wall of a room, one of a complex of rooms. The text has been reconstructed from fragments and there is much debate about the meaning of individual words or phrases and about the function of the rooms.[91] All suggestions, however, connect the context to cult, perhaps some sort of cult of the dead.[92]

The more easily deciphered portion of the inscription, so-called "Combination I," is a vision report. Balaam, "a seer of the gods," is visited by the gods, who reveal something of the future to him. He fasts and when the people ask him why he does not eat, he describes a set of reversals of proper order in the natural universe.[93] This passage and the more difficult to decipher "Combination II" are fascinating, leading to intriguing suggestions about the religious worldview behind the inscription and to the larger role played by the prophet Balaam in ancient Near Eastern traditions outside of the Bible. For our purposes, in exploring the place of monumental inscriptions on the oral-literate continuum, once again we find writing in a sacred-rendering, space-defining context. The writing, an activity on the literate end of the continuum, validates the space in a transformative magical way associated with oral-traditional culture. The vision report and the "world-altered" message included in it help those who enter the space to partake of Balaam's experience, to return to a sacred founding event of some sort. Need they be able to read the inscription to share in Balaam's experience and is this text thus proof of the worshiper's ability to read and of the role of literacy in the liturgy of those who would participate in

religious experience at Deir 'Alla, whatever that experience was? Not necessarily. One thinks of Jewish American women who would attend synagogue in the 1950s without being able to read Hebrew, who still knew that
the ten commandments were suspended over the ark containing the Torah
scrolls. Once again the writing is highly iconic and monumental, as well as
transformational.

The contents of the Deir 'Alla Inscription in the section including the descriptive series of reversals is quite stylized and uses a good deal of parallel content and syntax. The rest of the text is too broken for stylistic analysis. As McCarter notes, the material in "Combination I" belongs to an ancient
Near Eastern topos.[94] The divine council scene, the vision report, and the
sorts of predictions are all found elsewhere in ancient Near Eastern literature.[95] This text is thus traditional-style material, as Hackett notes implicitly.[96] The writing attached to walls gives the traditional material a role as
monument and icon.

CONCLUSIONS

The study of epigraphic material from ancient Israel places questions about
Israelite notions of literacy in excellent perspective. The vast majority of
texts and letters are pragmatic and brief—military, military-commercial, or
commercial in nature. Writing for such purposes appears to be much more
common in the second half of the monarchy than in the first, and available
to a variety of tradesmen, officials, and others. Even a poor corvée worker
could have a message written for him by a local professional. The writing
is usually, however, for circumscribed purposes, and the attendant literacy
in the modern sense needs to have been only limited in order for such writing to communicate meaningfully to the reader of the text. Indeed, the wide
use of sealings in this period is a substitute for the sender's writing while
the assumption behind letters is that they are written by scribes and sometimes read by secretaries.

Writing that is not for these limited military or commercial purposes has
an iconic, symbolic, monumental aspect, whether a brief blessing or dedication to bring the divine presence to accompany the dead, a curse to ward
away those who would disturb them, or a means in the case of the longer
Siloam inscription of literally investing oneself in one's project. Writing creates identity whether making a person immortal or rendering a space sacred. The power of writing is thus highly respected. Professional scribes
who would prepare writing on formal monuments no doubt could read
what they wrote. But the purpose of writing in these cases is not primarily

for record keeping or for future consultation or even in order that the inscription be read in its own time. Indeed, the Siloam inscription is hidden away in a dark tunnel. Such writing is monumental and iconic. It reflects a respect for the ways in which writing creates and transforms, a respect for writing more common among the illiterate than among those who are literate in the modern sense.

All of these examples thus find their place on the oral-literate continuum, and all of these examples of literacy in ancient Israel do not in the least overturn the suggestion that Israelites live in a world heavily informed by the oral end of the continuum as I and others have defined it.

CHAPTER 4

Logistics of Literacy

Archives and Libraries, Education,
and Writing Materials

In chapter 3 we discussed many of the nonbiblical Hebrew texts that are often cited as support for "general literacy" in ancient Israel. This study led to a more complex and nuanced understanding of Israelite literacy. The products of Israelite writing are to be appreciated in the context of an oral culture and as belonging somewhere upon an oral-literate continuum. The oral mentality frames writings, while the capacity of members of society to write or read influences the culture and its means of communication, composition, self-preservation and definition.

In this chapter, we expand our understanding of Israelite literacy by exploring three additional areas to which scholars point when making what I find to be too simple a case for Israelite literacy: archives and libraries, education, and the logistics of writing.

RECORD KEEPING:
ARCHIVES AND LIBRARIES

Do Thomas's and Clanchy's suggestions concerning the nature of and attitudes toward record keeping in oral-traditional cultures help us better to appreciate attitudes toward writing in ancient Israel and possible ancient Near Eastern parallels? This is an extremely difficult question because of the paucity of archival and library evidence from Israel itself and because of difficulties involved in interpreting and determining the relevance of comparative material from Israel's ancient Near Eastern neighbors.

At the "oral" end of the continuum, records are not easily retrieved and not made "for utilitarian purposes." They are "pledges to posterity," an assurance of cultural or familial continuity. And yet, we might add, they are not regularly employed for purposes of historical consultation in the style of a modern archive. Like inscriptions, they have a symbolic value. Allusions to them may be found in other writings, but the allusion or quotation relies on memory rather than verbatim copying.

At the literate end of the scale, records provide the possibility for immediate consultation concerning an ongoing transaction or the opportunity to refresh one's memory about an earlier one, a way to prove land rights or date of marriage or to estimate how much fodder is used per year by a farm. They are catalogued to provide access to later generations or to the historian who might consult them to verify information or to copy a section.

Relevant to this discussion as well is the distinction between libraries and archives, the former being repositories for literary and scholarly texts, the latter being holdings of letters, contracts, deeds, dockets, and other records, although within private holdings in the better-represented parts of the ancient Near East the distinction between archive and library is sometimes blurred. Literary texts housed in libraries also should be assessed in terms of an oral-literate continuum. Does the library preserve bits of culture in a symbolic fashion—a sort of literary time capsule—or are the library's holdings regularly read, consulted by people who want to read a particular story or to acquire knowledge of an astrological, medical, mathematical, or zoological nature?

Archives in Ancient Israel

Several sets of archaeological material may testify to the collecting and holding of written information in archives in ancient Israel. The Samaria ostraca were found in what archaeologists believe to have been the "royal administrative headquarters" of the northern kingdom.[1] These 102 documents dated to the eighth century B.C.E.[2] are essentially dockets, recording deliveries of wine and oil. These products possibly were received as taxes[3] or were supplies for the palace complex in the Israelite capital.[4] Here, then, in one appropriate location is a set of related written records.

The Lachish letters were found in a destruction level of a guardroom between the outer and inner gates of the city Lachish.[5] This collection of eighteen ostraca dealing with military matters and located in one appropriate place may perhaps be an archive of a sort. The letters concerned current matters of import to those who lived at the time of the writing of the letters, namely during the few years preceding the destruction of Jerusalem in 587/6 B.C.E. Similarly, scholars suggest that many of the Arad letters or ostraca pertain to the affairs of Eliashib, son of Ashiyahu, "commander of the fortress in its last phase."[6] Lindenberger suggests that Eliashib may have been a "quarter-master" rather than a commander and that letters 55–60 were found in his office.[7] For both the Lachish and Arad collections the term "official files" may be more accurate than "archive."

Also from the sixth century are the group of fifty-one inscribed bullae found in burnt remains of the residential quarter of the southeast portion of Jerusalem, the so-called City of David.[8] As discussed above, each clay bulla would have been attached to a string wrapped around rolled papyrus or leather—a letter or another sort of document. The impression in clay would identify the owner of the seal that had been used to identify the document. Could these bullae indicate the presence of some sort of family archive?

Finally there are two postexilic examples of possible archival material. One is a group of bullae published by N. Avigad that seem to have "originated in a single hoard and from the archives of the governor of the city-state of Yehud."[9] Again, the presence of bullae indicates the presence of documents that now have disintegrated and been lost. Indeed some of the bullae studied by Avigad retain impressions or tracings of the papyrus to which they had been attached or pressed while the little lump of clay was wet and sealable. A second example is a fragmentary collection of later Persian period/early Hellenistic texts published by F. M. Cross. The cache appears to include documents from a private family archive, having to do with property. Cross suggests the material belonged to Samaritan refugees hiding in the cave, in the Wadi ed-Deliyeh, where the documents were found.[10] Numerous skeletal remains suggest that the Samaritans never escaped their hiding place alive. Basing himself on a story told by the Latin historian Quintus Curtius, Cross suggests that members of the Samaritan aristocracy had revolted against Alexander the Great, who had them hunted down and executed. In any event, the documents may provide late examples of private archival material.

Such collections indicate that writing was not only available to convey information in the literate mode, as discussed above for letters, but that information contained in the documents could and would be saved, relevant letters or documents kept together, for future consultation or reference. Some cautions are in order, however. Sealed papyrus or leather documents containing information about property transfers, ownership rights, and other matters, though archived and held, would not necessarily be opened regularly and available for consultation, for the seal once broken was difficult to reseal. The logistics of sealing thus seem to argue against viewing archives in too modern and literate a mode. Archives of sealed papyrus and leather documents probably do not resemble the record departments of our town halls, places where research is conducted, facts checked, and files consulted. The record is available should it be absolutely necessary, for example, for a grandson to prove his rights to a piece of the family's land, but more often than not common local knowledge and the existence of the document, sealed and identified by that seal, may convey the grandson's rights. The "record keeping" is again on the oral-literate continuum.

When we write of collections of ostraca, another important question arises. Were sherds archived in the ancient Near East?[11] The ostracon, after all, is the scratch paper of the ancient Near Eastern world, cheap, plentiful, and expendable. It is not out of the question that the finds at Lachish, Samaria, and Arad reflect "waste basket" material or the stuff of recycle bins rather than archives. Records kept for the long term may have been written on more valuable and formal surfaces. The preexilic collections of ostraca do appear to have to do with current usage rather than with long-term, systematic record keeping. Indeed many other ostraca have been used as fill in building projects in an early sort of recycling. Then as now, not every note needed to be kept, or communiqués might be kept and then discarded when no longer useful or relevant. Long-term archives may well have existed in ancient Israel, as the caches of bullae suggest, but the actual evidence of a literate-style archival mentality is quite thin and must be treated with caution.

Libraries in Ancient Israel

As for libraries, there is no archaeologically recoverable evidence of their existence or, for that matter, specific reference to them in the Hebrew Bible. On the other hand, M. Haran goes too far in suggesting that Israelites had no libraries because their sacred literary documents were so few—being only books of the Torah![12] We can imagine the existence of individual scrolls, one prophetic oracle or several kept by disciples in a private archive, a copied version of some version of an ancient tale about the judges kept by a scribe in Josiah's palace, a briefer version of the Deuteronomistic history taken into exile. All of these remain possibilities, a matter to which we will return in a final chapter as we explore possibilities for the genesis of the Hebrew Bible. But neither such imaginings nor the probable existence of state archives in royal cities or fortresses alter the dominant image of a world in which the oral end of the continuum tends to dominate. Indeed, the much more elaborate and extensive archival findings from the great city-states of Mesopotamia and elsewhere often cited as models for Israel, in which it is argued much has been lost, testify to the ongoing importance of the oral-literate continuum in understanding those ancient cultures as well.

Ethnographic Parallels

In fact, Assyriologists have begun to ask questions about the oral-written continuum in Sumerian and Akkadian literature. While many of the essays in a recent anthology edited by Vogelzang and Vanstiphout are too heavily constrained by evaluating the validity of the Lord-Parry model for Mesopotamian literature, other valuable threads in the work beautifully describe in detail the ways in which some of the characteristics of metonymy operate in particular compositions or across the tradition. See, for example, Vogelzang on the use of episodic structure,[13] Vanstiphout on repetition and structure in the Aratta Cycle,[14] Shlomo Izre'el on parallelism and repetition and the use of recurring phrases or formulas,[15] and Westenholz on "variation" and "fixity."[16] As Jerold Cooper writes, nicely summarizing what I consider to be the best work of his colleagues: "The chief value of oral formulaic theory is that it shows us how traditional language and composition, whether oral or written, operate, and helps us to penetrate the esthetics of Mesopotamian literature."[17]

Many of the essays in this volume, moreover, touch on the interplay between oral and literary mentalities in the received literature and in its possible contexts.[18] The dominant message of the Vogelzang and Vanstiphout collection, however, is that the extant corpus of Mesopotamian literature, spanning thousands of years, several languages, and numerous dialects, collected from various geographically distinct sites, stems from cultures in which "the scribal arts were lauded."[19] Similarly, writing about the Sumerian tradition Cooper notes: "I would like to insist that we have a continuous tradition of writing and transmitting Sumerian literature from at least the Fara period through the Old Babylonian period and beyond."[20] Cooper points to a lengthy period of "continual editing, composition, redaction, and selection"[21]—a literate mentality.

It is the same conviction about the scribal motivation behind and literate nature of the material that one finds in scholarly examinations of the nature and role of archives and libraries in some of the city-states and empires of the ancient Near East.

Archives and Libraries in the Non-Israelite Ancient Near East

On the one hand, studies of ancient Near Eastern collections of documents seem to emphasize the literate end of the scale for many of these ancient societies. For example, the review and assessment of Ernst Posner enthusiastically suggests that "those before us were made as record conscious as we are forced to be. . . . When compared to the small volume of medieval archives, the archives of the ancient world seem to have much more in common with those of our own times."[22] Klaas Veenhof provides a masterful overview of a more recent scholarly meeting precisely on the topic of archives and libraries in the ancient Near East. He describes the use of storage repositories for current records and employs the term "central archives" to describe a collection located on the second floor of the palace at Ugarit.[23] He suggests that Room L 2769 of Ebla was "designed for systematically filing texts," while consulting and writing may have been done in connecting rooms L 2878.[24] He provides examples of conquerors apparently maintaining the palace archives of the conquered "in view of administrative continuity."[25] He describes large private archives that "owe their existence to the need of written documentation for evidentiary or informatory purposes, in order to control and steer the movement of goods and persons."[26] In addition, Veenhoff provides examples of virtual cataloguing and filing systems that made records available for consultation:[27] the use of labels attached by strings, short inscriptions on storage containers for clay tablets, and other markings.[28]

His overview is then supported by the more detailed evidence in particular cases put forward by his colleagues, for example, P. Matthiae concerning the Ebla evidence, who draws conclusions that support notions of ancient literate activity in a modern mode. He writes about the preservation and consultation of monthly accounts concerning the distribution of textiles.[29] W. H. Van Soldt suggests that various wings of the "palace archives at Ugarit were used for specific sorts of material,"[30] thus enhancing the portrait of carefully catalogued materials.

At first, one has the impression of veritable modern-style records in the literate mode, and yet when one reads the evidence brought forward by Veenhof and the others more closely, one is equally impressed with the continuing power of the oral mode, finding echoes of Thomas's and Clanchy's comments on attitudes toward record keeping in largely oral cultures.

Veenhof notes, for example, that in general, archives in the ancient Near East are not collections preserved for historical value but current records that have been preserved and found because the building holding them was destroyed, providing us a snapshot of what was going on in a particular slice of time. These disposable writings frequently deal with commercial matters—again in the category of brief pragmatic messages.[31]

In spite of his enthusiasm for cuneiform record keeping, even Veenhof has to admit that some of these collections do not seem to be records in the modern mode at all. The "lack of system or disorder" in "archival" material at Mari has motivated one scholar to suggest that the "apparent lack of system to some extent may have been intentional in order to limit access to vital written information to a small group of trusted officials."[32] Veenhof rejects this peculiar explanation. In commenting on the Mari situation, J. Margueron[33] takes note of the "astonishing heterogeneity" of the archives and admits that ancient archivists' "démarche intellectuelle," "their intellectual orientation," is not necessarily identical to ours. Not all cuneiform archives are thus at the same point on the oral-literate continuum, accessibility and systematization being, as Clanchy notes, traits closer to the literate end than the mere accumulation of documents. The Mari "archives" appear to be closer to the oral end of the continuum in this respect than other ancient Near Eastern examples. About the situation in ancient Israel one cannot know.

Libraries pose other questions. In a modern literate culture, libraries make available to an audience a range of works of fiction and nonfiction. Cataloguing systems are vital to make resources on specific topics retrievable. The libraries inform in an active way and do not merely preserve the arcane, an icon for posterity, a sort of time capsule of writings. What sort of material is contained in the cuneiform "libraries," who has access to them, and for what purposes? Again even for the Mesopotamian collections that have been designated as "libraries" by scholars one sees evidence of the oral world.

Olaf Pedersén provides a careful and nicely representative tally of holdings found in the archives and libraries of ancient Assur. His study of a series of private archives reveals the sort of records discussed by Veenhof and his colleagues: purchase documents, loan documents, lists of commercial items, deeds, judicial documents, and so on.[34] The combined library/archive of the Assur temple, containing texts dating from the thirteenth through seventh centuries B.C.E. includes records important to the temple, for example, an inventory of vessels, censors, and textiles; royal decrees concerning offerings at the temple, and various grants.[35] "Library" holdings at the same temple, that is holdings that we would call "literary," include inscriptions from various kings,[36] royal rituals, a lexical list, a catalogue of songs (perhaps hymns), a creation myth, a fable (again Pedersén is using modern Western terminology for these genres, but one would assume they are narratives), mathematical texts, incantations, omen texts.[37] Pedersén suggests that other libraries belonged to particular groups with particular interests. For example, a library of a family of scribes contains lexical lists (the largest amount of material), an astronomical compendium, incantations, the Dialogue of Pessimism, a Šamaš hymn, *Enuma elish,* the Erra epic, and purchase documents.[38] A larger private library belonging to a family of exorcists contains an exorcist's manual, incantations, prayers, psalms, omens, and a cultic commentary.[39]

The gathering of these materials in various libraries certainly does suggest the literate end of the continuum. We recognize the presence of what we would call "literary classics," available in various copies among the remains of ancient Near Eastern culture and the presence of what we would call "scholarly texts" of interest to special groups: exorcisms and omens for exorcists; lexical lists for scribes. Clearly the setting down of these texts in writing and their being gathered together on some level betoken a literate mentality. The hymns are not merely preserved in memory or produced extemporaneously; knowledge of words or means of cures or modes of telling the future have been collected and set down and preserved successfully for millennia in this fashion. Mogens Weitemeyer argues, moreover, that library texts were arranged and sometimes marked to allow for identification and retrieval;[40] he writes of catalogues.[41] Simo Parpola has published what he considers to be a catalogue list of a major acquisition to the palace libraries of Nineveh.[42] And yet as Weitemeyer notes, such libraries were used by a small circumscribed group of officials.[43] The private libraries may have had pragmatic function as aids in their owners' work but were also tributes to their work, identifying them as possessors of a special sacred arcane knowledge. The texts are on some level signets and markers of status.

Indeed some tablets[44] appear to have been offered as "votive gifts to the deity." The writing, like the words on monumental inscriptions or amulets, lends to the message a concrete reality. The writing is not simply a means of sending a message or of conveying a thought but is seen as a precious commodity worthy of a gift to the god. Such a notion is something other than an attitude to writing typical of modern literacy but is appropriate to a society in which writing is still regarded as special and unusual. Is it no coincidence that many of the private libraries discussed by Pedersén are located in a sacred space, the inner room of the house "which had the graves of the family under the floor."[45]

Additional evidence of the oral side of the oral-written continuum in these writing-conscious cultures is offered by Stephen J. Lieberman. In an essay that challenges the notion of canonical literature in an Assyrian context, canon being an improper import from the biblical field,[46] Lieberman explores the reasons why texts were collected. Assurbanipal's library is Lieberman's primary focus.

Inscriptional evidence (colophons on the tablets containing the cuneiform texts) indicates that some tablets were preserved in the god Nabû's temple "for the life of Assurbanipal," that is, "to cause the God Nabû to favor him"—again as an offering.[47] On the other hand, texts collected for Assurbanipal were apparently consulted not only by him but by his officials, the written form of the material making consultation possible. Is this not an indication of modern-style literacy at least on the part of an élite few? Yes, and yet the literature they collect and consult is largely in the realm of omens used for divinatory purposes to help the king decide when or whether to undertake certain projects.[48] Writing assists as a means of reading divine plans and accommodating human actions to them. The practical benefits of writing thus intermingle with oral-world assumptions about the efficacy of omens. Scribes, Lieberman notes, felt free to "correct" texts, and the texts themselves reflect numerous variants within the omen tradition.[49] Material preserved thus strongly admits of O'Keeffe's quality of visible song. Indeed if the king's consultants did not approve of the king's interpretation of or manipulation of written omen materials, they could cite oral tradition, which in turn could then be written down.[50] These library collections thus give testimony to the vibrant interaction of oral and written mentalities. In many ways writings are now available to serve as adjuncts to and facilitators of oral-traditional activities, while oral tradition contributes to the expansion of the written tradition.

Pedersén notes further that some of the texts in the private library of a family of exorcists are copies or excerpts of other texts. It is common to find notes upon them such as "quickly excerpted for a special performance."[51] In a similar vein Dalley writes:

> Akkadian literature in its written form is different in concept from later written literature. Through the study of several versions of one story, it has become clear that one version may omit an episode crucial to the sequence, or it may be so elliptical or telescoped as to be unintelligible without the help of another, more explicit version. This is a recognized feature of Sumerian literature, which preceded Akkadian, and is also true to a lesser extent of stories written in Akkadian. A later version is not necessarily fuller than an earlier one: for example, the latest version of *Ishtar's Descent* from Nineveh is slightly briefer than the earlier version from Assur, and less than half the length of the Sumerian story, which is even earlier. We should probably understand some of the abrupt changes of theme as bare skeletons which were fleshed out in practice by skilled narrators, rather as early musical notation gave only the guidelines needed to remind the musician of appropriate melody and rhythms, leaving embellishments and flourishes to his own skills and to popular tastes. . . .
>
> The primary purpose of recording stories in writing was not necessarily to supply individual readers with a coherent and connected ac-

count. Ancient stories were used for a multitude of purposes, often in extracts: attached to a ritual, to give authenticity or to provide an aetiology; to give the weight of some ancient tradition to a custom or to an incantation.[52]

One cannot but think of the folklorist Ruth Finnegan's comments on the Maori orators who had notebooks in which were copied favorite phrases and jottings, notebooks they would use to help enhance their oral performances.[53]

Finally we note Lieberman's point that tablets were collected and kept in Assurbanipal's library not only for the king's pragmatic use but also "to preserve tablets in Assurbanipal's name for the ages."[54] Concern for posterity and the preservation of writings is something we also do in a modern literate mode, but like a great philanthropist who founds a university or establishes a fellowship fund in his or her name, Assurbanipal is also establishing a monument to preserve his memory. So M. T. Clanchy writes of the monumental function of medieval collections, an example of participation in the oral end of the continuum that finds parallels in our own culture.

We have looked then at inscriptional evidence from ancient Israel, at thin but apparent Israelite archival remains, and at possible models for Israelite archives and libraries from the rich archaeological remains of cuneiform cultures of the ancient Near East. In all cases, we conclude that literacy in these ancient cultures is other than what we mean by literacy, that the oral and the written exist in tandem, and that the writing culture is in various ways framed by assumptions typical of oral worlds.

EDUCATION

Another important piece in the discussion concerning the oral and literate mentalities has to do with education. André Lemaire suggests that the new bureaucracy under Solomon established a veritable system of state schools to train servants for the state.[55] A. Demsky and M. Kochavi suggest that Israelites developed scribal schools for administrative purposes during the premonarchic period to assist in "tribal administration"![56] Few scholars nowadays accept old-style assumptions about a neatly organized tribal league or the like, let alone that such a league promoted the development of scribal schools.

Lemaire believes that schools not only produced state administrators early in the monarchy but created a situation of more general literacy late in the monarchy.[57] Schools, he believes, extended even to most villages in the eighth century B.C.E. and later.

Evidence for such school systems that contributes to arguments for "general literacy" in ancient Israel is slim, as Carol Meyers, David Jamieson-Drake, and James Crenshaw[58] have concluded. Such arguments are based on biblical texts that may be variously interpreted and on the sort of epigraphic material explored in chapter 3. Millard, Williams, and Lemaire,[59] for example, each cite Deut. 6:6–9 as evidence of general literacy in the late monarchy, for this famous passage, now incorporated into a prayer that is central in Jewish liturgy, commands that God's words be written "upon your doorposts and upon your gates." Thus, goes the argument, everyone must be able to read and write. An orally based perspective suggests that this is precisely the sort of iconic and monumental use of writing that is typical of traditional and strongly oral cultures. Not everyone need be able to write or read the words to know what they say and mean. Indeed, the previous verses demand that you "recite" or "repeat" these words to your children, "speak of them [the words of God] when you sit in your house or walk by the way, when you lie down or rise up" (Deut. 6:7). The emphasis is at the oral end of the continuum.

As Jamiesen-Drake notes, defining certain epigraphic finds such as the Gezer Calendar and the various "abecedaries" as school exercises, and therefore as evidence of the presence of a school where they were found, pushes the evidence beyond its limitations.[60] The "abecedaries" indeed may have held magical, symbolic importance.

One can assert that writing is in use early in the monarchy, but much more in evidence in the late monarchy, and that the writers, however simple their texts, did learn to write in some context. Some of the writing, for example, Hezekiah's tunnel inscription, is much more elegant than others, and certain members of the community were highly trained in writing skills. Such skills could have been acquired in schools or in a family setting passed on from parents to children, as Carol Meyers notes.[61] The writing and reading skills necessary in a commercial setting, for example, may well have been taught in the course of learning about or growing up in the family business.

Jamiesen-Drake uses a sociological-archaeological model to suggest that if scribal schools did exist to teach more sophisticated skills of writing and reading, they would have been found in certain likely urban centers such as Jerusalem in the late monarchy.[62] The numbers of epigraphic finds alone suggest that more writing of different varieties is found from the eighth century on than in previous centuries. To suggest more than this is to hypothesize. Did those who "searched out" and "arranged" and wrote down proverbs (to quote Eccl. 12:9–10) learn their skills in wisdom "schools" or were such schools like the Rabbinic academies, often composed of a teacher with his few close disciples?

It is at least as important to ask how people passed on the oral aspects of Israelite cultures, the oral mentality that makes itself so apparent in the very style, structure, content, and purposes of material now preserved in writing. Throughout, it seems clear that once writing is available, the oral and the written interact on a continuum, and that assertions about general literacy in the modern mode are as inappropriate to ancient Israelite culture as, in Lieberman's view, is the modern notion of canon to Assurbanipal's library.

LOGISTICS OF READING AND WRITING

In discussing modes of literacy in ancient Israel, questions about the sorts of instruments and materials used to make letters and the materials upon which texts are written are also important. What sort of materials are available in adequate quantities and to whom? Do materials used imply anything about attitudes to preservation—monumental eternity or quick consumption? How technically skilled did the writer have to be to use certain instruments or materials? How much training was necessary for one to read various examples of writing? How easy was it to find one's place in a written text? How portable was the writing surface? Do ancient examples of Israelite writing conform in any ways to our notion of "book," the term so often used to translate the Hebrew *sēper*?

Stone can provide a surface for monumental inscriptions. Basing themselves on Jer. 17:1 and Job 19:24, some suggest that an "iron pen and stone stylus could have been used as chisels to carve into the stone" although "no artifact or pictorial evidence of these tools in ancient Israel has yet been found."[63] Job 19:24 is better translated "iron stylus and lead," perhaps revealing something of another ancient Israelite writing technique.[64] The skill level for the beautiful, even writing on the Siloam inscription would be very high indeed. Incised or inked upon stone, writing in the personal "monuments" of graffiti could be of varying quality. The surface preparation would not require great technical skill. Stone covered with a thick layer of plaster that is then written upon was also available (e.g., Deir 'Alla; Kuntillet 'Ajrud). Preparation of and work with such surfaces would presumably require a greater degree of technical skill, the work of craftsmen, for special locations and purposes. Large stones and stone walls were, of course, not portable surfaces. Thus the very nature of the material is monumental in the ways we have described. This is an important point as we think of the logistics of literacy. It is frequently asserted that writing was familiar to people in ancient Israel because of such monuments and that the presence of this writing in part constitutes literacy. Even if people who were able to read paused to read the inscription (assuming the monument was not too high to be seen clearly or in a private cave or a dark water tunnel), information in the inscription would be reorealized and transported orally or would have to be copied on a smaller portable document. A monument or a graffito is a *sēper* but not a book in our sense. We have discussed the many seals and jar handles, portable writing impressed upon or inked upon clay, that give evidence of a particular variety of literacy in a commercial context and examples of brief writing have been found on metal and ivory,[65] but what about longer, more complex, but portable texts that might begin to approach "books" and literacy in the modern mode? In this category are ostraca, that is, broken sherds, wooden tablets, wax-coated writing boards, papyrus, and leather.

We have ample evidence of ostraca discussed above, available especially for practical communication in the military and commercial realms. Most ostraca were inked with a substance made of carbon (soot) and an organic gum. The pen was made of a rush "cut obliquely and then frayed at the end to form a brush or with a reed cut obliquely and split." Evidence of both sorts of pen is in the style of the letter-making itself.[66] Ostraca are good for letters, dockets, brief records, evidence again of the use of the technology of writing for pragmatic purposes.

As we explore the nature of Israelite literacy and evidence from the material culture of writing, important unknowns concern the use of the remaining surfaces: wood, wood and wax, papyrus, and leather. It is on such surfaces that one would expect to find more the sorts of Israelite writing that have been preserved in the Hebrew Bible: narratives, oracles, legal texts, and so on that some would describe as quintessential products of an Israelite literacy. "Wooden tablets, often coated with stucco," were frequently used as writing surfaces in Egypt. This material would not survive in Israel's climate, and only one example, a letter of the first century C.E., has survived.[67] In Anatolia, Syria, and Mesopotamia, wooden tablets covered with wax were linked together to form a diptych or polyptych.[68] Neo-Hittite reliefs of the eighth century B.C.E. portray scribes writing with stylus on these surfaces. Lemaire suggests such surfaces, easy to work with and correct, were useful for rough drafts that could then be copied onto papyrus or leather. No examples within Israel of this material have been found, though some have suggested that Isa. 30:8 and Hab. 2:2, which refer to writing on tablets, are references to waxed writing boards.

The most important surfaces to consider when thinking of longer literary or scholarly works that were both portable and preservable in the style of a book are papyrus and leather.

Papyrus, made from the stalk of a plant that grew particularly well in the watery inlets of the Egyptian Delta (Lower Egypt) was a major Egyptian resource and export used for various products including "paper," the English word that derives its name from the ancient Egyptian writing surface.[69]

Pliny the Elder, the Roman naturalist of the first century, describes the making of papyrus as follows:

> The raw material taken from the tall plants—some as high as 35 feet—consisted of strips cut lengthwise from the pith of the three-sided stalks. Strips of equal length and quality were then arranged on a flat surface, in the manner of lattice-work, in a horizontal and vertical layer, the former representing the recto and the latter the verso side of the sheet. Through the application of pressure and water from the Nile—perhaps with the occasional addition of glue—the layers were merged into a fairly homogeneous mass, which was then exposed to the sun. After drying, the sheets were rubbed smooth with shells or ivory and perhaps whitened with chalk. Excess moisture was forced out by additional pounding.[70]

There is no doubt that papyrus was exported to the Palestinian region.[71] We have mentioned the tracings on bullae that indicate the use of papyrus for letters and other documents in Israel and Judah in the eighth and seventh centuries B.C.E. The climate has prevented the survival of the actual documents. The only paleo-Hebrew piece that has survived is the seventh century B.C.E. palimpsest found at Wadi Murabba'at discussed in chapter 3. Aramaic documents on papyrus from the second half of the first millennium B.C.E. have survived. They are letters, deeds, contracts, and other archival sorts of material.[72]

It is entirely possible that literary and scholarly texts—even of significant length—might have been set down on papyrus. In Egypt individual sheets were glued together with a starch paste into rolls of twenty sheets. The longest individual roll ever preserved is the Harris Papyrus of the twelfth century B.C.E., currently held in the collections of the British Museum (Catalogue no. 10053). It is 133 feet long, $16\frac{3}{4}$ inches wide, and contains 79 sheets.[73]

Lemaire considers probable the use of papyrus scrolls to copy biblical texts during the first Temple period. Like M. Haran, he suggests a transition to the use of skins in the Persian period.[74] The argument has been made that papyrus was an affordable surface for those who would need it—government officials and scribes of various kinds. This suggestion seems reasonable, but so does A. Demsky's alternate view that the more familiar surface and the more readily available in ancient Israel in first and second temple periods would have been a parchment or leather product made from animal skins. This material need not be imported, after all.[75] The skins were treated with repeated processes of washing, liming, scraping, and stretching, the final process involving a dusting with chalk and a rubbing with pumice.[76] Like Egyptian rolls of papyrus, skins could be joined to create lengthy book-sized rolls as indicated by the Isaiah scroll (4Q Is[a]) found among the Hellenistic-period Dead Sea Scrolls. This, the fullest of the biblical texts found at Qumran, contains 54 columns of writing on 17 sheets of leather, an average of 29.9 lines per column, and is 7.34 m. or about 24 feet in length. With Qumran material as his model, Lansing Hicks suggests that between 1.25 and 1.75 Masoretic chapters would fit on each leather sheet with three or four columns of writing per sheet.[77] Hicks then links this calculation about average number of columns at Qumran with Jer. 36:23 to suggest that Jehoiakim is said not to cut the document in arbitrary pieces, but to slice off three or four columns (*dělātôt*) at a time by cutting the "sutures uniting the sheets."[78] Hicks thus suggests considerable continuity in the logistics of writing in pre- and post-exilic periods.

To write on papyrus or leather required training—knowing, for example, how to keep straight lines on papyrus by employing the texture created by the strips of the natural material or how to rule the leather surface.[79] The best leather surface could be tricky to work on, even for the experienced scribe.

Writing on these surfaces, like the chiseling upon the wall of Hezekiah's water tunnel, thus is done by a small, specialized group. When one thinks of the availability of animal skin surfaces, moreover, one thinks of priests and the sacrificial ritual that makes hides available, not to mention priestly skills in cutting and flaying (see Lev. 1:1–9, for example) that might make the manufacture of leather writing surfaces a logical extension of priestly activity. I do not make this argument to lead up to a suggestion that the Bible is a priestly and/or scribal work, though it does seem likely that such a small group is responsible ultimately for preserving the written collection we now have.

Even when those with access to the material culture of writing do compose or record compositions on skin or papyrus that may then be preserved in various archives or libraries, the oral culture frames the writing, not only in matters of aesthetics (discussed in chapters 1 and 2) so that, as A. N.

Doane has suggested,[80] the scribe becomes a sort of performer, not only in attitudes that consider the writing transformative and iconic (chapter 3), but also in the variants of texts that existed and in the very nature of the Hebrew writing itself.

Even as late as the Dead Sea Scrolls, texts exist in multiplicity, anonymous, and variable. Julio Trebolle Barrera, Emanuel Tov, and Eugene Ulrich have all pointed to the richness of "textual plurality"[81] evidenced by the variants of biblical texts found at Qumran. Ulrich points to two editions of Exodus; variant editions of Numbers; two literary editions of Jeremiah; two possible major editions of Psalms; and "variant editions of certain passages" in Samuel.[82] Emanuel Tov describes further the "reworked" biblical texts at Qumran, texts that evidence varying degrees of rewriting and elaboration upon biblical texts.[83] Tov regards such works not as variants granted the same respect as the "biblical text" but as exegesis on one particular variant of the "text" regarded as the "actual," real biblical text. Of course, one wonders if the distinction between paraphrase, reworking exegesis, and "actual text" was not much more fluid than Tov allows.

As Barrera notes after discussing "the textual plurality, which was "even richer than so far assumed":[84] "At the present state of research, practitioners of textual criticism and defenders of an authorized text should probably operate with a broader concept of what constitutes an original text vs. an authorized text."[85] In a similar vein, Ulrich writes:

> The Scriptures were pluriform . . . until at least 70 C.E. probably until 100, and quite possibly as late as 135 or beyond. Thus, we must revise our imaginations and our explanations . . . we can see now more clearly that there were multiple literary editions of many of the biblical books. And we can understand that, e.g., the Book of Jeremiah or Daniel was considered among the books of Scripture, but the specific textual form was not a consideration.[86]

As we explore the logistics of literacy, the "pluriform" nature of the biblical tradition is an important factor. Even traditions that are clearly written evidence in their multiformity qualities of an oral register. In a community's implicit acceptance of these variants as valid without "consideration" of "the specific textual form"[87] there is a quite different sort of literacy from our own. This line of thought in turn leads to questions about scholarly approaches to biblical texts. Ulrich writes, "Because the text of each book was produced organically, in multiple layers, determining 'the original text' is a difficult, complex task; and theologically it may not even be the correct goal."[88] Ulrich asks how one makes value judgments about which version is "better" or preferable. Attention to the oral side of the oral-literate continuum leads to even more radical questions. Is there a "correct" text or "best" text? Can one ever determine what an original text was? As text critics, we always work from a finite number of variants. The corpus of biblical variants, even as enriched by the Qumran corpus, is only partial, textual decisions being made on the basis of what has survived and been found, not on the basis of what once existed.

No matter how one responds to such questions, we do well even in working with written manuscripts of ancient Israelite literature to allow ourselves to think in an oral mode. An "orally" informed worldview provides a context for the writing and receiving of versions of the compositions now housed in particular forms in the Hebrew Bible.

Moreover, the very nature of unvocalized Hebrew, even allowing for markers between words that are found in inscriptional evidence and Qumran,[89] requires a sense of how the words usually go in order to read successfully. Ancient Hebrew is a language rich in O'Keeffe's quality of visible song.

Issues in material culture are relevant to understanding the way the oral world affects potential receivers of these written down, unvocalized variants kept in archives or libraries, many of which are small and belong to families. Many of the texts would have been brief—a single psalm, a page sampling of legal custom, a story. There may have been lengthier texts, the Hebrew equivalent to the Ahiqar narrative. Lengthy texts—a collection of prophecies or some version of the narrative that runs from Genesis to Numbers—are difficult to use. A lengthy papyrus or leather scroll may be rather heavy when unopened, unwieldy when fully opened. Indeed we have no evidence that Israelites used long tables either to write or to read and we assume that for either activity only a small portion of the scroll would be exposed at one time. This being the case one faces a real challenge if one wants to turn efficiently to a passage in the middle of a scroll, or if one wishes to compare two passages. One cannot simply turn to the tenth folio to reach a particular passage or use a bookmark to move back and forth between texts.

T. C. Skeat describes the way a papyrus scroll was read. He has made the case that the scroll offers advantages to a reader, providing in particular a "panoramic" rolling view of the text.[90] This advantage is apparent only if one wishes to read the scroll in order but quickly vanishes if one's interest is in turning to one story or passage.[91] Hence Dawson's suggestion that references to passages from books in antiquity, even the citing of specific texts, are frequently from memory.

The written text provides a portion of tradition that becomes set, an icon, perhaps a sacred object that may be ritually studied sequentially or read in for special occasions, or copied when the old papyrus begins to succumb to age. The stories, the customs, the rituals, and the proverbs live, however, in the oral culture, in the lives and words of people. A work such as the Hebrew Bible, richly traditional and informative as it is, is just a slice of, a collection of freeze frames in an even richer tradition. The transmission of this tradition may well have involved complex interplays between written and oral processes. We will return to this issue at the end of our study, but first we turn to the Hebrew Bible itself to explore what its writings reveal about their authors' attitudes toward orality and literacy.

CHAPTER 5

Attitudes to Writing
in the Hebrew Bible
The Oral End of the Continuum

Our study of the quality of the language and communication in the Hebrew Bible has revealed an aesthetic in the oral register. In a second chapter we explored some of the significant variation possible within this register and the continuum between orality and literacy upon which all extant Israelite literature belongs. Our study of nonbiblical Israelite literature supports the contention that while writing becomes an increasingly important resource in the late monarchies (eighth century B.C.E. on), the conceptual framework and social settings for this writing nevertheless must be understood in the context of an oral world. As Ruth Finnegan notes, in any writing culture orality and literacy coexist and interact, as each influences the other. There is no "great divide" between the oral and the written in the cultures of ancient Israel but a continuum. Texts may well seem to be at one or another end of this continuum, showing more the perspective of an oral mentality or of a literate worldview as we have described these attitudes. Alternatively, texts may fall right in the middle of the continuum, revealing an inseparable mix of oral and literate mentalities—as one might well expect in a traditional culture whose writing reflects the aesthetic of an oral register, but all of whose verbal productions are available to us, preserved through time, because of the technology of writing.

With these gradations in mind, we turn to the largest single corpus of extant Israelite writing, the compositions of the Hebrew Bible, our goal being to explore attitudes to writing expressed by the Israelites who produced these texts and found them meaningful.

To examine this large collection on the oral-literate scale, we will draw an artificial distinction between texts that most thoroughly suggest an oral mentality (chapter 5), those most suggestive of literacy in the modern sense (chapter 6), and those in which the two blend and intertwine in interesting, significant, and more inseparable ways (chapter 7). We emphasize in each of the next three sections, however, that in all cases the written informs the oral and vice versa. The situation in the Hebrew Scriptures thus beautifully parallels that of epigraphic, nonbiblical materials in which we emphasized the need to understand the written work in terms of the oral world and to appreciate the oral-traditional aspects of Israelite culture, fully aware of the existence and availability of writing especially to certain members of the community and for particular purposes. These somewhat circumscribed uses of writing nevertheless had significant influence on Israel's economic, political, and social worlds.

THE ORAL END OF THE CONTINUUM

One of the indicators of a traditional-style culture, in which modern literacy is not the norm, is the special sort of respect accorded writing, the aura that surrounds it, its links to the realm of the supernatural, its capacity to effect transformation, its magical properties and power.[1] Another is the way in which writing is treated as an icon, a memorial, or monument. We might consult ancient writing on a stone to glean information about a bygone culture. We write nowadays to preserve records and facts, our thoughts, or literary creations, making them available for future consultation. The written object in oral-traditional settings, however, serves a more fully symbolic function as a testament to a people's shared sense of the group, as a reminder of what is important. The function of writing in an oral culture is more "wholesale," than retail.

These magical and memorial aspects of writing in an oral world emerged in our study of epigraphic materials in the curses, blessings, and amulets on the one hand and in the monumental texts and graffiti on the other. Both aspects of an oral mentality are richly represented in the writings of the Hebrew Bible as well.

GOD'S WRITING

Bengt Holbek notes that even in cultures in which writing, its existence and possibilities, is quite familiar to the general population, nevertheless notions remain of "special" writing that are rooted ultimately in "what the illiterate think of writing"—in an oral culture.[2] In this category of special writing are the many biblical references to God's writing.

The two tablets of the testimony, tablets of stone given to Moses on Sinai, are written with the finger of God (Ex. 31:18). The power of the deity, anthropomorphized, is like an electrical current or a laser beam. The finger directs the power to etch in stone the message of God. The importance of the tablets, their role in linking God and Israel, in assuring God's presence and wishes among them, is greatly enhanced by this notion of God's own writing, a point emphasized at Exodus 32:16: "The tablets are the work of God, the writing is the writing of God engraved upon the tablets." Through the medium of writing, the laws shimmer with the power of the one who spoke them; through writing, God is invested in the tablets. (See also Deut. 9:10; 4:13; 5:22.) The tablets, moreover, are rewritten by God after they are broken (Deut. 10:2, 4; Ex. 34:1; see also 2 Kings 17:37.) The supramundane power of the oral event at Sinai when God speaks out the fire and the mountain burns with fire and is enveloped by darkness and cloud (see the description at Deut. 4:11) also attaches to the process whereby God's words become tactile, visible, and moveable.

The numinous power of writing emerges also in Daniel 5, a story set in the period of the neo-Babylonian Empire but composed or set down in its current form in the Hellenistic period when writing as a medium is a very familiar phenomenon, a tool used to compose and to write down a variety of genres. Indeed, the second century B.C.E. is the manuscript date of a small number of actual pieces of biblical text found among the Dead Sea Scrolls. While none of this is to suggest that modern-style literacy was common and general even in this late biblical period, it is to suggest that people would be quite familiar with writing and its various uses in their culture and yet that the concept of writing as infused with the otherworldly, special, and unfamiliar remained appealing and strong. The evidence of an oral world shines through the use of written words. As Holbek notes, in such cultures an otherworldly quality is attributed to special writing that is archaic (e.g., runes) or foreign or as in this case to writing that is familiar and yet unintelligible, like writing seen through a glass darkly.

The tale in Aramaic describes how in the midst of a royal banquet at the court of Belshazzar, all of a sudden the fingers of a human's hand appear and write upon the wall of the palace. The eerie scene unhinges the king, who calls to his enchanters and wisemen (note the use of one of the formulas discussed in chapter 1): "Any person who can read this writing and tell me its interpretation will be dressed in purple, have a chain of gold set upon his neck and have power as third in the kingdom (Dan. 5:7)." In accordance with the traditional narrative pattern found also in Genesis 41 and Daniel 2, the king's men can neither read nor interpret the writing. Daniel is called and reads the phrase aloud "MENE MENE TEKEL PARSIN" (5:25). The terms "*mene mene tekel parsin*" are monetary units in Aramaic. They have a rhythmical, incantation quality when spoken, an assonance based on the repetition of "e." Even these terms once read appear to be nonsense. It is as if one said "nickel nickel dime penny." It is very much within this orally based framework of magical letters and mysterious writing that the scene continues.

Daniel interprets the terms via wordplay, a technique used for dream interpretation throughout the Near East. That is, if one dreams of an image that is an elephant (*pil*), the interpreter may suggest that "wonders" (*pĕlāʾôt*) are in your future (see *b. Ber.* 56b).

Indeed, techniques of dream interpretation and word interpretation intermingle in Rabbinic literature. Dreamers dream of Torah passages that require explanation and application to their life situations, while the very exercise of midrash reflects techniques in wordplay and idea association typical of dream interpretation. The oral world does not cease with the close of the biblical canon even among the Rabbinic élite but continues with the very process of Rabbinic commentary, so seemingly scholastic and literate an activity. Thus the oral continues to inform the written.

Another example of the important interplay between the written and the oral in the worldview of Israelites having to do with "divine writing" is the motif of God's record book. In some texts God is perceived as keeper of the ultimate record, a book that seems to indicate each person's fate based upon their merit and God's choices (Isa. 4:3; Dan. 12:1; Ex. 32:32; Mal. 3:16; Ps. 69:29 [English v. 28]; Ps. 139:16; Isa. 65:6). On the one hand, the motif of God's record seems to belong at the literate end of the scale—even God keeps records, Santa Claus-like, to keep track of important information concerning his charges (e.g., Mal. 3:16). Most of these references to God's book are in late biblical passages. As we will show below, the chronological weight of biblical passages that seem to emphasize the "literate" end of the continuum (e.g., the use of letters, references to records, quotations of written texts) is postexilic. And yet the notion of a heavenly book puts this biblical example of record keeping on an oral and mystical plane. God's books in Dan. 12:1 and Ps. 139:16 have the quality of predetermination. The magic book predicts and brings about events, ensuring a particular future with knowledge beyond the mundane (139:6, 16), part and parcel of God's capacity as creator. Moreover the book appears to hold the person's life force within it. The inscribed name is a virtual life token like the many amulets, sacred swords, and secret jewels of traditional heroes. Break the sword or crush the amulet and the hero dies. So too, blot out the name and in a scribbler's form of sympathetic magic, the person dies. In Ex. 32:32, 33, "blotting out the name from the book" is an idiom for "kill" or "cause to die," an idiom rooted in a concept of divine writing informed by the oral end of the continuum even while it connotes writing in a more literate-style, record-keeping mode.

TRANSFORMATIONS

As discussed in connection with tomb inscriptions and graffiti, the name written down and iconized conveys the essence of the named person or group. Thus the blotting out of the name in the divine book erases the person, and in several passages the transformation or manipulation of the name effects a wider transformation.

Numbers 17 describes the aftermath of the Korah rebellion in which certain Israelites challenge the absolute power and leadership of Moses and Aaron of the tribe of Levi. God intervenes to settle the dispute. The names of the leaders of each ancestral house are to be written on separate staffs, one for each man. The staff of the man whom Yahweh chooses as leader will sprout or bud (Num. 17:17–20 [English vv. 2–5]). The one that blossoms is, of course, that of Moses's brother, thereby confirming his right to leadership. The blossoming staff is to be set up as a permanent warning of death to rebels (17:25; English 17:10). Thus through the writing upon them, the staffs become symbols of persons and markers of status, assuring Aaron's elevation as one chosen by God.

In Ezekiel 37:16, 17, God commands Ezekiel to write "for Judah" on one stick and "for Joseph" on the other and to join them together. The writing on sticks is thus involved in a prophetic sign act symbolizing, predicting, and in Israelite worldview helping to bring about the reunification of Northern and Southern Israelite kingdoms and the return of all exiles to the land. (See the interpretation at 37:21–28.) In Numbers 17 and Ezekiel 37 written names thus are involved in the representation of and manipulation of status, magically endowed, symbolic, and iconic.

The manipulation of written words to determine status is at the heart of the ritual for the woman accused by her husband of adultery. In this case no supporting witnesses are available and as in the situation in which a murdered person is found without evidence of the perpetrator (Deut. 21:1–9), through ritual actions God is asked to mediate and set matters to rest one way or another, thereby allowing the community to move on and set aside a cause for social rupture. In this androcentric culture, the wife's fidelity is central to social neatness and underscores the importance of traceable, well-maintained patrilineages. The family is a microcosm of society at large. Doubt and accusation are unhealthy and disruptive. One could write at length about possible implications of the ritual as described in Num. 5:11–31 for understanding the social position and status of women in ancient Israel or at least for understanding a particular priestly view of women as preserved in Numbers. For our interest in attitudes to writing, the key part of the ritual is the writing down on a scroll the curse to be suffered by a guilty woman. The writing is then to be washed off into a concoction called "the water of bitterness" (5:23, 24), which the accused is made to drink. If the curse has its effect, she becomes "an execration among her people," if not she is to be rehabilitated. The words are visceral and potent. The curse's potential is physically invested in the words. This ritual reflects the illiterate's attitude to writing and testifies to the power of words.

It is in this context that one needs to understand Ezekiel's swallowing the scroll (2:9–3:11). The scroll offered to Ezekiel in a visionary trance, appears in a stretched out hand. Note the passive "stretched out" that avoids mentioning whose hand it is. "He" or "It" (is it the source of the voice in 1:28, the likeness of the glory of the Lord [1:28], the owner of the hand [2:9]?) spreads out the scroll; it has writing on the front and back—words of lamentation and mourning and woe. He asks Ezekiel to eat the scroll, and the prophet eats. The scroll tastes sweet as honey. This is Ezekiel's initiation vision, a vision in which he is literally filled with words of God. The scene has the dreamlike quality of the visionary experience, and is expressed in metaphors for the numinous. The prophet sees not God but "the appearance of the likeness."[3] The details of the scroll, moreover, are obscure—the prophet can tell there are words of lamentation, mourning, and woe, but it is as if only bits can be seen from the corner of his eye.[4] The messages Ezekiel goes on to convey are varied and often more specific. The written scroll is to be absorbed and swallowed, not as Ellen Davis suggests because future communication is to be "swallowed," written and not oral,[5] but because the prophet is transformed into a medium through his literal absorption of God's words. Verse 4 orders the prophet to "*speak* in my words to them." Thus the scroll and its general message of lamentation have become one with the prophet. Like the woman accused of adultery, he is being physically acted upon by the words, his future status determined by the words within him. The words are transformative in a real, physical sense.

TRANSFORMATIVE
AND TESTIMONIAL

In addition to passages concerning "God's writing" and ones in which writing contains the essence of the person or effects her transformation, an Israelite oral mentality is revealed in a host of passages in which writing serves a testimonial, symbolic, or iconic function. In a number of these passages, the testimonial also is transformative, and in each case, literate and oral mentalities coexist although the oral in these cases dominates.

Ezekiel 24:2 begins in what seems to be quite a literate mode. With God in the role of boss and the prophet as secretary, the former asks the latter to take a memo. "Human, write down for yourself the name of the day, this very day. The king of Babylon has laid siege to Jerusalem on this very day." Does God want the prophet to record the date for future historians? Is he to write down a fact in order to allow for better remembrance than keeping the date in mind? All of this seems at first very much like record keeping in a modern literate mode, and perhaps on one level it is. And yet the written message is coupled with a ritually evocative *mashal* to be spoken, the *mashal* of the boiling pot that describes Jerusalem as an unclean, bloodied vessel, whose "filth" must be consumed by fire, and with this coupling the written message becomes more than a memo or record. It becomes a witness to, a signal of, and perhaps like the scene of the boiling pot, also an agent in the invasion, pressing it forward. Something big has happened and "I will judge you" (24:14).

Writing is linked to imminent or eventual military defeat in Isaiah 8:1. The catchy phrase "The spoil hurries, the booty hastens!" that the prophet is ordered to write on a large tablet "in the engraving of humans" (or "with a human's stylus") is to be witnessed by witnesses (Isa. 8:2). Again the literate world presents itself, a world of records and witnesses, but one quickly sees that legalese and incantation are one. The phrase on the tablet is also assigned as a name for the prophet's son, borne of a prophetess (the prophet's wife or a woman taken for the express purpose of creating a living symbol of the invasion). The writing here is not record keeping but performs a magical transformative purpose, a sign act in the symbols of writing. The tablet serves as icon and witness to the prophet's prediction, but it is also more transitive, helping to bring about the destruction itself through the power of written words (see also Jer. 51:60, discussed below).

The border between writing for remembrance that suggests a literate mentality and writing as icon and transformer evocative of the oral world is apparent also in Ex. 17:14–16. After the defeat of Amalek, one of Israel's archetypal enemies recalled in negative terms throughout the tradition, the Lord declares to Moses "Write this as a memorial in a register" (upon a document, *sēper*) and literally "put it in the ears of Joshua," that is, "say it aloud in the hearing of Joshua that I will surely erase the memory of Amalek from under heaven." On the one hand, the writing is an aid to memory—on the other, the words need to be said aloud to be comprehended and absorbed. That which is written ironically speaks of erasure, of wiping out. The term, moreover, for "remembrance," *zikkārôn,* also means "memorial" or "testi-monial" as in references to a variety of objects elsewhere in the Hebrew Bible (e.g., stones in the Jordan [Josh. 4:7]; stones of ephod [Ex. 28:12; 29]). Again strongly iconic nuances enter. The written down phrase serves to identify and encapsulate Amalek's status and indeed like a curse or bless-ing helps to make permanent Amalek's status as defeated enemy. It is not merely a matter of remembering but a matter of making physical, real, and lasting the Israelites' hopes concerning a group that threatens them.

A number of other brief references to writing in the Hebrew Bible testify to the testimonial roles writing is perceived to play. For example, at Job 19:23 the righteous sufferer Job says,

> Would, then, that my words were written
> Would that they were inscribed in a document
> With a pen of iron and with lead
> Forever upon a rock might they be carved
> For I know my redeemer lives.

This little text provides all sorts of reminders about modes of writing in an-cient Israel, materials and methods used, and the fact that a *sēper* is not a book but a text or document. But why does Job want his words to be writ-ten down? He goes on to say that his redeemer lives and that he will finally achieve vindication—perhaps only after his death. The Hebrew at this point is problematical. Is the writing a means of preserving his case, the argument for his innocence available even once he is gone? On one level this may be the case, but on another, perhaps deeper level, the writing also serves to preserve Job himself forever, a memorial and testimony, an eternal monu-ment to what he perceives to be truth.

This orally based nuance of the testimonial also attaches to the writing at Isa. 30:8:

> Now, go and write it on a tablet before them
> Upon a writing surface inscribe it
> And let it be for the time to come.
> Forever [or "as a testimony"] and [for] ever.

To what does the object "it" refer? In the NRSV the text has been set up to imply that this command is a rubric introducing the oracle that follows, a lawsuit accusing Israel of rebellion and promising punishment. Is it God's word (v. 12) that is to be heeded and written down? Or does the writing down refer to the difficult-to-translate epithet that precedes in verse 7? This phrase is applied to Egypt, Judah's sometimes ally that the prophet rejects as worthless. Protection money is paid to Egypt in vain for she is "Rahab who sits still." The writing down of this mocking name for Egypt serves as a metonymic standard critical of Judean foreign policy, a policy not sufficiently rooted in the Yahweh-trusting isolationism of the biblical prophets. This brief encapsulation of Israel's foolhardy faithlessness leads beautifully to the longer excursus in 30:9–17 in which they are said to ignore proper prophecy, trusting in oppression and deceit (v. 12), in military prowess (15–16).

The iconic function of writing allows for the metaphor at Jer. 17:1:

> The sin of Judah is written with an iron stylus;
>> With a diamond point it is engraved on the tablet of their heart,
>> and upon the horns of your altars.

Similarly, the opposite theme of faithfulness to God is represented in writing at Isa. 44:5. "This one will write on his hand 'For Yahweh' or 'belonging to Yahweh.'" In a similar category is the engraving on a ritual object for the clothing of the high priest (Ex. 28:36; also 39:30; 29:6). His turban is to have tied upon it a "rosette," possibly a shiny plate on which is engraved "Holy to the Lord," like the engraving upon a signet. Like the signet, the "rosette" identifies Aaron, is a metonymic marker of his identity, in this case a marker designed to reflect his status as a mediator between Israel and God (see Ex. 28:38), a marker that in a more transitive fashion makes him holy. More than a reminder, more than a symbol, the writing helps to remake Aaron in a visceral and real sense.

Perhaps the most important writing in all of Jewish tradition that underscores the tensions and continuities between oral and literate mentalities is the Torah itself. Surely the Bible's most prominent act of dictation is when Moses is commanded by God to write down the commandments on tablets (Ex. 24:4; 34:28); the "words of the Torah on a writing surface" (*sēper*, a more generic term than "tablet" or "scroll"; Deut. 31:24). Michael Coogan has suggested that the dictation texts contrast with those in which God is said to write the law with his own hand, the former being later in date and evidence of a growing literate mentality.[6] While I am not as confident about the source-critical assumptions that lie behind Coogan's dating of the texts or about the relative chronology itself, nevertheless these images of Moses as God's scribe do lie closer to the literate end of the continuum than God's own writing. On the other hand, attitudes to written Torah evidence the oral mentality as well, especially in the various echoes or imitations of the first setting down of the law. One thinks, for example, of Deut. 27:3. Upon crossing the Jordan and entering the land, the people are to set up large stones and cover them in plaster and then write upon them "all the words of this law [lit. Torah]" (Deut. 27:3). By "this law" the writer appears to mean some form of or portion of Deuteronomy (see also 17:18–19 where the phrase may mean laws pertaining to kingship).

Joshua 8:30–32 includes the fulfillment of Moses' commandment to write the law on stones. In this version as in Deuteronomy 27:8, "the stones" seem to be unhewn stones of the altar (see Deut. 27:5–6, 8). The stones then serve as an icon of the covenant, backdrop for the ritual of blessings and curses (28:33–35). Similarly, in Deut. 31:24–26 after Moses finishes writing down "the words of this Torah upon a writing surface until they were complete," he commands that the document be placed next to the ark of the covenant "that it be there a witness ['*ēd*] among you." The selection of the term "testimony" or "witness" is an interesting one seen before (Isa. 30:8) that underscores the memorial and iconic function of the writing. This way of looking at the function of writing sheds new light on the custom described at Deut. 6:9 and 11:20, the placing of the words of the Torah "on the doorposts of your house and upon your gates" to be discussed in more detail below. As Thomas notes with regard to some Greek epigraphic specimens, the writing in these cases is not to provide a record of the words in case they are forgotten. Rather everyone knows what the stone altar of Joshua 8 commemorates; the writing invests the stones with the power of Torah. The stones preserve the message of Torah but in a "wholesale" rather than "retail" fashion.[7] Thus the function of such written objects is more at the oral end of the continuum between orality and literacy. Proverbs 3:3 and 7:3 urge one to bind the commandments around your neck (on your fingers, 7:3) and to write them on the tablet of your heart, metaphorically playing on the iconic quality of writing.

The line between this iconic, symbolic, and suggestive function and a practical function of providing a record that can be retrieved, employed to preserve information, can, of course, be a thin one (see Ex. 17:14; 1 Sam. 10:25; Deut. 31:19). When Samuel tells the people the rights and duties of kingship, "he wrote it down in a document and laid it up before God" (1 Sam. 10:25). On the one hand, information is preserved, a code of conduct created, but is this not the preparation of a covenantal witness of iconic significance? A monumental nuance is present as perhaps in all our great documents, for example, the Bill of Rights or the Constitution. Deuteronomy 31:19 seems to describe a process in the literate mode whereby a song, which is to be orally delivered (see v. 30 and use of the term "to speak"), is to be written down in order that it be taught to the people, who can then recite it and know it. The technology of writing ensures that the song will not be lost and allows it to be passed on. But the written text as in oral cultures is an aid to oral performance and again is called a testimony or witness (*'ēd*), underlining its monumental function.

An interesting mixture of writing as an icon and writing in a more literate mode is found at Joshua 24, the covenant-making scene at Shechem. In mimesis of Moses, as so often in the Book of Joshua, Joshua makes statutes and ordinances, and writes these words in "the document [*sēper*] of the Torah of God" (24:26). Then he sets up a large stone that he declares to be a witness or testimony, *'ēdāh* (24:26–27). One wonders if Joshua is imagined to be writing a next installment on the very Torah written down by Moses. (Of course it is never entirely clear if each of these mentioned Torahs is the same one or what "torah" means [see chapter 6].) The instructions to Joshua do seem to imply the concept of teachings preserved in writing.

Our study of the "oral" end of the continuum thus leads full circle to the literate end. Throughout we have found that the oral and the written interact in important ways and that appreciation for this interaction is essential for understanding the Israelite worldview. Israelite writing is set in an oral context. Biblical passages that present "God's writing," that emphasize the magical and transformative capabilities of writing and the iconic, monumental, or testimonial functions of written texts all testify to the liveliness and importance of the oral mentality. We turn now to a selection of passages that emphasize the literate end of the continuum, but again the quality of the oral emerges in these texts as well.

CHAPTER 6

The Literate End
of the Continuum

SIGNATURES, LEGAL DOCUMENTS

The Hebrew Bible presents a most basic use of writing in a literate mode in the signing or preparation of legal documents. The signing and sealing of a deed of purchase at Jer. 32:10, 12, 44 provide an example.

God commands Jeremiah to buy his cousin's field at Anathoth, his to redeem by purchase from his kinsman. The buying of this field in the land of Benjamin is a sign act, representing in the midst of Babylonian invasion (32:36) God's promise that the people will return to their land and holdings. It represents, moreover, the prophet's confidence in the future and the ultimate survival, stability, and fulfillment of God's covenant through the land (32:21–22). While defeat and exile appear to be on the immediate horizon, the land will be repossessed, ancient clan holdings kept intact.

A written deed of purchase is signed by Jeremiah, sealed, and witnessed (32:10). The sealed deed of purchase is said to contain terms and conditions. There is as well an open copy, as appears to have been customary in deed keeping elsewhere in the ancient Near East.[1] The open copy could be available for easy reference. Jeremiah gives the deed and its copy to Baruch, son of Neriah, in the presence of the witnesses and his cousin and the Judeans sitting in the court of the guard. Then Jeremiah charges Baruch to place the sealed deed and the open deed in a clay jar for long-term storage in accordance with God's wishes.

This scene offers great insight into the use of writing in the literate mode: A document is made in duplicate, signed before witnesses in a judicial setting, the original is sealed, and both copies are stored for future reference. The scene, of course, serves the symbolic purposes of representing Israel's hopes for the future even when facing defeat. Nevertheless the use of writing is at the literate end of the continuum. The writing of a certificate of divorce (Deut. 24:1, 3) is another example of use of the technology of writing for legal purposes.

This notion of putting one's name on a binding legal document or setting down in writing a legal exchange carries over into a text such as Neh. 10:1 (9:38 in English) in which the people sign a new agreement to follow God, a sealed document. The question even with this basic use of writing, as Thomas would remind us, is whether such documents carry the modern nuance of simple record keeping or something more: the magical use of writing to bring about and ensure what is in the writing, the physical placement of the self in an agreement through the use of the name in letters or the signature on a scroll that is an aspect of, a physical continuation of, or a representation of the self. Perhaps such nuances even nowadays attach to signatures and certain life-passage documents such as marriage licenses and birth certificates. It is interesting that the author of Neh. 10:1 envisions the makers of covenant to participate in a legal, written agreement, whereas the author of Ex. 19:8 has the people agree only orally. In Josh. 24:21, 22, 24 also people agree orally, although the oral agreement is followed by writing in a document (v. 26).[2]

LETTERS

Another set of texts employing the term "to write" that seem appropriate to modern notions of literacy are letters. One need not take a position on the authenticity of one or another letter, but the writers who refer to these letters assume that they are a means of communicating across geographic distances[3] as are our own letters. Some references are to the official correspondence of royalty, for example, Huram (Hiram) of Tyre's letter to Solomon written in connection with plans to build the temple in Jerusalem (2 Chron. 2:10 [v. 11 in English]), or public decrees. (These include, for example, Esth. 3:12, the edict to kill the Jews; 2 Chron. 30:1, Hezekiah's invitation to celebrate the Passover in Jerusalem; Esth. 9:20–23, Mordecai's letters to the Jews concerning the celebration of 14 Adar; see also 9:29, Esther's letter, and Esth. 8:8; 8:5; 8:10; 1:19.) Some are accusatory; for example, Ezra 4:7–16, the letter written by Bishlam, Mithredath, Tabeel, and their comrades to King Artaxerxes to derail the returned exiles' building projects, and the king's response (Ezra 4:17–22). Such an accusatory letter relates to another genre of written communication, the *lettre de cachet:* the communiqué to place Uriah in the forefront of the battle (2 Sam. 11:14, 15); Jehu's communiqué to the elders of Jezreel to dispatch with Ahab's seventy sons (2 Kings 10:1, 6, 7); the false accusation against Naboth (1 Kings 21:8, 9). (See also Job 31:35; perhaps also Job 13:26.) Partaking of the interplay between oral and written discussed by Finnegan, Thomas, and others are texts such as

Ezra 1:1 (2 Chron. 36:22) referring to a written edict of Cyrus that is also spread in the land orally by herald. Similarly, Elijah is said to engage in a long-distance form of prophecy, sending a letter to King Jehoram of Judah. This passage at 2 Chron. 21:12–15 is not represented in the Deuteronomistic corpus (see at 2 Kings 8). At 2 Chron. 32:17 Sennacherib is pictured to have written letters to "deride" God—letters that are read aloud as a public proclamation to frighten the Israelites. Here communiqué, curse text, oral and written merge.

It is worth noting that this intertwining of written and oral communication with special emphasis on the former is found particularly in postexilic material (see also the written agreement to the covenant discussed above [Neh. 10:1]). Indeed the vast majority of references to letters are late. Note, for example, that Hiram's response to Solomon in the Deuteronomistic passage parallel to the story of the building of the temple in 2 Chronicles 2 does not introduce Hiram's words of response with reference to a letter or writing (1 Kings 5:21–22 [English vv. 7–8]; cf. 2 Chron. 2:10 [English v. 11]). The later writer of Chronicles frequently adds the accoutrements of a more literate mentality to the earlier version in the Deuteronomistic History. The epigraphic corpus offers many actual examples of letters from the period of the monarchy. One does not mean to imply that letters are a postexilic phenomenon or the like. Nevertheless, late biblical authors of Ezra-Nehemiah, 1 and 2 Chronicles, and Esther certainly refer to letters as recordlike documents on file, as proof for certain claims of reliability, or as testaments to the importance and factuality of certain decrees. Are not dreams and visions used for similar purposes in other, more orally informed biblical texts?

RECORDS, ANNALS

Another group of texts employing the term *ktb*, "to write," that appear to be closer to the literate than oral end of the continuum involve references to records and annals.

In the priestly text of Num. 11:26, Eldad and Medad are said to be among those "written." The reference is to a list or genealogical record, an issue important to the book of Numbers. Similarly in Neh. 7:5, the governor Nehemiah states in his memoir that he found the "document of the genealogy" of those who first returned (to the land) and that written in it was a long list provided in verses 7–60. Nehemiah also cites those who could not prove their descent from these records (vv. 61–64). In a genealogy of 1 Chronicles certain ancestors (those who came in the days of King Hezekiah and exterminated native inhabitants of the land, displacing them) are described as "written by name" (1 Chron. 4:41). 1 Chronicles 4:22 should possibly be translated "the records [*haddĕbārîm*] are ancient." Frequently one finds the rubric *dibrê ḥayyāmîm,* literally "the matters or acts of the days," or the rubric *dibrê* and a named person: for example, the matters of the prophet Nathan (2 Chron. 9:29), of the prophet Shemiah (2 Chron. 12:15; see also 2 Chron. 20:34; 33:18, 19), or the formula and variations upon it "written in the document (*sēper* = document) of the matters of the days of so and so" (Esth. 2:23; 10:2; Neh. 12:23; 1 Kings 15:31, 14:19, 11:41, 16:5; 2 Kings 21:17), or more briefly "the document of the kings of Judah and Israel" (2 Chron. 16:11; 27:7).

Within a story such as Esther, the king is pictured to be able to retrieve and consult records in a very modern way. Thus Ahasuerus is pictured on a sleepless night, having his court "annals" read to him, literally "the document of remembrances," "the acts of days" (Esth. 6:1). Is he searching for the cause of his insomnia or catching up on his "paperwork," seeking entertainment or engaging in a form of counting sheep? He does not read to himself—again the oral world presents itself—but it is assumed that the writing down of happenings provides an aid for memory. Writing is for purposes of record keeping.

In works presenting themselves as historiographic chronicles, the reader is offered an impression that the written text is an epitome of a fuller record that can be consulted, proof, as in some of the references to letters, of the veracity of the report, conveying an impression of reliability. It matters not if such works existed or not, except to those who attempt to portray biblical writers as early historical researchers. For our question of orality and literacy, such references imply a respect for written records. The author thinks he should refer to them.

Equally interesting within some of these rubrics is the implication that prophets such as Nathan, Samuel, and Gad are the keepers of records/acts or at least that records/acts are said to have gathered around the names of the prophets. (See 1 Chron. 29:29; 2 Chron. 9:29; and the difficult to translate 2 Chron. 33:19, on the "records" of the "seers"[?].) The parallel place in the Deuteronomistic corpus, 2 Kings 21:17–18, contains no such references to the seers' records. In a similar vein, 2 Chron. 26:22 refers to the "remaining acts/matters/chronicles of Uzziah, the first ones and the last ones wrote Isaiah ben Amoz, the prophet." See also 2 Chron. 32:32, "the good acts of Hezekiah written in the vision of the prophet Isaiah son of Amoz in the Book of the Kings of Judah and Israel." Compare to Isa. 1:1. "The *vision* of Isaiah, the son of Amoz, which he saw concerning Judah and Jerusalem in the days of Uzziah." These late biblical authors not only allude to records and show themselves of a reading, history-keeping mode but even transform oral transmitters of oracles and ecstatic seers of visions into archivists. The worldview here is at the literate end of the continuum, even while the tales reported or expanded continue to exhibit traditional style. It is, of course, tempting to speculate on what the Chronicler understands the Book of the Kings of Judah and Israel to be, a version of the Deuteronomistic History, a large work that once included what we now call Isaiah, some part of the tradition. Ultimately it is something kept in writing.

In the work of the Chronicler one also finds two intriguing references to materials "written upon the *midraš* of the document of the kings" (2 Chron. 24:27); "written in the *midraš* of the prophet Iddo" (2 Chron. 13:22). How is the root *drš* used here? The NRSV translation at 2 Chronicles 13:22, a "story," does not really do justice to the biblical root "to search" or "to seek" and is perhaps a back formation based on our knowledge of later Jewish use of the term. Midrash does become, in part, story or narration. The root meaning suggested by the term is, in fact, somewhat more scholastic and interpretative. "Commentary" (NRSV, 2 Chron. 24:27) seems better. Was there a Book of Kings, referred to also frequently in the Deuteronomistic History, and a commentary upon it? Were commentaries attributed to the prophet Iddo? References to a derivative literature, whether or not the Book of the Kings or a commentary on it existed, nevertheless, again suggest in this late work of the Chronicler a literate mentality. Of course it would have been possible for an oral commentary to exist on a reasonably fixed earlier oral tradition. The classical Rabbis would contend that midrash was an oral elaboration of a written Torah. These passages, however, refer to "*writings upon/in*," "things *written* in." Second Chronicles 35:25 also refers to material written in "the laments." Is this another collection of written materials? In 2 Chron. 35:4 are instructions to follow the writing of David the king and the writing of Solomon, his son. Clearly here is an author who believes that writing serves to preserve and hand on information and that kings would leave such written instructions behind.

Such instructions provide directions for a current situation, for example, how to celebrate the Passover in the time of Josiah. Reference to a written work validates an author's account of a piece of the tradition at Josh. 10:13. Poetry about the sun standing still for Joshua must be true: "Is it not written in the document of Jashar?" Again what interests us is not whether the Book of Jashar existed as a source for a biblical historiographer but that the preserver or composer of this piece of tradition feels called upon to make reference to a written account. This does appear to be a worldview in which written is better, in which tradition preserved in writing is tradition to be believed.

Also interesting in this context is 2 Sam. 1:18. The mourning song for Saul and Jonathan, the Song of the Bow, is said to be composed by David or "intoned" ("to compose a lament" NRSV; literally "to lament a lament"). An oral context is assumed. David says to teach "The Bow" to the Judahites. "Behold it is written upon the document of Jashar." This line may mean that it is recorded that David said to teach the song or that the lament has now been written in the Book of Jashar, in which case the author is imagining a process of oral composition and/or performance, oral transmission and fixing in memory, and writing down for preservation, which bring us to our next category.

COMPOSITION IN WRITING AND THE
WRITING DOWN OF ORAL COMPOSITIONS

Another large set of biblical material employing the term *ktb* specifically refers to the writing down of oral material or to an act of composition in writing, whether the writing is creative or expository.

The teacher of Eccles. 12:10 is said to write words of truth plainly (MT *kātûb;* other manuscript traditions: *wĕkātab*), while Proverbs 22:20, one of the so-called "words of the wise," inquires, "Have I not written for you (the day before yesterday [so the consonantal, written tradition (K)]; thirty measures of [so the vocalized, read tradition (Q)]) counsels and knowledge." References to enumeration and list making in writing are found at Judg. 8:14; Isa. 10:19; 1 Chron. 24:6; Ezra 8:34. Joshua 18:8, 9 refers to the "writing up" of a description of the land, its cities, and suggests a surveyor's report or record: literally "write down the land." Similarly, at Num. 33:2 Moses is said to write down the Israelites' travel itinerary by command of the Lord. The rubric "and these are their stages" is followed by an outline or list. As we have seen earlier, reference to a written source—in this case a composition commanded by God under particular circumstances—is used to validate the tradition, to imply that this really is the way things were. Isaiah 38:9 provides another case of writing down that is close to the literate end of the oral-literate continuum. Hezekiah composes a poem upon the occasion of his recovery from illness. The rubric for this personal lament is *miktāb lĕḥizqiyyāhû,* "a writing of Hezekiah," not a "song" but a "writing." Perhaps the term *miktāb* need not literally refer to writing any more than the *dbr* root need refer to speech. Nevertheless, the rubric implies that compositions can be thought of as written.

One of the clearest examples of oral material that is written down is Jeremiah's dictation of prophecy to Baruch (see also Jer. 45:1). We will have more to say about the famous passage in Jeremiah 36 and its implicit attitudes to oral and written in a moment. Another interesting example discussed above with references to writing in testimonial and transformative modes is Exodus 17:14.

REFERENCES TO WRITTEN TORAH

Perhaps the most frequent recurring use of "to write," *ktb,* is in reference to torah. In each case, the question arises whether the reference to torah is a general wholesale appeal to the right way, acknowledged to be preserved in a written sacred source, or to torah as record, a means of ascertaining how to perform a ritual, or the date of a holiday, or what exactly David did say concerning the temple. Is the rubric "as it is written" a wholesale reference to validate a position or a request to examine a specific source for details? In either event, it is significant that the appeal is to what is treated as a set, written tradition. Such appeals imply a mentality at the literate end of the continuum. Yet even in this case, given what Gene Ulrich has shown about manuscript variations in the postbiblical Qumran corpus, "set" needs be understood in terms of an "oral register" as described by Foley and O'Keeffe. That is, various versions of the "text" are considered to be the same text. This is a different sort of appeal to literacy and the written tradition than our own, one grounded in an oral mentality.

A general reference to the tradition that is considered to be enshrined in writing is found at Dan. 9:11: "The curse and the oath that are written in the Torah of Moses, the servant of God, have been poured out upon us because we sinned against him" (see also 9:13). Similarly, David advises Solomon, his son, to keep God's laws, commandments, ordinances, and testimonies as it is written in the Torah of Moses (1 Kings 2:3), and Josh. 1:8 declares "This Book of the Torah shall not depart out of your mouth, meditate upon it day and night in order that you take care to do all that is written in it." The written torah is to be spoken (reoralized) and thought about. The assumption may well be that all reading is done aloud. Thus to read is to speak, as is typical of premodern literate cultures.

The reference at Deut. 28:58 to "the words/matters of this Torah that are written in this document" also appears to be a general appeal to biblical law. Does "this document" refer to the writing upon the plastered stones that provide the monument on Mount Ebal (27:2–8), to some version of Deuteronomy, or to some notion of the larger Torah? (See also Deut. 29:20, 28 [English v. 27]). It is also ambiguous as to what Jer. 25:13 refers to: "I will bring upon that land all my words that I spoke against it, all that is written on this document [*sēper*] that Jeremiah prophecied against all the nations." Is the text an implicit written collection of Jeremiah's prophecies (Jer. 30:2), a more specific reference to curses uttered against Babylon? In any event, the writtenness of the material is assumed and lends credibility to the predictions of Jeremiah.

Another set of references to what is "written in the document" (*sēper,* often translated "book") refers to the document said to be found by the priest Hilkiah that influences the Judean king, Josiah, and his reform: the curses written within it (2 Chron. 34:24); the ancestors not acting in accordance with what was written in it (2 Chron. 34:21); the need to follow commands written in the document (2 Kings 23:3; 24). Once again this is a general reference to the Yahwistic agenda outlined in Josiah's reforms in 2 Kings 23 that is assumed to be written down. We will have more to say about the place of this interesting text in the oral-literate continuum in chapter 7.

MORE SPECIFIC REFERENCES
TO DETAILS OF TORAH

In a somewhat different category closer to the literate end of the continuum are references to specific laws in the Torah, the quite conscious use of what is often presented as quotation from scripture to encourage or support an action by the community.

Deuteronomy 17:18 declares explicitly that a king will himself write or have a copy of this torah written for him in the presence of Levitical priests. He will read in it (not have it read to him) so that he will know what to do (see further in chapter 7). Joshua 8:31 makes reference to written prescriptions concerning an altar of whole stones upon which no one has wielded iron (Ex. 20:24, 25; esp. Deut. 27:5, 6 with the references to "whole"). Second Chronicles 30:5, 18 and 2 Kings 23:21 refer to keeping the Passover as prescribed in "the document [*sēper*] of the covenant. " Josiah, as described in 2 Kings 23, but especially in the account in 2 Chronicles 30, is organizing a Jerusalem-based, centralized Passover celebration as prescribed in the Deuteronomic tradition (Deuteronomy 16), one at odds with the home-based Passover enjoined in Exodus 12. Thus this "book of the covenant" (2 Kings 23:2) or keeping Passover as is "written" (2 Chron. 30:5, 18) refers to Deuteronomic Torah. Hence scholars' understandable, if historicist, suggestion that the "found book" in 2 Kings 22:8, the guide to reform, was some actual version of Deuteronomy. It is interesting that in both versions of the account of Josiah's Passover, it is Deuteronomic tradition that provides the written validation. Not everyone in Israel is portrayed as convinced or impressed by Deuteronomic prescriptions for a centralized Passover celebration, as 2 Chron. 30:10 indicates.

Equally interesting is that rules for distributing burnt offerings said to be written in the *sēper* of Moses are not found explicitly in Deuteronomy or any other place in the law (2 Chron. 35:12). It is not important that the rule be written but that it be *believed* to be written and that its being believed to be written is an aspect of the worldview of this author. Other references to written prescriptions as justification for action in the events being narrated are, however, found in the current Book of Deuteronomy or elsewhere. Thus 2 Kings 14:6 (2 Chron. 25:4) quotes Deuteronomy 24:16 concerning a matter of legal ethics during the reign of King Amaziah of Judah: "The fathers shall not be put to death for the children." Nehemiah 13:1 describes the Levites reading from "the *sēper* of Moses" in the hearing of the people. The interesting implication is that while the text is written and its writings a guide for action, the people themselves do not read. They receive the contents in oral communication from a scroll, a process of communication that again reveals the continuum between oral and written. It is found that no Ammonite or Moabite should ever enter the assembly of God and so the Israelites "separated out from Israel all mixed company" (13:3). This proscription is found quite precisely in Deut. 23:3–5. First Chronicles 16:40 describes David's maintaining the ritual pattern of the continual offering in accordance with what is "written in Torah Yahweh." Appropriate material is preserved in Num. 28:3 and Ex. 29:38 although 1 Chron. 16:40 does not contain the precise complete parallels in language to a Deuteronomic or other Pentateuchal text, suggesting quotation as in Neh. 13:1 and 2 Kings 14:6 (2 Chron. 25:4). For our study, what matters is that these writers, again primarily writers who can be dated late with confidence, make reference to a supposed proof text, to what is written, thereby valorizing written texts and showing their participation in the literate end of the continuum.

CONCLUSIONS

The Bible offers ample evidence of an Israelite literate mentality: writing on deeds and decrees; letters; references to genealogical and other written lists or surveys; rubrics that cite royal and other annals; some references to the composing of literature in writing or to the writing down of oral compositions; the importance of the concept of a written Torah; specific references to details of a written Torah and quotations that can be found in the Pentateuch as it now stands.

While some of these indications of the literate mentality are in preexilic texts, the majority are in late passages. The Chronicler, for example, provides letters where the Deuteronomistic historian has none; the references to annals, *dibrê hayyāmîm,* are more plentiful in 1 and 2 Chronicles than in the Deuteronomistic History, and, most interesting, these late writers employ "record" rubrics to assign annals even to the traditional prophets of Israel. The writers of Ezra-Nehemiah, 1 and 2 Chronicles, and Esther project a literate mentality. They validate scenes and statements by an appeal to written sources. Their writings imply the valorization of writing as a practical technology.

And yet even in the passages at the literate end of the continuum are nuances of orality, a reminder of the oral context that frames the use of writing, even in the postexilic period. In the Hebrew Bible, the written and signed deed serves as symbolic action; written edicts are read aloud by heralds; it is assumed that written materials will be reoralized ("The Bow"); the king has his records read to him; the written Torah belongs in the mouth; quotation from a written source is not from one uniform tradition, "a book," but from one of a number of variants all of which are the tradition. Thus even at the literate end of the continuum, the oral mentality is present and active, informing the way writing is used. Exploring the interplay between orality and literacy is essential to understanding the social contexts of reading and writing in a traditional culture.

CHAPTER 7

The Interplay between Orality and Literacy

Case Studies

A number of scholars have taken the position that literacy was general in ancient Israel[1] perhaps even earlier than the eighth century B.C.E. date suggested for an increase in writing by epigraphic finds and other patterns of archaeological evidence.[2] Our position throughout this study is not that ancient Israelites knew little of writing, but rather that Israelite literacy in form and function is not to be confused with modern literacy and that ancient Israelite literacy has to be understood in the context of an oral-traditional culture. Literacy and orality are part of an ongoing continuum even in the latest biblical period. This point is emphasized by the very style of biblical literature, by the nature and function of nonbiblical examples of Israelite writing, and by attitudes to writing exhibited by the writers of the Hebrew Bible itself. In this chapter we examine closely some biblical examples of the oral-literate interplay. A number of these texts interest us in particular because they are so often cited simplistically as supposed proof of a too-modern literacy in the ancient cultures of Israel.

DEUTERONOMY 6:4–9

Deuteronomy 6:4–9 remains an important, indeed central, expression of Jewish worldview that reaches back into the traditions preserved by the composer of Deuteronomy, a thread in religious outlook that may be as old as Northern Levitical circles of the ninth or eighth centuries B.C.E. Alan Millard[3] and others note that in verse 9 the average person is urged to write "these words that I [God] command you" on "the doorposts of your house and upon your gates." Hence it is assumed that the average Israelite, perhaps in a quite early period, writes and is, in short, literate. We ask, however, what is the nature, function, and context of this writing and again find strong indication of the vibrancy of the oral culture. The words are to be taught to one's children, literally to be repeated: *wĕšinnantām.* "Speak of them when you sit in your house and when you walk on the way, when you lie down and when you rise up." In homiletical style, the authors of Deuteronomy always try to present in an accessible fashion what they understand to be Torah, the essentials of Israelite values and the proper way to live the life of covenant with God. They identify with their audience, picturing men and women trying to live the law on a pragmatic, day-to-day basis, internalizing Israelite ethics in the ordinary course of their lives. The words are to be spoken, talked about, passed on to future generations.

And what are these *dĕbārîm,* literally "words"? They are most likely verses 4 and 5 concerning Yahweh God's oneness and the covenantal obligation to love Yahweh, but are these words not themselves merely metonymic markers of the larger ethos of the Book of Deuteronomy? The part can stand for the whole in this traditional culture.

And what of the writing? The command to write on the doorposts and gates is parallel to a command to "bind the words as a sign upon your hands" and "they shall be as bands between your eyes." These words have been interpreted in classical Judaism to require the wearing of phylacteries, just as the command to write on doorposts and gates have been interpreted to require the custom of attaching a small box containing Deut. 6:4–9 and 11:13–21, the mezuzah, to the side of the doorway entry. It has been suggested by some scholars that originally the writing was literally to be incised into or tattooed upon the body. In both cases, the doorway writing or the body writing is metonymic and symbolic, a means of reminding one who sees or wears the writing of God's larger demands, the essentials of Israelite religion.

We cannot know if Israelites generally did the writing themselves or had it prepared by craftsmen, as we currently do when we buy a mezuzah or a pair of phylacteries, "tefillin." Thus even on a basic level, this text is not easy proof of general literacy in ancient Israel as Millard and the others define it. In any case, the writing is best understood in an oral-traditional context: symbolic, a witness, iconic like the sacred tablets of ten "words" themselves. The words, moreover, are to be repeated and spoken. The oral world provides their elaborative and living context.

DEUTERONOMY 17:14–20

Another passage cited as proof of Israelite literacy is Deut. 17:14–20, a set of rules for Israelite kings.[4] The Book of Deuteronomy barely mentions the monarchy, and the king is discussed in terms of a code that ideally should curtail his power and pretensions. It is to be assumed that while participants in Deuteronomy's ideal world have to put up with kings, nevertheless the power of kings is to be circumscribed. This code may be as early as northern Deuteronomic thinkers of the period of the Israelite kingdom or a late-biblical reflection on the abuses of kingship, now nevertheless accepted as a feature of Israelite social structure, a sort of necessary evil. The code requires the king not to acquire too many horses or wives or too much gold or silver, and above all to follow and uphold the covenant, not exalting himself over his brethren (17:16, 17, 19, 20). Warnings thus include specifics and more sweeping comments on hubris.

For our study of the oral-literate continuum, verse 18 is most interesting. When he accedes to the throne, the king is to write for himself a copy of "this torah" upon a *sēper* (a writing surface) before the priests and Levites. It is to be with him, and he is to read in it all the days of his life so that he learns to fear Yahweh, God, to pay heed to all the words of this torah and these statutes (17:18–19). Thus writing, reading, and studying a text are fundamental responsibilities and indicators of kingship—all of which seem to reveal a worldview at the literate end of the continuum. But we fail to appreciate the larger cultural context if we ignore aspects of the oral. What exactly is to be copied and kept with him? The suggestion that he is to copy the whole Book of Deuteronomy and keep it with him is unlikely.[5] Such a scroll would be quite heavy and long and require a large commitment of the king's time to prepare, even assuming his erudition as a scribe. In worries about his horses and wives, the writerly authors of Deuteronomy do not seem to assume the king is one of them. One could assume, as does the NRSV translation, that the king has the scroll copied for him. The work would then be carried by his aides when he went to war and the like, similar to the black box that travels with American presidents. It seems more likely that the text is brief, perhaps the ten commandments. See the parallel terminology in Deut. 4:44–45, the introductory preface to the Bible's second presentation of the ten commandments that gives the Book of Deuteronomy its Greek name. Or is the king to copy the laws pertaining to kingship? In any event, the copying more likely refers to a brief and metonymic snippet of the larger law, like the writing on the doorposts or the body, that actually can be kept "with" the king, a part of his insignia as mediator of God's covenant with Israel. The author of Deuteronomy urges kings ceremonially to copy a biblical text (or have it copied for them) as an initiation ritual, a part of their elevation to kingship. The piece of text is to be a sort of rosary to them, a marker of their status and their obligations, a source of meditation perhaps as well. Understood in this light, Deuteronomy 17:18–19 presents another use of writing in an oral world. This act of writing is special, ritually framed, and testimonial. We err to overliteralize this use of writing, to see it as a mundane indicator that "Deuteronomy expects a degree of literacy to permeate society."[6] The king who writes down law is in the view of the authors of Deuteronomy one who continues in the tradition of Moses, who himself is shown mimetically to follow in the footsteps of the divine writer of Torah.

2 KINGS 23

Even more complex in intertwining nuances of orality and literacy is another passage involving a king who reads in the law. The king is the seventh-century Josiah, leader of a religious and political reform whose guiding principles were those found in the book of Deuteronomy and stemming from pre-Josianic, probably Levitical circles. The emphasis of these reformers is upon Torah faithfulness, which for them implies a radical monotheism, aniconism, condemnation of fertility ritual, of cults of the dead and of human sacrifice, and a notion of holy war that allows for purging the body politic of non-Yahwistic elements. In Josiah's reform these elements combine with a strongly pro-southern, pro-Davidic, and pro-Jerusalem emphasis on centralization of worship in the great temple of Jerusalem built by Josiah's ancestor Solomon. The Deuteronomistic writers' favorite leader is Josiah, whom some modern scholars regard as patron of a major historiographic project that brought us the so-called Deuteronomic or Deuteronomistic History, running from Deuteronomy through 2 Kings. Whether or not we accept theories of Josianic-period composition of this central portion of the Hebrew Scriptures—I am sympathetic to the notion of various traditions coalescing in some form under Deuteronomic influence in this period—chapters 22—23 that artfully create the background to the reform, come from strongly pro-Josian Deuteronomistic authors who express the essentials of the zealous reforming worldview described above together with the southern monarchic emphasis on the importance of the Jerusalem Temple.

Josiah, with appropriate kingly concern for the well-being of the great Temple, orders that funds be dispersed for repairs on the ancient building (2 Kings 22:3–7). The priest Hilkiah, who is one of the officials charged to undertake the project, announces to Shaphan the scribe, another official involved in the undertaking, that he has found a *sēper* Torah, a Torah document in the house of the Lord. This written Torah as interpreted is then said to become the basis for Josiah's reform. Josiah himself reads the Torah aloud to the people (see also 2 Kings 23:2 and Deut. 17:19).

Scholars frequently cite this text as further evidence of a literate mentality. It is suggested that the Jerusalem temple, like other ancient Near Eastern temples, housed a library. Hence the possibility of finding such a document. The reform is after all said to be based on a written document, and thus it reveals much about the respect accorded written words by the presenters and receivers of this thread in the tradition. The king, moreover, is able to read the holy writing, testifying to his education in the skills of literacy (2 Kings 23:2).

The story of the found "book" might be read as implying a literate orientation in that the written work preserves the pure wisdom of olden times that had been somehow lost or forgotten, preserved and waiting to be rediscovered, like a Tibetan treasure text. Indeed it is suggested remarkably that Passover has been improperly celebrated in all the years since the days of the judges, presumably in the home-based family rituals enjoined by Exodus 12 rather than in the culticly centralized fashion suggested by Deut. 16:5–6 (2 Kings 23:22–23). Has the book been lost so long? Implicit is the need to consult writings in order properly to perform ritual. The written is preferable to custom—all of which implies a most modern-style worldview. The very nature of the source buried and hidden, however, suggests that a written tradition is not generally assumed to be available in an easily accessed form. See again how ongoing and complex is the interplay between oral and written in the worldview of ancient Israelites and how far their notion of Torah as "book" is from ours: The found document is read *aloud* to Josiah by Shaphan the secretary. The king then commands that inquiry be made to a prophet, Huldah, to find out the full meaning and significance of the discovered written words. The supramundane must be consulted. Daniel 5, the scene of the handwriting on the wall, comes to mind. Only after hearing about the significance of these words for understanding Israel's failings and defeats does the king mourn and take action. The king himself then reads aloud to the people all the words of "the 'book' of the covenant," binding them to the covenant (2 Kings 23:3) as had Moses and Joshua.

For us questions about whether a document was really found or not in the time of Josiah or if such a work was a form of Deuteronomy or if participants in later tradition assumed the work to be Deuteronomy are moot. As Wolfgang Speyer has shown in his book *Die literarische Fälschung im heidnischen und christlichen Altertum,* the "found book" tradition is a cross-cultural one that has not to do with real books but with contemporary needs to validate an action or political or theological position. Nevertheless, even as literary and religious motif, the found written document in the tale of Josiah's reform reveals much about the attitudes toward written words held by the author of this account. The respect shown for written words, the trust in writing, is necessary for literacy, but the respect here is of those who do not take the written word for granted. This text, like the tablets from Sinai, is endowed with mystery and aura. It validates reform not only because it is written and true but because it is unusual, mysterious, and divinely sent.

To suggest that the document is found in the library reduces the account to an everyday event in our terms—the experience of an archivist who is helping to ready the rare book room for redecorating. Rather the event is to be understood as unusual and extraordinary, another example of attitudes toward writing in an oral world.

EXAMPLES FROM JEREMIAH

Partaking of aspects of writing in the oral register while evidencing some of the practical benefits of literacy in the modern sense is Jer. 51:60–64. Jeremiah dictates a doomsday prediction to Seraiah, an aristocrat going into Babylonian exile with King Zedekiah. Writing "on one document," he describes the disasters that will eventually befall Babylon itself. Seraiah is to read the doom-saying once he arrives in Babylon. Like the flying scroll of the curse in Zechariah 5:1–4, Seraiah in a more mundane way is a moveable curse, a messenger service for incantations. As with the letters discussed above, this is a literate use of writing to send information across distances (cf. the prophecy by letter in 2 Chron. 21:12–15). Presumably the on-site curse is more potent than the one uttered miles away. Yet the act of writing and reading a curse, using words for magical, transformative purposes, is in itself an act in the oral register. Moreover, the document becomes part of a prophetic sign act, for after reading the message of doom, Seraiah is to attach a stone to the document and throw it into the Euphrates and say "Thus will Babylon sink and rise no more because of the disaster I am bringing upon her" (51:64). The document helps to bring the disaster about.

Jeremiah 36 provides another example of communication through the written word that allows the composer not to be there in order for the communication to succeed, a literate enterprise. God commands Jeremiah to prepare a text on a scroll document. The text consists of all the words spoken by God to the prophet (v. 2) since the days of Josiah, messages received by Jeremiah directly from God, the heart of the message being to submit to certain defeat by Babylonia (36:29). Yet here the oral (36:29) is to be rendered written, a writing down not done directly by the prophet himself, for he in turn calls to Baruch, who actually writes down on the scroll God word's from "the mouth of Jeremiah." The tale, like Jeremiah 51, thus provides an interesting comment on the interplay between orality and literacy.

Jeremiah, who has been declared an unpatriotic subversive by the government of King Jehoiakim, is denied access to the Temple district and the public pulpit it affords, and so he sends Baruch to read aloud God's message against Judah and Israel. When the court officials hear of these activities, they summon Baruch to the palace and order him to read also to them (perhaps they cannot read such a complex document, again providing a view into the world of orality). The scroll is left behind for the moment but must be brought to the king while Jeremiah and his scribe are told to hide by sympathetic officials. The king and his inner circle are unimpressed by the document that one official, Jehudi, reads to them. The king slices off sections of the parchment or papyrus with a knife and tosses them into the fire.[7] But, of course, in this world of inspired improvisation and memorization, the contents of the scroll have not been destroyed; they are in Jeremiah's mind and mouth, and he dictates a second copy. The burned scroll has in fact become an implicit sign act symbolic of the land and the king. God declares that Jehoiakim and his line will be destroyed; the land will indeed be burned and destroyed by Babylonia. Thus orality and literacy intertwine in interesting ways in this passage: the oral prophecy is dictated, written down in ink and read. The prophet does not do the writing nor the listeners the reading—these skills either being beneath the holy man and the king and most of his officials or considered the purview of special technicians, perhaps both. Moreover, the writing allows for the dissemination of a message but is not necessary for its preservation, at least while the prophet lives. Finally, this written scroll helps to bring about a change in status, the king's and Babylon's, through its transformative capacity as sign act.

NEHEMIAH 8

As we explore the ways in which attitudes to orality and literacy emerge in the Hebrew Bible, Nehemiah 8 presents an important scene. The setting is the fifth-century B.C.E. return of exiled Judeans to Judea, the second wave of returnees, who with the support of the Persian government seek to rehabilitate Jerusalem and stabilize the Jewish community there.

The Yahwism of these former exiles is an uncompromising extension of the Deuteronomic worldview described above with new emphases on keeping the Sabbath and the strict avoidance of intermarriage, indeed with a narrowing definition of who is the true Jew.

In the scene in Nehemiah 8, all the "people," that is, those in Judea sympathetic to Ezra's radical-conservatism, his brand of Yahwism—all who count as Jews in the eyes of the author—gather together "as one man" and ask Ezra, "the scribe," to bring the Scroll of the Torah of Moses that Yahweh had commanded to Israel (v. 2). This gathering takes place on the first day of Tishre, the important New Year's month. He does read in it in the open square from dawn until midday. The people's ears literally are "at" the scroll of Torah—attentive, connected. Ezra opens the scroll and displays it as he stands on a wooden dais. The people stand when he opens it. The ceremonial context already includes aspects of synagogue worship. Even nowadays the lifting and exhibiting of the Torah iconizes it, treats it as symbol. So too in Nehemiah 8.

Verses 7–8 describes how named Levites read in the Torah of God as interpreted, and "with the setting forth the sense," the people understood the reading. Again Torah is mysterious writing in need of interpretation and clarification, hidden either because of a language barrier—these Jews may use Aramaic and not Hebrew as their vernacular—or because of the complexity of the material or because such texts, especially legal rather than homiletical ones, are unfamiliar and not easily digestible.

On the second day of this Torah festival, a select group of heads of ancestral houses and Levites gather to Ezra the scribe in order to gain insight into the words of the Torah. Again the scribe is the guide and teacher of this arcane and holy material. In their studies, they (presumably including Ezra) find enjoined the festival of tabernacles. Leviticus 23:33–42, especially 40–42, provides the closest parallel to the description of the festival found in Nehemiah 8. Once again we see appeal to a written source to justify or explain current religious action. As in the story of Josiah's found text, the existence of the holiday and the way it is to be celebrated seem to be news to Ezra and his flock—the found book pertains here as well, for information is to be gleaned from the difficult-to-translate, difficult-to-understand text that is not wholly known or regularly read even by an élite. While the fact that a written scroll is drawn upon to guide ritual life is somewhere within the realm of literacy, it is clear that the social setting assumed for Nehemiah 8 is still very much within the world of orality.

CONCLUSIONS

The biblical case studies in chapters 5–7 support the notion that writing played important roles in Israelite daily life and consciousness and that the practical benefits of reading and writing were well recognized. Writing preserves thoughts and compositions and allows for the accurate transfer of information across distances. Writing is respected, and words that can be read in a Torah are valorized as validating religious practice and belief. And yet this very valorization points to an attitude toward writing that regards it on some level as extraordinary and sacred. Some written texts serve as curses with the capacity to transform. Many are monumental or testimonial. Frequently the texts are partial metonymic symbols of a larger tradition. They are holy words posted on doorways or worn on the body (Deuteronomy 6) or kept by the person (Deuteronomy 17). The term "Torah" itself is variously employed. Torah in 2 Kings 22—23 seems to refer to a form of Deuteronomy, in Deuteronomy 17 to a smaller passage, in Nehemiah 8 to a different corpus. Two of the passages, 2 Kings 22—23 and Nehemiah 8, strongly emphasize that the written text needs to be interpreted to be understood. The quality of "lost text" applies to them, for even the erudite scribe finds new hidden information within the text. The written text is read aloud, an aid to oral presentation.

In these ways, the world of orality frames and colors a world of writing. We employ the term "literacy" in exploring ancient Israel with great caution. Israelite worldview and the Israelite literary tradition have been shaped, in part, by a complex interplay between oral and literate mentalities.

Chapter 8

The Oral Mentality and the Written Bible

A particular oral-style aesthetic characterizes the literature of the Hebrew Bible and many nonbiblical writings in ancient Hebrew as well. Attitudes to writing and reading in ancient Israel differ significantly from modern conceptions of literacy. We have emphasized the continuum between Israelite orality and literacy, noting that examples of writing in ancient Israel have to be understood in terms of an oral-traditional context in which writing is often believed to have magical transformative qualities and in which writing has symbolic and monumental significance. We have suggested that some passages dealing with writing and reading in the Hebrew Bible seem closer to our conception of literacy than others. An implicit chronology in biblical and nonbiblical works suggests that the practical and technological benefits of writing, for example, the use of letters and records, come to be appreciated more and more over the course of Israelite history. Even the most orally imbued biblical passages are available to us because of this technology and the value its users placed upon it. And yet even the latest biblical works still give evidence of orally based aesthetics and attitudes. Epigraphic finds testify, moreover, both to ongoing iconic and transformative uses of writing and to the pragmatic uses of writing in political, military, and commercial arenas.

We have tried to explore what we know of archives and libraries in Israel and have taken soundings in the ancient Near East in order to deal with questions of retrieval and possibilities for consultation of written material and have sought to understand where such collections fit in Israelite attitudes to literacy. Again we find a sliding scale or continuum between oral and written mentalities and the apparent accoutrements of what we would call literacy framed by some orally based attitudes and contexts. We have also sought to understand some of the logistics of literacy and orality. We know a good deal about materials used in writing but still know little for certain about the transmission of skills of reading or writing. We know little about scribal education or the nature of schools, and still less about the transmission of the skills of oral composition and oral performance of written or oral works.

We are now, however, prepared to bring these many observations about the complex relationship between orality and literacy in the products of Israelite culture and the attitudes of ancient Israelites to questions concerning the genesis of the Hebrew Bible. Just as many discussions of Israelite culture take it as a given that Israelites during the monarchy were literate in too simply defined a manner, notions about Israelite literacy and especially notions about the literate mentality of a courtly or scribal élite inform many of the theories about the origins and formation of the Hebrew Bible, theories that this study leads us to question.

ORAL ROOTS

Interest in the "oral" has been strongly represented in biblical scholarship. As discussed in chapter 1, it has long been suggested that oral works lie behind many of the written works of scripture. Except for a few scholars such as I. Engnell,[1] most suggest that the "oral" lies deep in the prehistory of biblical texts. The oral world that supported such prebiblical forms, moreover, is frequently grounded in a nineteenth-century romanticism about nomads and the rural or pastoral life. In this view, the actual Bible has moved beyond whatever was oral about it. As Yair Zakovitch writes: "The Bible is not traditional literature, but sophisticated refined literature written down to cope with the traditional literature, and to make it appropriate for its 'Sitz im Buch' in Scripture."[2] Brian Peckham, who has his own complex version of the way the Bible coalesced, writes: "The traditions [of the Bible] like the collection, began as literature. They can be attributed to authors who composed them according to the rules of grammar and syntax and prosody and rhetoric and with the language, style, and structure of a 'written text.' "[3] I hope to have proven quite the opposite about biblical language, style, and structure in chapters 1 and 2 and to have complicated readers' views of what "the traditional" entails.

Peckham's and Zakovitch's insistence that the literate mentality shapes the Bible and dominates it is common among biblicists. Peckham writes further:

> Prophecy was the heir to and of a popular oral tradition, but it was written; and although it is poetry, drama, and oratory composed in direct discourse, all the signs of oral composition and transmission and the clues to an oral society are missing. The traditions appeared at once

> alive and fully formed. Their beginning is obviously not their origin but
> is relatively late in a literate world.[4]

If I understand Peckham correctly, he asserts that the Hebrew Bible is a product of a literate world, signs of oral roots now being subsumed or erased. I hope to have offered a more nuanced argument about the oral and literate mentalities behind prophetic and other biblical works. Peckham's description is a useful introduction to a review of major theories concerning biblical composition and the Israelite contexts behind the literature. The theories that have dominated scholarly discourse approach the Bible with the presuppositions of modern literate readers and writers.

SOURCE CRITICISM

Julius Wellhausen's grand theory of Pentateuchal sources, the documentary hypothesis, itself based on the work of earlier scholars,[5] led to suggestions of two major corpora in the large portion of the Bible that preserves versions of myths of Israel's foundation and subsequent experiences under the monarchy and in the exile that followed it. One corpus was said to be from the sixth-century B.C.E. exilic period and priestly in orientation (*P*). Running from Genesis through Numbers, it contained earlier layers from eighth-century B.C.E. northern (Elohist: *E*) and ninth-century B.C.E. southern (Yahwist: *J*) monarchic contributors. The other corpus, headed by the Book of Deuteronomy (the *D* source of the Pentateuch) ran from Deuteronomy through 2 Kings and was suggested to be from a seventh-century B.C.E. writer from the court of the Judean king Josiah. Wellhausen's scheme for J, E, D, and P has been refined and debated over the years. The tenth and ninth centuries B.C.E. are deemed by most as better dates for the Pentateuchal sources J and E than those of Wellhausen. Some regard J as an individual, others as a school. Some doubt the possibility of distinguishing between J and E sources and prefer to describe an epic JE source to be contrasted with a P priestly source. Some regard P as a source, others as a supplemental thread or tradent. Some scholars suggest earlier and later priestly layers; others provide layers for the "Deuteronomic" or "Deuteronomistic" corpus, allowing for early materials, a major seventh-century B.C.E. Josianic composition, and an exilic revision.[6] Others posit sources in addition to JEDP. Nevertheless the basic scheme has survived. Richard Friedman's *Who Wrote the Bible?*[7] is a modern version of Wellhausen's thesis.

Implicit in the documentary hypothesis are particular views of the composition of the Hebrew Bible and of its relation to actual social periods and historical circumstances. (These views dominate a substantial set of works that accept the existence of a Yahwist source—usually treated as a specific author. This author is argued to be the composer of great early history of Israel, an ideological tour de force in support of either Davidic or Solomonic claims to the monarchy. Even material in the primeval history, argues Walter Brueggemann, is presented by a writer loyal to the Davidic royal house who shapes world-creation in terms of Davidic family history.[8] R. E. Clements's monograph *Abraham and David* and Coote's and Ord's *The Bible's First History* explore how J reflects a courtly Davidic writer's worldview and concerns, attitudes supportive of Davidic policies and ideologies.[9] Coote has also produced studies of E and P, excerpting verses assigned to each source and suggesting a social background and setting for each Pentateuchal corpus as delineated.[10]

Another work that briefly became popular among general readers is Harold Bloom's commentary on David Rosenberg's rather free translation of portions of Genesis deemed by them to be *The Book of J*. Bloom suggests that J is an aristocratic woman writing during the reign of Rehoboam, Solomon's son, in reaction to and conversation with the courtly author of the "authorized" court history of David in 1 Samuel.[11]

For our interest in orality and literacy, the documentary hypothesis suggests a number of things:

1. As early as the court of David there existed a lengthy written historiographical narrative of Israel that is preserved pretty much intact for centuries presumably on leather or papyrus.
2. The writer is either a collector in the style of the Brothers Grimm who reshapes raw material or a modern-style literateur familiar with folk tradition. Alternatively, the J work is prepared by a school—a committee of collectors or literati who argue over how best the story should go and reach a consensus.
3. The original writer or writers of J are courtly and aristocratic, trained in their writerly and readerly skills.
4. This early work is combined at some later date, cut-and-paste style, with other written sources.
5. A readerly and writerly redactor or redactors combine the pieces into an ever-enlarging tradition in accordance with particular worldviews and aesthetics, preserving side by side clashing styles and ideological disparities.

6. The work of combining sources takes place in some library work room or scriptorium where the sources can be laid out partially or fully side by side on tables or benches or on the floor; a third or fourth roll is also laid out for preparation of the new, revised edition.

7. The scholar redactors match the episode in J to its counterpart in E, finding the right location in each roll, and make decisions about what to include or exclude.

8. The sources are then discarded or lost.

9. Others like J prepare the material in Deuteronomy through 2 Kings some three hundred years later, a written text on leather or papyrus that is then expanded and adapted in the exile, the original written version, like J, available to be altered and touched up.

I suggest that the above imagining comes from our world and not from that of ancient Israel. Apart from questions about orality and literacy, the documentary hypothesis has always seemed to me untenable. The Scandinavian School exemplified by scholars such as Eduard Nielsen has shown how the key identifying traits of this or that source—for example, the use of the God-name Yahweh exclusively by the J source in Genesis—proves to be inconsistently and inconclusively in evidence. Another issue is the simple discouraging fact that in their studies of the Pentateuch scholars differ in their assignments of verses to particular sources. Thus a story that is significant for one scholar's understanding of the life-setting, worldview, and identity of J may not even be in another scholar's reconstruction of the source. Similarly while many scholars are not convinced that E is a separable, reconstructible source, Robert Coote claims to be able to list the verses of E and to show quite specifically how this E reflects concerns of the late tenth century B.C.E. northern king Jeroboam. Coote suggests, for example, that E's stories about endangered sons reflect Jeroboam's worry about ("his fixation with") dynastic succession.[12] How can one author such as J be the composer of Genesis 12 and 26?[13] The styles of these two stories of the patriarch who tells the foreign ruler that his wife is his sister are so different, the attitude to authority so different, that they cannot be from the same writer. Do we, then, want to consider J a collector more up-to-date in his or her scholarly techniques than the nineteenth-century Grimms, for unlike the Grimms who homogenized their retold tales in line with their own Victorian tastes and times, this J preserves the various styles of his sources, their attitudes and not his.

It is theoretically possible that a rich narrative or narratives of the people's history were written down at the court of David or Solomon by an author sensitive to and influenced by oral aesthetics. Portions of what I have called the bardic war tradition in interest and content may owe its promulgation or preservation to such authors,[14] though oral means seem more likely than written. Such tales of David and earlier bandit chiefs are manly tales of battle and conquest, of booty and bravery, of treachery and vengeance, exalting Israel's leaders and seem the appropriate purview of courtly composers. It seems, however, highly unlikely that the tales of small things, of famine and family, of barrenness and flight, of sibling rivalry and parental preference, come from an official Davidic court historian or literateur. Realizing this and agreeing with this portrait of what is generally assigned to J, Westermann points to earlier roots of these stories that are then collected by J.[15] But again if J so carefully preserves the flavor of these stories of the patriarchs and matriarchs, then he pays more attention to the preservation of his sources than the nineteenth-century European collectors. It seems much more likely that many of the patriarchal traditions took shape apart from a courtly setting but that they or strings of them came to be regarded eventually as a part of pan-Israelite history and culture. The written narratives we have inherited may be a selection from or creations based upon many oral variants, strings of the tales that would have appealed to Israelites. Such a selection was included and combined in the little library of works we call the Hebrew Bible.

Specific issues in the logistics of literacy further argue against the documentary hypothesis. The notion of written composition by committee seems unlikely on the face of it, though a committee of the whole could have influenced the oral form these stories take, as audiences react to and reinforce certain tellings (see below).

At the heart of documentary hypothesis, either Wellhausen's or modern versions that tend to date the sources later in the monarchic or postmonarchic period, is the cut-and-paste image of an individual pictured like Emperor Claudius of the PBS series, having his various written sources laid out before him as he chooses this verse or that, includes this tale not that, edits, elaborates, all in a library setting.

If the texts are leather, they may be heavy and need to be unrolled. Finding the proper passage in each scroll is a bit of a chore. If texts are papyrus, they are read held in the arm, one hand clasping or "supporting" the "bulk" of the scroll, while the other unrolls.[16] Did the redactor need three colleagues to hold J, E, and P for him? Did each read the text out loud, and did he ask them to pause until he jotted down his selections, working like a secretary with three tapes dictated by the boss?

Without worrying about logistics, David Damrosch suggests that one source, the author of the David story, looks at J in order to write his work, and that the author of the Davidic court narrative then influences P's "reworking of the Pentateuch."[17] Was J so thoroughly set by the tenth century B.C.E. when Damrosch dates the Davidic material? Did the author of the court narrative receive J "hot off the presses"? Is J being transmitted orally? Genre analysis, moreover, is important to Damrosch's study of the genesis of the Bible, yet his definitions of epic, chronicle, and history are all based upon Western scholarly categories, external to the ancient Israelite world.[18] This is not to deny that many sources, oral and written, lie behind the Hebrew Bible but to suggest that the hypothesized scenario behind the documentary hypothesis is flawed.

Doyne Dawson's point about the nature of texts in ancient cultures is relevant here. The library may be held in the memory. But how do the works of the implicit library come to be? Questions about orality and literacy are extremely relevant in this matter.

Another major theory of biblical composition that is also rooted in modern notions of literacy is the historiographic approach. Some scholars share basic aspects of the sort of source-critical methodology associated with Wellhausen, but unlike R. Friedman, R. Coote, and other modern scholars, do so with interesting nuances and datings, departures and new twists.

In *In Search of History,* John Van Seters eschews some of the dicing and splicing source-criticism of old-fashioned Wellhausenism still employed by Richard Friedman and others, though admittedly his work with "pre-Yahwist," "Yahwist," and "post-Yahwist" layers in his more recent book looks like the old-style source analysis.[19] Van Seters regards the Deuteronomistic History as a sweeping and innovative historiographic work that integrates various literary forms, including the king list, the royal inscription, the chronicle, and material "in the popular storytelling mode" in order to set forth within one work the whole foundation of Israelite society."[20] Similarly J is an "antiquarian historian who drew upon a range of [such] primeval and national traditions to create his 'prologue' to the history of Israel."[21] Van Seters discusses genres of "antiquarian" material, which sections of the Deuteronomistic History approximate.[22] This suggestion in itself might raise a flag of caution, for as Dan Ben-Amos has shown[23] genres are ethnic phenomena particular to the culture and group. That is, would an ancient Israelite have recognized the genres Van Seters describes? Did he distinguish, for example, between popular storytelling and the "Chronicle"? What is "a chronicle of the king of Israel/Judah" cited as a source so often in 1 and 2

Kings—the same as genres found elsewhere in the ancient Near East or not? In his book on the Yahwist, Van Seters uses terms such as "legend" and "myth" with no attention to issues in ethnic genres.[24] He does not and cannot describe the nitty-gritty world in which the collecting, copying, and incorporating takes place. Van Seters promises to address how the histories were written and how these units were drawn together.[25] He mentions an editor and "author or authors," mentions "official" and "unofficial sources."[26] He talks of a core Deuteronomistic History later attracting traditions as if it exudes a magnetic force and says that a "rather drastic effort was made" later to reshape the history as if some superorganic force works upon it.[27] He never really addresses "how" the work comes to be, and one is left falling back upon old wooden source-critical images of the scholar surrounded by scrolls. Does the historian visit archives and copy down monuments onto leather? What are the logistics that make possible the historiographic work Van Seters imagines? Where do the popular stories come from? One's parents, "folk," "oral tradition"? Again they arrive superorganically without recourse to actual human beings or social contexts. How does J, whom Van Seters views as creating a companion history for DtrH,[28] have the Deuteronomistic History available to him? Does he carry it into exile? In what form? Has he fixed the text in his memory? Similarly, Van Seters imagines the Yahwist to quote directly from a Babylonian account of Marduk's creation and suggests "the Yahwist's account of creation and the paradise story is the product of research (historia) that includes both biblical and foreign sources."[29] How does such a writer have access to such sources? Does he copy cuneiform tablets, rely on memorization, informants' or his own? Does he own scrolls?

In contrast to Van Seters and Damrosch, R. N. Whybray rejects source-critical theories to explain who wrote the Bible and raises doubts about tradition-history to account for the prehistory of the Pentateuchal traditions and eventual formation of the Bible.[30] He carefully critiques scholars' loose use of categories such as "saga" as variously defined[31] and the application of work by Olrik and Jolles to biblical materials and appears, therefore, to be more sensitive to ethnic genres than Van Seters and Damrosch.[32] Moreover, he makes good use of previous work by Wilson and Long, who emphasize the possibility for innovation upon traditional forms by individual artists.[33]

Whybray ultimately concludes, however, that one ancient historian of the postexilic period is responsible for composing the Pentateuch, "a history of the origins of the people Israel, prefaced by an account of the origins of the world."

> He had at his disposal a mass of material, most of which may have been
> of quite recent origin and had not necessarily formed part of any an-
> cient Israelite tradition. Following the canons of the historiography of
> his time, he radically reworked this material, probably with substantial
> additions of his own invention, making no attempt to produce a smooth
> narrative free from inconsistencies, contradictions and unevennesses.[34]

For him, as for Van Seters, this theory rests upon comparisons with the histories of Herodotus and with the works of Herodotus's predecessors that
survive only in fragments. The author of the Pentateuch (Whybray) or the
Yahwist (Van Seters) is suggested to be an antiquarian historian like
Herodotus or his predecessors. In this way, Whybray, like Van Seters, falls
back into the trap of ignoring ethnic genres, issues of logistics (how did this
historian obtain his sources?), and issues of social context.

One of the central weaknesses in Whybray's and Van Seters's approaches
is the appeal to Herodotus. In a recent work that explores the interesting
interplay between oral and literate mentalities in Herodotus' historiography,
Mabel Lang carefully examines the special and unifying characteristics and
techniques of Herodotus' discourse. For example, she points to Herodotus'
use of the first person.[35] She discusses Herodotus' use of complex rhetorical questions of various types[36] and his use of certain other devices such as
the "transition-by-knowledge," which she demonstrates is "a Herodotean
device and not merely that of his sources."[37] Lang studies "the extent to
which Herodotus' style makes his history and how it affects his historicity."[38]
Throughout, her point is that these various devices unify Herodotus' *History*.

If any biblical work bears comparison with Herodotus' *History,* it may be
1 and 2 Chronicles, which at least has a dominant and unifying point of
view, but comparisons with a hypothesized Yahwist or Deuteronomistic historian or author of the Pentateuch simply do not work. The great variety in
style and worldview, the very anonymity of the biblical works argue against
such comparison with Herodotus and against the view of biblical composition derived from this comparison.

Rather than think of the Bible as a book, we do well to think of the Bible
as a library. This library contains what came to be regarded by the Jews of
the Second Temple period as essential shared expressions of a people's
worldview and self-definition. Various portions of the library were preserved in various ways, states, and locations before the coalescing of the library we now call the Bible. Some may well have been written pieces kept
in the archive of a particular interest group or party. Such written pieces
may have been composed in writing or dictations from oral works. Some

might have been abbreviated written aids to longer oral performances or, as in a case of legal texts, a sampling of the tradition of case law as a writer understood it. Some works may have taken shape through an oral process of recitation and receiving and could have been or could not have been written down in various editions years earlier. Some may have become more or less set without the need for writing. For all of these works, understanding the interplay between the oral and the written is important. The written-down works of the Hebrew Bible were various in origin and would have existed in variants, written and/or oral, that came to be regarded as typical of the Israelite library. Let us imagine some of the options, some of the ways in which portions of the pan-Israelite library took shape.

In exploring models for the genesis of various portions of the biblical corpus, the oral-literate continuum remains extremely useful. Not all works will have taken shape in the same fashion. In some cases, the process of becoming may have approached in some respects modern notions of literacy, while the genesis of other works may have been much closer to the oral end of the scale. In the question of aesthetics, the continuum applies as well. Some of the works produced are more oral-traditional in style than others.

ORAL TO WRITTEN—PERFORMANCE DICTATED AND COPIED: MODEL 1

While we have rejected Gunkel's romantic model, it is possible that some works of the Hebrew Bible were composed in oral performance in accordance with certain conventions of composition, content, structure, and style. By no means do we suggest that a Lord-Parry model underlies all of the traditional literature of the Bible, nor do modern students of early and oral literatures agree with all of Lord's and Parry's theories about the social contexts that gave life to such works. In particular, modern scholars emphasize the interplay between orality and literacy even in modern traditional cultures, whereas Parry and Lord, in his earlier years, envisioned a "great divide" between oral and literate mentalities.

Nevertheless, especially for the compositions of the classical prophetic corpus, oral performances that are written down through dictation or later recreated via notes by someone at home in the oral-compositional medium seems a distinct possibility, not only because of the style of the works of the classical prophets—which, granted, could have been created by a writer familiar with formulaic composition—but also because of the assumed life setting or social context behind the literature.

As I have shown, for example, Isaiah 1 strongly evidences the fresh manipulation of formula patterns in language and the use of conventionalized themes or "literary forms" to create the conceptual building blocks of the oracle. Isaiah combines a woe oracle with a cult polemic to chastise an eighth-century B.C.E. Judean audience. The phrase "I hate" + "terms for offerings or festivals" that helps to build the cult polemic is a formula pattern found widely in the tradition.[39] Such formula patterns, along with coventionalized patterns of content, provide the oral composer ready means of producing his message. Conventionalized metrics, moreover—the limping meter of the lament and the staccato call to change one's ways—contribute to the poet's traditional medium.[40] Metrics, words chosen formulaically, and recurring themes may well be the stuff of oral composition for the classical prophets who speak aloud and publicly. Their message is not to be sealed away and hidden until the time is ripe, in contrast to late and postbiblical rubrics, but rather to be spoken to the people. The classical prophets are the mouthpieces of Yahweh, their muse, and can be imagined to have addressed groups gathered for the very public Sabbaths, feasts, and new moons that Isaiah and Amos condemn, thus rendering the cult polemic particularly stinging, ironic, and effective. One can see the crowd gasp, the shock is palpable. Such occasions would also provide settings for more upbeat and crowd-pleasing condemnations of Israel's enemies and for messages of ultimate salvation. How would a work such as Isaiah 1 or Amos 5 move from oral performance to written text?

John Niles suggests in his study of Beowulf that there are various ways in which an oral performance could be set in writing in a traditional culture: (1) "Intervention by an outsider." Niles suggests that "when a tradition of oral poetry is in flower, people who live within the tradition feel little impulse to write it down. The impulse to preserve poems in writing comes chiefly from outside the oral culture, when another interested party happens upon the scene."[41] (2) "Intervention by an insider." A person born into the oral culture knows the technology of writing and wishes to preserve the tradition for some reason. Reasons may include the desire to share the work with those outside the immediate context or pride in the work stemming from nationalism; another sort of enthusiasm for the author and his message (as in outsider intervention); or a fear that the traditions, be they narrative, oracular, or proverbial, may be lost because of a disruption or evolution of the "old" culture that had sustained the forms in a live context.[42]

Of course under other circumstances the writing down may preserve a snapshot or moment in what continues as a lively oral tradition. The writing down of material need not necessarily signal the end of the production of oral versions of such works.

How does the insider/outsider distinction apply in the case of recording prophetic speech acts? The modes and media of prophecy would have to be learned, involving in some cases a discipleship between older and younger prophets (e.g., Elijah and Elisha; Jeremiah and Baruch), in other cases a larger guild or band. Such a guild could constitute the insiders. It is possible that prophetic speech acts were recorded and preserved by those within the group. Only the group, initially, might want to preserve the often controversial and difficult-to-accept messages of God mediated through the prophets. On the other hand, as Robert R. Wilson notes, prophetic groups generally have support groups within the larger population.[43] It is possible that such a supporter records prophecy. The recording, the keeping of prophetic oracles, and perhaps their subsequent revision in any event comes from a member of the group or a sympathetic outside supporter. Indeed, once a prophet is believed by a group to be a "true prophet," it becomes especially important to write down and preserve his/her variously interpretable messages so that they may be available for future validation, confirming and perhaps helping to bring about the events they predict.[44]

One might expect such oracles to be kept in a private archive belonging to a family or a guild of prophets or in the private archive of a person who is part of the support group of the prophet. In time the collected oracles become a part of the classical Israelite library, reflecting as they do essential aspects of Israelite worldview mediated through the eyes of those whom Morton Smith labels "Yahweh-aloners,"[45] those who place their stamp finally on the pan-Israelite library.

John Niles suggests that the very process of recording a performance alters it.[46] The performer, in this case the prophet, may produce or reproduce his work specifically for the writer or at least is aware of his presence. This in turn may affect content and style. The performer may "ham it up" or do a particularly effective performance. The poet may have to slow down considerably in order that copying be accomplished. This may give him the time to think of particularly good images and lines or may have a negative impact on his rhythm.

In all these speculations about prophecy as performance we need also to consider the possibility that prophetic works were oral performances based on written notes or fuller compositions.[47] Basing themselves on biblical rubrics and many scenes in which the biblical "book" is treated as a libretto for oral recitation, Gitay and Conrad each suggest that, like the written works in many traditional societies, prophetic oracles are meant to be recited or performed from texts or notes. Therefore they contain the rhetorical features expected in oral performance, and it is impossible to know in which medium, oral or written, they were composed. This sort of possibility needs to be considered alongside a model that describes a process from oral composition to written preservation. If there are dictated, written versions of oral performances in the Hebrew Bible, the poetry of the classical prophets seems a likely possibility.

ORAL TO WRITTEN AND WRITTEN TO ORAL—THE PAN-ISRAELITE STORY: MODEL 2

What of longer narrative compositions that provide a slice of essential Israelite myth, the stories of ancestors, heroes, and the formation of the early history of the group that help to express and formulate Israel's self-definition? There are a number of candidates for such oral compositions: some of the stories about the patriarchs and matriarchs; portions of the exodus story; some of the tales of the judges. We suggest that portions of these traditions were performed to audiences, taking basic shape in content and theme in response to the audiences who hear the performances.[48] At some fairly late date in the formation of the biblical tradition, several of these "stories" are written down by a gifted writer who like most Israelites knows how the stories go. It is also possible that as in many traditional cultures, written notes or abstracts aided the more elaborate performances. In this way, we imagine not only a process whereby oral becomes written but also a process whereby the written becomes oral and then that oral production is eventually recreated in fuller written form.

A partial model for this sort of compositional process is provided by Gregory Nagy. Nagy suggests that the Homeric and Hesiodic poems, which he sees as strongly evidencing the traits of oral composition as laid out by Lord and Parry, "crystallized" gradually and over time as "a direct response to the exigencies of a pan-Hellenic audience. . . . By way of countless such performances for over two centuries, each recomposition at each successive performance could become less and less variable."[49] In Nagy's view, the locus for such "recompositions" that tend to flatten out regional differences and begin to constitute the larger group's shared myth may have been the competitive performances held at pan-Hellenic festivals such as the eighth-century B.C.E. Olympic Games. He suggests that the carriers of the traditions were the rhapsodes, who by the time of Plato were not oral poets composing and performing simultaneously but performers who inherited oral traditions and participated in their systematization.[50] Nagy suggests that as time went on the poems became more "fixed" and were generated, as are the Indian Vedas, through the "mnemonic techniques that had been part of the oral tradition":[51]

> Recalling the testimony of Herodotus and others to the effect that Homer and Hesiod provide a systematization of values common to all Greeks, we may go so far to say that "Homer" and "Hesiod" are themselves the cumulative embodiment of this systematization—the ultimate poetic response to pan-Hellenic audiences from the eighth century onward.[52]

> In theory, though, written texts of the Homeric and Hesiodic poems could have been generated at any time—in fact, many times—during the lengthy phase of rhapsodic transmission.[53]

What is perhaps most striking about the Israelite traditions now contained in the Hebrew Bible is the way in which they present a unifying pan-Hebraic portrait of a people whose origins, whatever modern model we accept, is agreed to be various and complex. Except for the few references in Exodus to Israel as a "mixed multitude" and except for our careful reading between the lines as scholars, the biblical portrait of the Israelites emphasizes their wholeness as a group. Genealogies that trace origins back to Abraham, Isaac, and Jacob help to create this unified image, as does the panoramic sweep of the tales that picture Israel as a whole, enslaved or conquering or demanding a king. In contrast to many national founding myths in which a conflict between feuding brothers ends in the death of one sibling, the Israelite tale of twelve brothers ends in reconciliation, as Joseph and his brothers reunite. Even the political realities of the schism between northern and southern kingdoms described in 1 and 2 Kings and the southern bias of the literature as preserved does not alter this notion of the people's wholeness. The northerners are regarded as kin who have gone astray, but the national myth links Ephraim/Manasseh with Judah.

Nagy writes of traditions with strict prosodic rules, and when he suggests texts become "fixed," he refers not only to the very words with which they are presented but also to their meter and syntax. The extant traditional literature that Nagy studies, Homer and Hesiod, has such a format. This is not the case with extant Israelite literature. When writing of systematization and the gradual fixing of the tradition, we refer to essential contours of content and character and to frequently used expressions for the pieces of content. In writing of essential contours, one allows for variations in patricular tellings of portions of the tradition, versions, for example, of Moses' call or of Israel's crossing of the Red Sea. But Moses is everyone's hero, who was called by God, the passage through the sea a shared and foundational miracle account. We also think it entirely possible that the telling of pan-Israelite stories was aided by notes or some sort of written texts. Even allowing for these nuances and differences, Nagy's model is an excellent one for the Israelite case, allowing for the traditional style of the material, helping to explain the particular pan-Israelite interests of the narratives and the way in which once disparate traditions coalesced into the people's story.

It is possible that an individual working in a scriptorium, J or Whybray's historiographer, created the biblical portrait of Israel, offspring of Jacob, slaves liberated from Egypt, but Nagy's model is more convincing. A J did not "collect" traditions in Genesis through Exodus, a tenth-century B.C.E. Brother Grimm. Rather the traditions took shape beginning with the monarchy and its centralized pan-Hebraic festivals in Jerusalem. Who would be the Israelite equivalents of the Greek rhapsodes? The likely candidates would be Levites, traditionally considered the teacher clan, more portable and less territorially bound than the members of other tribes (Josh. 14:3, 4; 18:7), more vulnerable in the view of the author of Deuteronomy 12 and 1 and 2 Chronicles (Deut. 12:12, 18, 19; 14:27; 16:11, 14; 26:11). Such Israelites could have also brought northern traditions with them to incorporate into the southern. When the Temple is destroyed and the option for live sharing of the stories is interrupted, writing Levites might have produced fuller written versions of some of these threads in the people's story, versions closer to what is now collected in the library we call the Bible.

Information about the actual roles of Levites in ancient Israel is somewhat limited. Scholars have long debated about how or whether those called "Levites" are to be distinguished from other priestly groups and during which periods, about their status as a tribe or other ethnic entity. Recognizably priestly material in the Hebrew Bible tends to be from those said to be of the Levitical tribe who conduct ritual and are concerned with laws of purity, information about cultic accoutrements, and other matters preserved in Leviticus and Numbers that pertain to the successful mediation between divine and human realms (Num. 8:5–26; 3:9–39; 4:4–15; 10:8; 31:30, 47; Ezek. 45:5; 1 Chron. 15:11–15). The lengthiest descriptions of the roles and assignments of the Levites that look beyond roles related to the sacrificial cult itself come from 1 and 2 Chronicles and Nehemiah, late biblical works.

One interesting role for some Levitical groups involves singing and playing musical instruments. In 2 Chronicles 29:30 Levites are described as singing praises to the Lord; in Neh. 12:8, 27–28, they are in charge of songs of thanksgiving (see also 1 Chron. 6:32; 9:33; 15:16; 23:30; 25:6, 7; 2 Chron. 35:15). They are also associated with skill in playing musical instruments (2 Chron. 7:6; 34:12). One is not about to leap to the suggestion that the Levites were Israel's singers of tales, extemporaneous performers of traditional narratives. These references in particular refer to the performance of praise songs and songs of thanksgiving, perhaps the sort of material preserved in Psalms or included in 1 Chron. 16:8–36 and attributed to Asaph and his kindred, Levitical singers whose appointment the Chronicler attributes to David.

On the other hand, even songs of praise and thanksgiving that have been preserved in the tradition frequently do include renditions of key threads in essential Israelite myth. In 1 Chronicles 16:14–22, for example, is an interesting version of Israel's early history, alluding to the covenant with the patriarchs and Israel's prestate marginal status. Material in 1 Chron. 16:8–22 parallels Ps. 105:1–15 with a minor variation (1 Chron. 16:13: Israel; Ps. 105:6: Abraham)—as both perhaps share a fixed block of traditional narration. Psalm 105 continues with the story of Joseph, Israel's enslavement in Egypt, the plagues and exodus account, the wanderings in the wilderness (notice that in this account the quails incident is a positive experience, proof of God's generosity and fecundity [Ps. 105:40; compare Num. 11:31–34 and Ps. 78:18, 27–31]), and the taking possession of the holy land.

Psalm 106, another thanksgiving psalm, reviews Israel's acts of wrongdoing and, in contrast to Psalm 105, casts some of the key periods or events in the Israelite myth in negative terms: Israel rebelled at the Red Sea (106:7; Ex. 14:10–11), they had wanton cravings in the wilderness, a version of the quails incident that agrees with Numbers rather than the rosy account in Ps. 105:40. The Korah rebellion (Numbers 16) is listed, as are the incidents of the golden calf (Exodus 32) and Baal Peor (Num. 25:1–13), and at the waters of Meribah (Ex. 17:1–7; Num. 20:2–13). This psalmist knows well the outline of Numbers and Exodus in its current canonical form. Is his or her work a later version of Israelite myth than that of the author of Psalm 105, or does each artist give his or her own rendering? (Compare also Psalm 78 with its pro-Davidic bias.)

For each work, however, an essential outline of Israel's founding myth is found albeit with variations. The songs of thanksgiving and praise performed by Levites can thus have much in common with the narratives in Genesis through Numbers. They are keeping and producing in its essentials the same pan-Israelite tradition whereby the group is descended from the patriarchs, Abraham, Isaac, and Jacob, whereby they experience slavery, liberation, a wilderness trek, and receive the promised land. Psalm 136, another hymn of thanksgiving, begins with the creation, moving on to the killing of the firstborn, the exodus and drowning of Egyptians in the sea, and the victories over Sihon, Og, and others.

Do these singers produce such narrative patterns and motifs in their songs because the Hebrew Bible is by their time a set, written book that is read much as we read it? We might consider rather that such songs are versions of or slices of the pan-Israelite history that various Levites produce in various forms in community settings. Some of these renditions were at some point committed to writing. Some may have been composed in writing, memorized, performed often, lost in writing, and written down again for preservation years later. Some may have been extemporaneous performances as described for prophetic oracles. Some may have been guided by written notes or outlines. But the essential pan-Israelite story may well have taken shape in interactions with audiences over years. A semblance, a taste of these sorts of performances is provided by the psalms we have in the Psalter and by the longer stories and cycles of stories in Genesis through Numbers that were eventually included in the pan-Israelite library.

What would these settings be? Again why associate the Levites with such settings? Two biblical passages are especially important in this context, Deut. 31:9–13 and Neh. 8:7.

In Deuteronomy 31, Moses is said to write down this Torah (all of Deuteronomy or some portion) and to give it to the Levites. Moses commands that every seventh year in the Sabbatical "when all Israel comes to appear before the Lord your God in the place that he will choose," the Levites are to assemble all Israel—men, women, and children, and the alien residents—and read the Torah to them so that "they may hear and learn to fear the Lord your God and to take care to do all the words of this Torah" (31:12). The emphasis on doing Torah implies that the term here refers to the law as NRSV translates. Would such an occasion for reading not also be an occasion to tell of the history of the people, to reinforce essential myth, the narrative context for Torah? Nehemiah 8:7 describes the way at a ritual gathering of the community in the seventh month Tishre—the New Year's festival month—the Levites read from the document, in the Torah of God, interpreting and making sense so that the people comprehended the reading (Neh. 8:8).

As discussed in chapter 7, these passages evidence a rich interplay between the oral and the written. Torah is written, *sēper,* and yet is read aloud to the people so that they can hear and learn. In Nehemiah 8 the reading requires an oral interpretation to be comprehensible. Nevertheless the precious texts are written texts. What does Torah constitute? Is the written

Torah "law" whereas the story is provided orally? There is no way to know for certain what the term "Torah" means in these passages.

We consider it at least a possibility that Levites are cast in these teaching, tradition-delivering, and preserving ways by authors of the second temple period because they were the preservers and promulgators of the tradition even in the first temple period. It is for this reason that 2 Chron. 17:7–9 portrays the southern king Jehoshaphat as sending Levites throughout the cities of Judah to teach among the people. Again, they are pictured with document of Torah in hand, and we cannot be certain what the Second Temple writer of this passage considers Torah to be, law code, Pentateuch, or version of Deuteronomy as in other places in the Deuteronomistic History. Traditions concerning the Levites as composers of psalms, the founding-myth content of several extant examples, and traditions about the Levites' teaching among the people combine to suggest an Israelite parallel to Nagy's model.

Models 1 and 2 both emphasize the way in which strands of Israelite tradition might take shape in live performance settings. The response of an audience helps to shape the performance. In the case of model 2, responses of audiences over time help to establish the contours of Israel's foundation myth.

LITERARY IMITATION: ## MODEL 3

A third model will strike biblicists as less radical and more compatible with literacy-based theories about biblical composition. John Niles uses the phrase "literary imitation" to describe the way in which some oral-style literature has been composed.[54]

Niles offers this model as one way to explain the particular aesthetic of Beowulf, that is so clearly grounded in a metonymic, oral-traditional style: "It sometimes happens that people who are not born into a dominantly oral culture, or whose education has led them into very different realms, imitate the style and content of an oral poetry and compose new songs that read like traditional ones."[55] Such poets who imitate the oral style often "do so naturally and unselfconsciously, for oral modes of expression are a large part of what they know."[56] It is possible that some works of the Hebrew Bible were composed in writing by authors who are fully conscious of and immersed in the oral culture. It is, of course, extremely difficult if not in many cases impossible to distinguish between oral-traditional imitative written works and orally performed works that were then set in writing. If the written work that imitates oral style is composed specifically for performance and regularly performed, then as Gitay has suggested, the written work, created with an oral rhetoric in mind, has a strongly oral context. Such a psalm, for example, might be stored in a priestly singer's archive and preserved, leaving no need to consider dictation or reproduction from memory of a specific performance as the means by which it was written down. Of course, if a work becomes extremely popular, any archival version becomes superfluous for purposes of preservation or transmission since anyone who can write in the culture or folk group could produce it for themselves at any time without looking at an earlier written draft.

The plagues account in Exodus is interesting to contemplate in terms of model 3. This account is rich in recurring rubrics, its plot structured on a repeating frame, with the dramatic build-up based upon important nuances in what is repeated. First, Pharaoh refuses to let the people go to the wilderness to worship (Ex. 5:4; 7:13), Moses' see-through means of initiating the escape (5:1). Then admonished by plagues, Pharaoh relents, saying he will let them go, but only if they stay in the land (8:21; English v. 25). A second time he says he will let them go to the wilderness if they do not go far (8:24; English v. 28). Another time he relents but allows them to go only if they do not take their children (10:8–11). A fourth time he relents, but only if the flocks and herds remain behind (10:24). The magicians at first can produce the same plague tricks as Moses (7:22; 8:3; English v. 7); then they cannot and express anxiety (8:14–15; English vv. 18–19). The magicians are afflicted themselves (9:11); some begin to admit that God's power is greater than theirs (9:20). Finally, they urge capitulation: "Egypt is ruined" (10:7). A similar pattern of increasing self-doubt characterizes Pharaoh's reactions, paralleled ironically and inversely by his inability to alter his "hardheartedness" because he is merely a tool in God's hands.

The plagues account leading up to the exodus is thus strongly characterized by an oral style. Models 1 and 2 would suggest that the piece was delivered orally in community settings—the Passover festival seems a likely candidate. Model 3 suggests rather that the author writes this account influenced by and immersed in the aesthetics of an oral world.

As George A. Kennedy has shown for classical rhetoric, aesthetics that govern speechmaking in the ancient Greek and Latin worlds come to influence literary, written forms as well. Kennedy coins the term "Letteraturizzazione" to describe this phenomenon.[57]

Kennedy points out that one of the most important aspects of this shift from orality and actual speech making to the writing of literature is the movement from the public function of rhetoric to the personal use of rhetorical features in written literature. He contrasts the public function of speeches for example with "the romantic and personal poetry of the nineteenth and twentieth centuries in which a poet seems alone in the universe."[58] The distance between oral and literate in the continuum of the modern developed world is a much greater one than the distance between oral and literate in traditional cultures, as we have discussed. However, if the plagues account or any of the other slices of the biblical tradition that are strongly characterized by an oral-traditional style were not meant to be public, performed orally in a community setting of some sort, what then is the social context for these works? The compositions of the Bible suddenly appear to be a rather élite corpus shared among a small group who can read autograph copies or works that individual authors share orally with a circle of colleagues. Such in fact is the context (whether real or fictionalized) assumed for works such as the vision reports of Daniel and other late or early postbiblical works. The important question is for whom would "nonpublic" works be created and for what purpose? The Daniel texts are mysterious, encoded messages to be preserved until the time of its fulfillment. This is not true of the greater biblical myth. In a world without print and mass media, the myth is promulgated orally even once versions are written down. The national myth is not a message created by the one for the few but the shared tradition that defines and helps to create the community as a whole. Thus for large narrative threads of the Bible, we prefer model 2.

On the other hand, other sorts of biblical compositions even while still invoking and imitating the traditional are products of a more literate and "contextualizing" mentality. In this category I would place, for example, Ecclesiastes. The author of Ecclesiastes is clearly familiar with traditional Israelite sayings and saying patterns, a literary form rooted in an oral, interactive context, but he has reformulated many of the sayings and contextualized large blocks of them in a particular philosophical literary context. Thus his work partakes of the traditional but in a mode more at the literate end of the scale.[59] This is not to say that a written work such as Ecclesiastes might not have been read aloud within a circle of like-minded intellectuals, some of whom may have memorized portions of it to reuse in contexts of public rhetoric. Ecclesiastes is simply less traditional than the plagues account of Exodus.

WRITTEN SOURCES FOR
WRITTEN COMPOSITIONS: MODEL 4

The Bible does offer one fairly certain example of composition in a literate mode, the use of a manuscript to produce another written work, namely the author of 1 and 2 Chronicles's use of a history of the kings of Israel and

Judah preserved in 1 and 2 Samuel, 1 and 2 Kings, portions of what we call the Deuteronomic or Deuteronomistic History.

First and 2 Chronicles is wonderfully uniform in ideology. A particular worldview governs which part of the ancient Israelite tradition is preserved in the work and how, one that is strongly pro-Temple and pro-priestly, concerned with Levites and their rights and duties. First and 2 Chronicles is Judean in outlook but open to reunification of north and south and to the notion that northernness can be good or rehabilitated. The work is strongly idealizing of David, developing the concept of God as Israel's rescuer in miracles, often negating the need for humans to wage war.[60] This point of view fully informs the whole work, which more than any other historiographic work in the Hebrew Bible might be compared to Herodotus' *History* as Mabel Lang has described it—unified, built upon recurring structural and thematic features, framed by a particular author's intentions and viewpoint.

The Chronicler uses many sources of varying genres such as psalms, genealogical lists, and narratives. He[61] may well have created and composed many of the pieces or have provided a particular rendering of older traditions, written and oral. The Chronicler includes, for example, a section on David's plans for the Temple, divinely sent information about this microcosm of the divine realm on earth to be built in Jerusalem, center of the Israelite cosmos. He also includes a lengthy set of information about groupings of Levites and their various duties.

We can conjecture, however, that the Chronicler probably also had laid out before him or that a colleague read aloud to him a set written text, that is portions of a version of the Deuteronomistic History. This writer no doubt had available more of the material of the Deuteronomistic History than he uses. In this sense the Chronicler engages in a truly modern variety of editing. He excludes on purpose, for example, passages that make David and his family look bad, the scene in which Michal criticizes David when the ark is returned to Jerusalem (2 Sam. 6:20–23; compare 1 Chron. 15:29); the entire Bathsheba episode (2 Sam. 11:1–12:23); the unfortunate rebellion of David's own son, Absalom, that follows a tale of rape and incest in 2 Samuel 13.

The least that the author of 1 and 2 Chronicles had are those passages that reflect verbatim the text of 1 and 2 Samuel and 1 and 2 Kings as represented in one or more of the extant manuscript traditions.[62] While other briefer biblical examples of supposed direct quotation or inner textual allusion might well be examples of oral-traditional style in which certain images call for certain phrases (see chapter 1), in 1 and 2 Chronicles the repeated language is so extensive, following the very order of chapters in Samuel and Kings, that the author's use of a set text cannot be doubted.

Is it possible that the Chronicler's source was quite set in memory in the style described by Nagy for Panhellenic myth and not written down? While such a process may lie behind the crystallization of some of the narratives found in the Deuteronomistic History itself, the exact sharing of language between the Deuteronomistic History and 1 and 2 Chronicles makes less probable such a process in the work of the Chronicler. Rather in a more modern style literacy, 1 and 2 Chronicles transmits a written source. Yet even in this case we must be aware of the oral-literate continuum. The author of 1 and 2 Chronicles is not a modern historian who consults the best sources available to him for purposes of accurately recording what happened in the past but a preeminent transmitter of essential story who excerpts and expands at will to provide his view of the truly true, his concept of Israelite myth, his vision of the workings of God in the human cosmos, his version of the underlying frameworks of Israelite identity.

Nevertheless, he uses verbatim written material. Some time before the fifth century a written account of the kings of Israel and Judah is available to the Chronicler. It would have been no less than twenty biblical chapters in length, probably longer and perhaps would have fit upon one scroll. Such a scroll, perhaps in more than one copy or edition, might have been written down at the time of the imminent Babylonian threat and hidden for safekeeping by Levitical groups, some of whose elderly members or offspring returned with Cyrus' decree, participating in the rebuilding of the Temple and the repeopling of Jerusalem.

CONCLUSIONS

This discussion of some of the possible ways in which literature of the Hebrew Bible was composed and preserved is offered not as a definitive explanation of the genesis of the Hebrew Bible. The process of biblical composition was so complex and the interplay between oral and written so complicated that any reconstruction based upon the four models offered above risks as much imprecision as the work of the theorists I have criticized in this chapter. Moreover it is important to state that these hypothetical models do not account for the formation of the Pentateuch, the Hexateuch, or the larger Hebrew Bible. In the case of Genesis through 2 Kings, for example, conscious efforts, however sometimes awkward, have been made by the ancient authors to link materials together. The study of this process or the production of a model for it is not the goal of my project.

The descriptive study in chapters 1–7 in this book does not rise or fall with the accuracy of my suggestions about the composition of biblical threads. However, if one allows that the descriptive portion of the study has merit, then many earlier theories about biblical composition must not be solid, for they are based upon outmoded notions concerning Israelite literacy. They either assume incorrectly a simple trajectory early in the biblical process from oral literature to written texts or largely ignore altogether the significance of oral aesthetics and oral contexts.

I hope in this chapter to have encouraged new thinking about the ways in which various processes rooted in oral and literate aspects of Israelite culture may have interacted in the creation of Israelite literature. I have offered four models: (1) the oral performance, which is dictated to a writer who preserves the text in an archive, creating a fixed text out of an event; (2) the slow crystallization of a pan-Hebraic literary tradition through many performances over centuries of increasingly pan-Israelite tales to audiences with certain expectations and assumptions about shared group identity; late in the process authors write down the shared stories; (3) a written imitation of oral-style literature to create portions of the tradition; (4) the production of a written text that is excerpted from another written text by a writer who deftly edits or recasts the text in accordance with his own view of Israelite identity. What is most interesting about the latter case is the way in which 1 and 2 Chronicles becomes a part of the Israelite tradition. First and 2 Samuel and 1 and 2 Kings are not discarded or replaced. Rather in good oral-traditional style, variants are allowable and accommodated.

Conclusion

The romantic portrait of the medieval monks pictures intellectuals preserving classical literature, passionately devoted to their work of copying texts, skilled in reading as well as writing. Denise A. Troll seeks to shake us from this portrait:

> Many of us have an image of medieval scribes as silent, dedicated monks producing illuminated manuscripts at tilted desks. We value their work because it preserved the treasures of antiquity. We feel certain that, as the monks worked, they absorbed the meaning of what they copied and themselves became storehouses, "veritable libraries" of the genius that preceded them. We envy their freedom to concentrate on every word, to commit each one to parchment or vellum so painstakingly that they must have memorized certain passages and been able to recall them at will. We believe that the monks were religiously devoted to preserving and translating the best intellectual and literary efforts of the past, and that they valued the technology of writing, knowing that they were paving the way for social literacy by providing the basic necessity: texts.[1]

Behind such a portrait "lurks the pervasive notion that reading and writing were always experienced and appreciated as they are in the twentieth century."[2] In fact, the situation was as follows:

> Manuscript technology and medieval monasticism constrained the scribes' experience and conception of writing. Writing was not a matter of self-expression or intellection, but a manual labor that produced a pleasing visual product. The monk was obliged to perform this labor by religious duty. Writing was a way to have sin forgiven, to partake manually in mystery and missionary effort. Evidence suggests that the scribes had no respect for learning, regardless of monastic rule or the mandate that they teach.[3]
>
> In summary, the second period of craft literacy was populated by what we would consider illiterate or semiliterate scribes who connected writing with art and religion. The period of scriptorial literacy was

populated by artistic serfs who manufactured textual notation from raw materials; like a factory assembly-line, their work was subject to many kinds of corporate and government regulations. The medieval scribes were valuable, diligent, oppressed, and often mediocre talents unaware of their contribution to the transition from an oral to a literate culture. They were writers—what a child would call "copycats"—not composers; more slaves than scholars. Still, their efforts created a manuscript culture that lasted a thousand years. Medieval literacy was an institution to preserve what was known, an institution erected on the bent backs of silent, anxious men. More often than not the scribes did not understand or appreciate the intellectual genius they preserved and transmitted, and they did not comprehend or respect the psychological and epistemological ramifications of the technology with which they worked.[4]

Students of human societies tend to identify with their subjects of study and to understand them and their world in terms of their own experiences. In the case of ancient Israel, this is often a valid way to proceed. The authors of the Hebrew Bible and the people behind the letters, inscriptions, and other epigraphic finds describe a range of familiar emotions: love, jealousy, loneliness, fear. They present sets of familiar human relationships and the complications these entail: mourning over deceased spouses or children; rivalry between brothers and sisters; the respect granted elders or the generation gaps that produce tensions; the need to follow authority, and the desire to rebel. They have to cope with famine and infertility, political insecurity and oppression, war and defeat. They begin to look like us, their world not so different from our own. We need to pay heed, however, to biblical polemics and to a recent spate of new examinations of Israelite religion and the social world that provides its contexts. Such studies suggest, for example, that polemics against child sacrifice in the Hebrew Bible are not merely heightened rhetoric, a way of describing the enemy within, nor a dim remembrance of a primitive long-ago past, nor evidence of the renegade practices of a few. Rather child sacrifice may have been regularly practiced in Israel, indeed a feature of state-sponsored ritual, until the seventh century B.C.E. reforms of the southern king Josiah.[5]

The Israelites practiced slavery. They may have engaged in rituals to placate the restless dead, believed to dwell in an underworld called Sheol comparable to the Greek Hades.[6] They allowed for an ideology of war in which God demands the killing of all enemies—men, women, children, and infants—a warview, I suggest, that is related to notions about the efficacy of human sacrifice and a deity's appreciation of such offerings.[7] The Israelites' world is then not ours, their worldviews in some respects radically different from our own.

It is with this respect for differences and an awareness of a tendency to paint the Israelites in our own image that we approach questions concerning Israelite literacy and the orally based attitudes that framed the use of reading and writing in Israelite culture. We have pointed to an aesthetic grounded in orality and have shown some of the various ways in which the qualities of "immanent art" or metonymy inform the written works of scripture. We have reexamined the evidence in paleography and material culture and the ethnographic parallels frequently cited to support the notion that in general the Israelites were literate in our sense. While indeed there is much evidence of the increasing importance of reading and writing in ancient Israel, especially in commercial, military, and political realms, we have shown how even such texts and practices provide evidence not of modern literacy but of a continuum or sliding scale in which the aesthetics, purposes of, and attitudes to writing are circumscribed by an oral mentality. Nonpragmatic texts frequently evidence the transformative and magical qualities ascribed to the products of literacy by the nonliterate. Writing describing events is less historiographic than testimonial, and monumental identity is invested in writing, events immortalized. At the same time, however, writing offers the opportunity to preserve orally created and employed compositions. Aspects of the literate end of the continuum clearly shape and influence oral works as well. Written works in turn may be reoralized and the new works then written down and so on.

This complex interplay between oral and literate mentalities emerges beautifully in the writings of the Hebrew Bible. In this corpus, as in the epigraphic corpus, examples of writing at the literate end of the scale increase over time: the use of letters, the references to annals and records, the purposeful use of writing to preserve information or orally generated compositions. Even in such cases, the oral world presents itself as letters or annals are read aloud or as in the case of Jeremiah 36, when the best preserver of an oracle turns out not to be the written text that is destroyed but the memory and capacity orally to recreate the message. As the Yoruba proverb goes, "The white man who created writing also created the eraser."

The Hebrew Bible, moreover, is a rich repository of texts at the oral end of the continuum. Writing transforms by blessing or curse, by making so what is written. Writing is the means by which the deity may communicate. Like God, writing is mysterious, powerful, and numinous.

Most interesting are those passages such as 2 Kings 23, Jeremiah 36, and

Nehemiah 8 in which oral and literate aspects of Israelite culture are seen richly to intertwine and interact. The interplay between orality and literacy is a central feature of Israelite self-expression and as such is a vital thread in ancient Israelite culture. Recognition of Israelite attitudes to orality and literacy and of the complex interplay between the two forces us to question long-respected theories about the development of the Israelite literary traditions preserved in the Bible.

We reject the romantic notion of an oral period in the history of Israel followed by the time of literacy in which Israelite literature becomes written and bookish. The oral and the literate interact throughout Israel's literary history, as is true also of the ancient Near Eastern cultures of Mesopotamia and Egypt often drawn upon as models for understanding evidence of Israelite culture that has been lost due to climate and the devastations of conquest.

Given this assessment of Israelite aesthetics and the importance placed on the ongoing oral-literate continuum, source-critical theories become suspect, as do other theories about the composition of the Hebrew Bible that are grounded in modern-style notions about Israelites' uses of reading and writing. We offer no easy answer to questions about the genesis of the Hebrew Bible, but we do provide some hypothetical alternate models for the composition and preservation of works contained in the pan-Israelite library we call the Bible.

Whether any of these particular models seem viable, the theme of the larger study stands: that an appreciation of Israelite culture and of the literature that the Israelites produced is possible only with an appreciation of the interaction between orality and literacy. To study Israelite literature is to examine the place of written words in an essentially oral world and to explore the ways in which the capacity to read and write in turn informs and shapes orally rooted products of the imagination.

Abbreviations

ABD	*Anchor Bible Dictionary.* 6 vols. New York: Doubleday, 1992.
BAR	*Biblical Archaeology Review*
BASOR	*Bulletin of the American Schools of Oriental Research*
BDB	F. Brown, S. R. Driver, and C. A. Briggs, *A Hebrew and English Lexicon of the Old Testament.* Oxford: Clarendon Press, 1968.
CBQ	*Catholic Biblical Quarterly*
DtrH	Deuteronomistic Historian
HSM	Harvard Semitic Monographs
HTR	*Harvard Theological Review*
HUCA	*Hebrew Union College Annual*
IDB	*The Interpreter's Dictionary of the Bible.* Nashville: Abingdon Press, 1962.
IEJ	*Israel Exploration Journal*
JAF	*Journal of American Folklore*
JANESCU	*Journal of the Ancient Near Eastern Society of Columbia University*
JBL	*Journal of Biblical Literature*
JNES	*Journal of Near Eastern Studies*
JSOT	*Journal for the Study of the Old Testament*
JSOTSup	Journal for the Study of the Old Testament, Supplement Series
JTS	*Journal of Theological Studies*
NRSV	New Revised Standard Version of the Bible
OBO	Orbis biblicus et orientalis
PEQ	*Palestine Exploration Quarterly*
RB	*Revue biblique*
RSV	Revised Standard Version of the Bible
SBLDS	SBL Dissertation Series
UF	*Ugarit-Forschungen*
VT	*Vetus Testamentum*

Notes

Introduction

1. See Edward Nielsen, *Oral Tradition: A Modern Problem in Old Testament Introduction* (London: SCM Press, 1954), 22–23, 24; see also the review in Douglas A. Knight, *Rediscovering the Traditions of Israel*, SBLDS 9 (Missoula, Mont.: Scholars Press, 1975), 260–399.

2. Hermann Gunkel, *The Legends of Genesis* (New York: Schocken Books, 1966; German original, 1901), 41.

3. Hermann Gunkel, *Genesis*, 3d ed. (Göttingen: Vandenhoeck & Ruprecht, 1910; 1st ed., 1901).

4. Hermann Gunkel, *The Folktale in the Old Testament* (Sheffield: Almond Press, 1987; German original 1917).

5. Axel Olrik, "Epic Laws of Folk Narrative," in *The Study of Folklore*, ed. Alan Dundes (Englewood Cliffs, N.J.: Prentice-Hall, 1965; Danish original, 1908; German translation, 1909), 129–41.

6. Gunkel, *The Folktale*, 33, 176.

7. Gerhard von Rad, "The Joseph Narrative and Ancient Wisdom," in *Studies in Ancient Israelite Wisdom*, ed. James L. Crenshaw (New York: KTAV Publishing House, 1976; German original, 1953), 440.

8. Nielsen, *Oral Tradition*, 31.

9. New York: Atheneum Publishers, 1968.

10. John Foley, "Word-Power, Performance, and Tradition," *JAF* 105 (1992): 286–89.

Chapter 1: Oral Register in the Biblical Libretto: Toward a Biblical Poetic

1. Gunkel, *The Legends*, 38–39.

2. John R. Kselman, "The Recovery of Poetic Fragments from the Pentateuchal Priestly Source," *JBL* 97 (1978): 161–73; Stanley Gevirtz, *Patterns in the Early Poetry of Israel*, Studies in Ancient Oriental Civilization, 32 (Chicago: University of Chicago Press, 1963); William Whallon, *Formula, Character, and Context: Studies in Homeric, Old English, and Old Testament Poetry* (Washington, D.C.: The Center for Hellenic Studies, 1969); and Perry Bruce Yoder, "A–B Pairs and Oral Composition in Hebrew Poetry," *VT* 21 (1971): 470–89. See also M. O'Conner's comments on oral composition as it relates to his complex classification of Israelite poetics in *Hebrew Verse Structure* (Winona Lake, Ind.: Eisenbrauns, 1980), 42–28, 96–109, 159–63.

3. Susan Niditch, "The Composition of Isaiah 1," *Biblica* 61 (1980): 509–29.

4. Robert Culley, *Oral Formulaic Language in the Biblical Psalms,* Near and Middle East Series, 4 (Toronto: University of Toronto Press, 1967).

5. Susan Niditch and Robert Doran, "The Success Story of the Wise Courtier," *JBL* 96 (1977): 189–90.

6. Susan Niditch, *Underdogs and Tricksters: A Prelude to Biblical Folklore* (San Francisco: Harper & Row, 1987), 126–28.

7. James Kugel, *The Idea of Biblical Poetry: Parallelism and Its History* (New Haven, Conn.: Yale University Press, 1981), 69–70.

8. Dan Ben-Amos, "Analytical Categories and Ethnic Genres," in *Folklore Genres,* ed. Dan Ben-Amos (Austin: University of Texas Press, 1976), 215–42.

9. See John Foley, *The Singer of Tales in Performance* (Bloomington, Ind.: Indiana University Press, 1995), 15–17.

10. Niditch, *Underdogs and Tricksters;* Susan Niditch, "Samson as Culture Hero, Trickster, and Bandit: The Empowerment of the Weak," *CBQ* 52 (1990): 608–24.

11. Dorothy Irvin, "The Joseph and Moses Stories as Narrative in the Light of Ancient Near Eastern Narrative," in *Israelite and Judaean History,* eds. John H. Hayes and J. Maxwell Miller, (Philadelphia: Westminster Press, 1977).

12. Ronald S. Hendel, *The Epic of the Patriarch: The Jacob Cycle and the Narrative Traditions of Canaan and Israel,* HSM 42 (Atlanta: Scholars Press, 1987).

13. Albert B. Lord, "Patterns of the Lives of the Patriarchs from Abraham to Samson and Samuel," in *Text and Tradition: The Hebrew Bible and Folklore,* ed. Susan Niditch (Atlanta: Scholars Press, 1990).

14. David Gunn, "Narrative Patterns and Oral Tradition in Judges and Samuel," *VT* 24 (1974): 286–317; David Gunn, "The 'Battle Report': Oral or Scribal Convention?" *JBL* 93 (1974): 513–18.

15. Niditch and Doran, "The Success Story."

16. Niditch, *The Symbolic Vision in Biblical Tradition,* HSM 30 (Chico, Calif.: Scholars Press, 1980).

17. Niditch, "Composition."

18. Niditch, *Chaos to Cosmos: Studies in Biblical Patterns of Creation* (Chico, Calif.: Scholars Press, 1984); Susan Niditch, "Ezekiel 40–48 in a Visionary Context," *CBQ* 48 (1986): 208–24.

19. A. B. Lord, "Characteristics of Orality," *Oral Tradition* 2 (1987, A Festschrift for Walter J. Ong): 57–62.

20. John Miles Foley, *Immanent Art: From Structure to Meaning in Traditional Oral Epic* (Bloomington, Ind.: Indiana University Press, 1991), 7.

21. Ibid., 11.

22. Ibid., 13.

23. Ibid., 252, 217, 133, 33.

24. Ibid., 32–33.

25. Ibid., 30.

26. Ibid., 33.

27. Ibid., 141.

28. Ibid., 33.

29. Ibid., 95.

30. Ibid., 69–70.
31. Ibid., see also 111–18.
32. Michael Fishbane, *Text and Texture* (New York: Schocken Books, 1979), xii, 50–54; and Joel Rosenberg "Bible," in *Back to the Sources: Reading the Classic Jewish Texts* (New York: Summit Books, 1984), 38.
33. G. S. Kirk, *Myth: Its Meaning and Functions in Ancient and Other Cultures* (Berkeley, Calif.: University of California Press, 1970), 120.
34. See Niditch, *Symbolic Vision,* 121–24, and the discussion in these pages of the horn as a metonymic symbol in Zechariah 2:1–4 (1:18–21 in English) and 1 Kings 22:11.
35. Niditch, "Ezekiel 40–48 in a Visionary Context," *CBQ* 48 (1986): 221; Niditch, *War in the Hebrew Bible: A Study in the Ethics of Violence* (New York: Oxford University Press, 1993), 38–40.
36. Niditch, *Folklore and the Hebrew Bible* (Minneapolis: Fortress Press, 1993), 49.
37. See J. Kugel, "The Adverbial Use of *kî tôb*," *JBL* 99 (1980): 433–35.
38. Claus Westermann, *Genesis 37—50* (Minneapolis: Augsburg Publishing House, 1986), 233–34.
39. Hendel, *The Epic of the Patriarch;* Gunn, "The 'Battle Report'"; Niditch, "Composition"; Niditch, *Symbolic Vision;* Carole R. Fontaine, *Traditional Sayings in the Old Testament: A Contextual Study,* The Bible and Literature, 5 (Sheffield: Almond Press, 1982).
40. Robert C. Culley, *Themes and Variations,* Semeia Studies (Atlanta: Scholars Press, 1992). See also Robert Alter, *The Art of Biblical Narrative* (New York: Basic Books, 1981).
41. See, for example, Paul D. Hanson, "Zechariah 9 and the Recapitulation of an Ancient Ritual Pattern," *JBL* 92 (1973): 37–59; and Frank Moore Cross, Jr., *Canaanite Myth and Hebrew Epic: Essays in the History of the Religion of Israel* (Cambridge, Mass.: Harvard University Press, 1973), 99–104.
42. See Cross, *Canaanite Myth,* 108, 144.
43. See Foley, *The Singer of Tales,* 39–44.
44. See Culley, *Themes and Variations,* 47, 169–71, on the importance of shared themes and individual variations upon them.
45. Niditch, "Ezekiel 40—48."

Chapter 2: Variations in the Oral Register

1. Julius Wellhausen, *Prolegomena to the History of Israel* (Edinburgh: Adam and Charles Black, 1885; reprinted, Atlanta: Scholars Press, 1994; German original, 1878).
2. Alexander Heidel, *The Babylonian Genesis* (Chicago: University of Chicago Press, 1951), 129.
3. Phyllis Trible, "Depatriarchalizing in Biblical Interpretation," in *The Jewish Woman,* ed. Elizabeth Koltun (New York: Schocken Books, 1976), 223.
4. Phyllis Trible, *God and the Rhetoric of Sexuality* (Philadelphia: Fortress Press, 1978), 88–90.
5. Niditch, *Folklore,* 33–47; Niditch, *Chaos to Cosmos,* with bibliography.

6. On this theme in ancient Near Eastern literatures, see Paul D. Hanson, "Rebellion in Heaven, Azazel, and Euhemeristic Heroes in 1 Enoch 6—7," *JBL* 96 (1977): 195–233.

7. Carol A. Newsom, "A Maker of Metaphors: Ezekiel's Oracles against Tyre," in *Interpreting the Prophets*, eds. James Luther Mays and Paul J. Achtemeier (Philadelphia: Fortress Press, 1987), 198.

8. Ibid.

9. John D. Niles, "Editing *Beowulf:* What Can Study of the Ballads Tell Us?" *Oral Tradition* 9/2 (1994): 461.

10. Ibid., 460–61.

11. Ellen F. Davis, *Swallowing the Scroll: Textuality and the Dynamics of Discourse in Ezekiel's Prophecy* (Sheffield: Almond Press, 1989), 27, 37–39.

12. Dell Hymes, "Ethnopoetics, Oral-Formulaic Theory, and Editing Texts," *Oral Tradition* 9 (1994): 331.

Chapter 3: New Ways of Thinking about Orality and Literacy: Israelite Evidence

1. Amihai Mazar, *Archaeology of the Land of Israel* (New York: Doubleday, 1992), 515.

2. Gabriel Barkay, "The Iron Age II–III," in *The Archaeology of Ancient Israel,* ed. Amnon Ben-Tor (New Haven, Conn.: Yale University Press for The Open University of Israel, 1992), 349.

3. William V. Harris, *Ancient Literacy* (Cambridge, Mass.: Harvard University Press, 1989), 114.

4. Mogens Trolle Larsen, "What They Wrote on Clay," in *Literacy and Society,* ed. Karen Schousbee and Mogens Trolle Larsen (Copenhagen: Akademisk Forlag, 1989), 134.

5. J. Baines and C. J. Eyre, "Four Notes on Literacy," *Göttingen Miszellen* 61 (1983): 65–74.

6. Carol Meyers, *Discovering Eve: Ancient Israelite Women in Context* (New York: Oxford University Press, 1988), 152–53; see also Barkay, "The Iron Age II–III," 349.

7. Meyers, *Discovering Eve,* 153.

8. Joseph Naveh, "A Palaeographical Note on the Distribution of the Hebrew Script," *HTR* 61 (1968): 73–74.

9. Mazar, *Archaeology,* 515.

10. Barkay, "The Iron Age II–III," 349.

11. See also Alan R. Millard, "An Assessment of the Evidence for Writing in Ancient Israel," *Biblical Archaeology Today: Proceedings of the International Congress on Biblical Archaeology, Jerusalem, April 1984* (Jerusalem: Israel Exploration Society, 1985); and Alan R. Millard, "The Question of Israelite Literacy," *Bible Review* 3 (1987): 26, 29, for an upbeat assessment of Israelite literacy in the modern mode.

12. Rosalind Thomas, *Literacy and Orality in Ancient Greece* (Cambridge: Cambridge University Press, 1992), 10–11.

13. Rosalind Thomas, *Oral Tradition and Written Record in Classical Athens* (Cambridge: Cambridge University Press, 1989), 30–32; see also P.J.J. Botha, "Greco-

Roman Literacy as Setting for New Testament Writings," *Neotestamentica* 26 (1992): 202.

14. Thomas, *Literacy and Orality*, 3. On the Israelite case, see Edgar Conrad, "Heard But Not Seen: The Representation of 'Books' in the Old Testament," *JSOT* 54 (1992): 45–59, who argues that written works are perceived not as ends in themselves but as the basis or foundation for oral presentation and proclamation.

15. Katherine O'Brien O'Keeffe, *Visible Song: Transitional Literacy in Old English Verse* (Cambridge: Cambridge University Press, 1990), 25.

16. O'Keeffe, *Visible Song,* 5–6, 14, 21–23.

17. O'Keeffe, *Visible Song,* 76.

18. See also Botha, "Greco-Roman Literacy," 201.

19. Doyne Dawson, *Cities of the Gods: Communist Utopias in Greek Thought* (New York: Oxford University Press, 1992), 89.

20. Thomas, *Literacy and Orality*, 96.

21. Thomas, *Oral Tradition and Written Record,* 73.

22. Felix Jacoby, *Atthis: The Local Chronicles of Ancient Athens* (Oxford: Clarendon Press, 1949), 205.

23. M. T. Clanchy, *From Memory to Written Record: England 1066–1307* (Cambridge, Mass.: Harvard University Press, 1979), 125; see Thomas, *Oral Tradition and Written Record,* 37.

24. Clanchy, *From Memory to Written Record,* 147.

25. Thomas, *Oral Tradition and Written Record,* 61.

26. Thomas, *Literacy and Orality,* 83–84.

27. Ibid., 86.

28. Peter Machinist, "Assyrians on Assyria in the First Millennium B.C.," in *Anfänge politischen Denkens in der Antike: Die nahöstlichen Kulturen und die Griechen,* ed. Kurt Raaflaub (Munich: R. Oldenbourg, 1993), 101.

29. See also ibid., 102.

30. See also Botha, "Greco-Roman Literacy," 209.

31. Barkay, "The Iron Age II–III," 350; André Lemaire, *Les écoles et la formation de la Bible dans l'ancien Israël,* OBO 39 (Fribourg: Editions Universitaires; Göttingen: Vandenhoeck & Ruprecht, 1981), 7–9, 12–13, 20–21.

32. Mazar, *Archaeology,* 362.

33. Barkay, "The Iron Age II–III," 350.

34. See Klaas A. D. Smelik, *Writings from Ancient Israel* (Louisville, Ky.: Westminster/John Knox Press, 1991), 21–25, and bibliography, 171.

35. See the critique by David W. Jamieson-Drake, *Scribes and Schools in Monarchic Judah: A Socio-Archaeological Approach,* JSOTSup 109 (Sheffield: Sheffield Academic Press, 1991), 156–57.

36. Lemaire, *Les écoles,* 20–25.

37. Barkay, "The Iron Age II–III," 342.

38. Kyle P. McCarter, "Aspects of the Religion of the Israelite Monarchy: Biblical and Epigraphic Data," in *Ancient Israelite Religion: Essays in Honor of Frank Moore Cross* ed. Patrick D. Miller, Jr., Paul D. Hanson, and S. Dean McBride (Philadelphia: Fortress Press, 1987), 139.

39. Mazar, *Archaeology,* 449; McCarter, "Aspects," 143.

40. Mazar, *Archaeology,* 448.

41. Ibid., 516–17; Gabriel Barkay, *Ketef Hinnom: A Treasure Facing Jerusalem's Walls,* Israel Museum Catalogue, 274 (Jerusalem, 1986), 34–35.

42. Barkay, "The Iron Age II–III," 371.

43. N. Avigad, "The Epitaph of a Royal Steward from Siloam Village," *IEJ* 3 (1953): 137–52; see also the possible curse terminology in the preexilic inscription found in a burial cave near Khirbet Beit Lei and published by J. Naveh, "Old Hebrew Inscriptions in a Burial Cave," *IEJ* 13 (1963): 88.

44. P. Bar-Adon, "An Early Hebrew Inscription in a Judean Desert Cave," *IEJ* 25 (1975): 231, 227, 232.

45. Ibid., 230.

46. Ibid., 232.

47. Frank Moore Cross, Jr., "The Cave Inscriptions from Khirbet Beit Lei," in *Near Eastern Archaeology in the Twentieth Century: Essays in Honor of Nelson Glueck,* ed. James A. Sanders (Garden City, N.Y.: Doubleday, 1970), 304, 302.

48. Ibid., 301.

49. Ibid., 304.

50. Itzhaq Beit-Arieh, "A Literary Ostracon from Ḥorvat 'Uza," *Tel Aviv* 20 (1993): 55, 63.

51. Barkay, "The Iron Age II–III," 346.

52. Mazar, *Archaeology,* 455, 457, 458.

53. André Lemaire, "Writing and Writing Materials," *ABD* (1992): 6:1002.

54. Barkay, "The Iron Age II–III," 346.

55. See, e.g., Barkay, "The Iron Age II–III," 320.

56. Mazar, *Archaeology,* 515.

57. Ibid., 410.

58. See Smelik, *Writings,* 55–57.

59. Barkay, "The Iron Age II–III," 350.

60. Ibid.

61. Lemaire, "Writing and Writing Materials," 1003.

62. Mazar, *Archaeology,* 518.

63. Barkay, "The Iron Age II–III," 351.

64. Itzhaq Beit-Arieh, "A First Temple Period Census Document," *PEQ* 115 (1983): 105–8.

65. Dennis Pardee, "Letters," *ABD* (1992): 4:202; Dennis Pardee, *Handbook of Ancient Hebrew Letters: A Study Edition* (Chico, Calif.: Scholars Press, 1982), 4.

66. Pardee, *Handbook,* 152.

67. Pardee, "Letters," 284.

68. Pardee, *Handbook,* 164.

69. Ibid., 145–52.

70. For details about original publication and additional bibliography, see Pardee, *Handbook,* 15–21.

71. André Lemaire, *Inscriptions hébraïques I: Les ostraca,* Littératures anciennes du Proche-Orient, 9 (Paris: Cerf, 1977), 231–35; Pardee, *Handbook,* 28.

72. Pardee, *Handbook,* 92.

73. Smelik, *Writings,* 94; Pardee, "Letters," 23.

74. Pardee, "Letters," 20–21.

75. See Pardee, *Handbook,* 237; on such conversational qualities of letters in an oral world, see also Botha, "Greco-Roman Literacy," 207, 209.

76. Pardee, *Handbook,* 87. See also Michael D. Coogan, "Literacy in Ancient Israel," in *The Oxford Companion to the Bible,* eds. Bruce M. Metzger and Michael D. Coogan (New York: Oxford University Press, 1993), 437–38.

77. Pardee, *Handbook,* 87.

78. See detailed discussion in the major sources listed in Smelik, *Writings,* 174–75, and brief discussion in ibid., 70–71; and more recently Simon B. Parker, "Siloam Inscription Memorializes Engineering Achievement," *BAR* 20 (1994): 36–38.

79. Smelik, *Writings,* 90.

80. Barkay, "The Iron Age II–III," 350.

81. Mazar, *Archaeology,* 515; see Joseph Naveh, "A Fragment of an Ancient Hebrew Inscription from the Ophel," *IEJ* 32 (1982): 195–98.

82. Avraham Biran and Joseph Naveh, "An Aramaic Stele Fragment from Tel Dan," *BAR* 43 (1993): 81–98. Avraham Biran and Joseph Naveh, "The Tel Dan Inscription: A New Fragment," *IEJ* 45 (1995): 1–18.

83. Patrick M. Graham, "The Discovery and Reconstruction of the Mesha Inscription," in *Studies in the Mesha Inscription and Moab,* ed. A. Dearman (Atlanta: Scholars Press, 1989), 50.

84. Ibid., 72 (figure on 307).

85. Ibid., 89.

86. On the genre see Joel Drinkard, "The Literary Genre of the Mesha Inscription," in *Studies in the Mesha Inscription and Moab,* ed. A. Dearman, 131–54, esp. 140–42.

87. Graham, "The Discovery and Reconstruction," 87.

88. Drinkard, "The Literary Genre of the Mesha Inscription," 154.

89. Martin Goodman, "Sacred Scripture and 'Defiling the Hands,'" *JTS* 41 (1990): 99–107.

90. Jo Ann Hackett, *The Balaam Text from Deir 'Alla,* HSM 31 (Chico, Calif.: Scholars Press, 1980), 12.

91. See discussions in ibid., 3–4, 21–89.

92. Ibid., 80–89.

93. See ibid., 75, for ancient Near Eastern parallels; see also Ecclesiastes 12.

94. P. Kyle McCarter, "The Balaam Texts from Deir 'Alla: The First Combination," *BASOR* 239 (1980): 58.

95. Hackett, *The Balaam Text,* 75.

96. Ibid., 75, note 81.

Chapter 4: Logistics of Literacy:
Archives and Libraries, Education, and Writing Materials

1. Mazar, *Archaeology,* 410.

2. Ibid., 409–10.

3. Ibid., 410.

4. See Smelik, *Writings,* 57.

5. Mazar, *Archaeology,* 435.

6. Ibid., 440–41.

7. James M. Lindenberger, *Ancient Aramaic and Hebrew Letters,* ed. Kent Harold Richards (Atlanta: Scholars Press, 1994), 101.

8. Mazar, *Archaeology,* 418, 518–20.

9. Jonas C. Greenfield, "Aspects of Archives in the Achaemenid Period," in *Cuneiform Archives and Libraries: Papers Read at the 30th Rencontre assyriologique internationale, Leiden, 4–8 July 1983,* ed. Klaas R. Veenhof (Leiden: Nederlands Historisch Archaeologisch Institut, 1986), 295; Avigad, *Bullae and Seals.*

10. Greenfield, "Aspects of Archives," 295; Frank Moore Cross, "Papyri of the Fourth Century B.C. from Daliyeh," in *New Directions in Biblical Archaeology,* eds. David Noel Freedman and Jonas C. Greenfield (Garden City, N.Y.: Doubleday, 1969), 51–52.

11. Oral communication from Robert R. Wilson.

12. Menahem Haran, "Archives, Libraries, and the Order of the Biblical Books," *JANESCU* 22 (1993): 52, 55.

13. Marianna E. Vogelzang, "Some Aspects of Oral and Written Tradition in Akkadian," in *Mesopotamian Epic Literature: Oral or Aural?* eds. Marianna E. Vogelzang and Herman L. J. Vanstiphout (Lewiston, N.Y.: Edwin Mellen Press, 1992), 278.

14. Herman L. J. Vanstiphout, "Repetition and Structure in the Aratta Cycle: Their Relevance for the Orality Debate," in *Mesopotamian Epic Literature,* eds. Vogelzang and Vanstiphout, 247–64.

15. Shlomo Izre'el, "The Study of Oral Poetry: Reflections of a Neophyte," in *Mesopotamian Epic Literature,* eds. Vogelzang and Vanstiphout, 173–92.

16. Joan Goodnick Westenholtz, "Oral Traditions and Written Texts in the Cycle of Akkade," in *Mesopotamian Epic Literature,* ed. Vogelzang and Vanstiphout, 132.

17. Jerrold S. Cooper, "Babbling on Recovering Mesopotamian Orality," in *Mesopotamian Epic Literature,* Vogelzang and Vanstiphout, 122.

18. Bendt Alster, "Interaction of Oral and Written Poetry in Early Mesopotamian Literature," in *Mesopotamian Epic Literature,* ed. Vogelzang and Vanstiphout, 53; Cooper, "Babbling on Recovering Mesopotamian Orality," 117; see also Marianna E. Vogelzang, "Some Questions about the Akkadian Disputes," in *Dispute Poems and Dialogues in the Ancient and Mediaeval Near East: Forms and Types of Literary Debates in Semitic and Related Literatures,* eds. G.J. Reinink and H.L.J. Vanstiphout (Leuven: Department Orientalistiek, 1991), 54.

19. Westenholz, "Oral Traditions and Written Texts," 143.

20. Cooper, "Babbling on Recovering Mesopotamian Orality," 119.

21. Ibid.

22. Ernst Posner, *Archives in the Ancient World* (Cambridge, Mass.: Harvard University Press, 1972), 1–2, see details in 12–70.

23. Veenhof, ed., *Cuneiform Archives and Libraries,* 4, 24.

24. Ibid., 6.

25. Ibid., 8.

26. Ibid., 10.

27. Ibid., 13.

28. Ibid., 14; see also Mogens Weitemeyer, "Archives and Library Technique in Ancient Mesopotamia," *Libri* 6 (1956): 221.

29. P. Matthiae, "The Archives of the Royal Palace G of Ebla: Distribution and Arrangement of the Tablets According to Archaeological Evidence," in *Cuneiform Archives and Libraries,* ed. Veenhof, 70.

30. W. H. Van Soldt, "The Palace Archives at Ugarit," in *Cuneiform Archives and Libraries,* ed. Veenhof, 199–200.

31. Veenhof, ed., *Cuneiform Archives and Libraries,* 7.

32. Ibid., 20.

33. Jean Margueron, "Quelques remarques concernant les archives retrouvés dans le palais de Mari," in *Cuneiform Archives and Libraries,* ed. Veenhof, 145.

34. Olaf Pedersén, *Archives and Libraries in the City of Assur: A Survey of the Material from the German Excavations,* Part II (Uppsala: Almqvist & Wiksell, 1986), 85–136.

35. Ibid., 12–17.

36. Ibid., 15.

37. Ibid., 14–19.

38. Ibid., 29–33.

39. Ibid., 41–47.

40. Weitemeyer, "Archives and Library Technique," 227–28, 231.

41. Ibid., 231.

42. Simo Parpola, "Assyrian Library Records," *JNES* 42 (1983): 4.

43. Weitemeyer, "Archives and Library Technique," 229–31.

44. See ibid., 229.

45. Pedersén, *Archives and Libraries,* abstract, 140–41.

46. Stephen J. Lieberman, "Canonical and Official Cuneiform Texts: Towards an Understanding of Assurbanipal's Personal Tablet Collection," in *Lingering over Words: Studies in Ancient Near Eastern Literature in Honor of William L. Moran,* ed. Tzvi Abusch, John Huehnergard, and Piotr Steinkeller (Atlanta: Scholars Press, 1990), 305–6.

47. Ibid., 318.

48. Ibid., 312–20.

49. Ibid., 334, 325–26.

50. Ibid., 327.

51. Pedersén, *Archives and Libraries,* 47.

52. Stephanie Dalley, *Myths from Mesopotamia* (New York: Oxford University Press, 1989), xvi.

53. Ruth Finnegan, "Oral Literature and Writing in the South Pacific," in *Oral and Traditional Literatures,* ed. Norman Simms (Colorado Springs, Colo.: Three Continents Press, 1982), 23–25; Ruth Finnegan, *Literacy and Orality* (Oxford: Basil Blackwell Publisher, 1988), 11; see also Ruth Finnegan, "How Oral Is Oral Literature?" *Bulletin of the School of Oriental and African Studies* 37 (1974): 56–57.

54. Lieberman, "Canonical and Official Cuneiform Texts," 311.

55. Lemaire, *Les écoles,* 47, 78–79; see the clear summary of his position in Jamieson-Drake, *Scribes and Schools,* 12.

56. A. Demsky and M. Kochavi, "An Alphabet from the Days of the Judges," *BAR* 4 (1978): 23–30.

57. Lemaire, *Les écoles,* 58; see also R. J. Williams, "Writing and Writing Materials," *IDB* (1962) 4:915; Millard, "An Assessment of the Evidence," 26, 29.

58. Meyers, *Discovering Eve,* 152; Jamieson-Drake, *Scribes and Schools;* and James Crenshaw, "Education in Ancient Israel," *JBL* 104 (1985): 612–15.

59. Millard, "An Assessment for the Evidence," 31; Williams, "Writing and Writing Materials," 915; and Lemaire, *Les écoles,* 58.

60. Jamiesen-Drake, *Scribes and Schools,* 156–57.

61. Meyers, *Discovering Eve,* 154.

62. Jamiesen-Drake, *Scribes and Schools,* 156.

63. A. Demsky, "Writing," *Encyclopedia Judaica* 16 (1971): 664.

64. See Marvin H. Pope, *Job* (Garden City, N.Y.: Doubleday, 1965), 144, for a discussion of Job 19:24 and ancient Near Eastern parallels.

65. André Lemaire, "Une inscription paléo-hébraïque sur granade en ivoire," *RB* 88 (1981): 236–39.

66. Lemaire, "Writing and Writing Materials," 1002.

67. Ibid.

68. See the description and discussion in Lansing R. Hicks, "Delet and Megillah: A Fresh Approach to Jeremiah *xxxvi,*" *VT* 33 (1983): 49–51.

69. See Naphtali Lewis, *Papyrus in Classical Antiquity* (Oxford: Clarendon Press, 1974), 3–20, 104–14.

70. Trans. Demsky, "Writing," 658, col. 2; on the manufacture of papyrus, see also Lewis, *Papyrus,* 34–69.

71. Demsky, "Writing," 658; Lemaire, "Writing and Writing Materials," 1003.

72. See chapter 3 and Lemaire "Writing and Writing Materials," 1003, for a quick overview.

73. Leila Avrin, *Scribes, Script, and Books: The Book Arts from Antiquity to the Renaissance* (Chicago/London: American Library Association and the British Library, 1991), 85, 87.

74. Lemaire, "Writing and Writing Materials," 1003; Menahem Haran, "Book-Scrolls at the Beginning of the Second Temple Period: The Transition from Papyrus to Skins," *HUCA* 54 (1983): 111–22.

75. Demsky, "Writing," 660; see also Hicks, "Delet and Megillah," 57–61.

76. Demsky, "Writing," 660.

77. Hicks, "Delet and Megillah," 62–66.

78. Ibid., 61.

79. Bruce M. Metzger, *The Text of the New Testament: Its Transmission, Corruption, and Restoration* (New York: Oxford University Press, 1992), 8.

80. A. N. Doane, "The Ethnography of Scribal Writing and Anglo-Saxon Poetry: Scribe as Performer," *Oral Tradition* 9 (1994): 420–39.

81. Julio Trebolle Barrera, "The Authoritative Functions of Scriptural Works at Qumran," in *The Community of the Renewed Covenant: The Notre Dame Symposium on the Dead Sea Scrolls,* ed. Eugene Ulrich and James VanderKam (Notre Dame, Ind.: University of Notre Dame Press, 1993), 108.

82. Eugene Ulrich, "The Bible in the Making: The Scriptures at Qumran," in *The Community of the Renewed Covenant,* ed. Ulrich and Vanderkam, 85–91.

83. Emanuel Tov, "Biblical Texts as Reworked in Some Qumran Manuscripts with Special Attention to 4QRP and 4QPara Gen-Exod," in *The Community of the Renewed Covenant,* ed. Ulrich and VanderKam, 124, 127–28, 113.

84. Barrera, "The Authoritative Functions," 108.

85. Ibid., 110.

86. Ulrich, "The Bible in the Making," in *The Community of the Renewed Covenant,* ed. Ulrich and VanderKam, 92.

87. Ibid.

88. Ibid.

89. Alan R. Millard, "Were Words Separated in Ancient Hebrew Writing?" *Bible Review* 3 (1992): 44–47.

90. T. C. Skeat, "The Origin of the Christian Codex," *Zeitschrift für Papyrologie und Epigraphik* 102 (1994): 265–66.

91. Metzger, *The Text of the New Testament,* 6.

Chapter 5: Attitudes to Writing in the Hebrew Bible: The Oral End of the Continuum

1. See Bengt Holbek, "What the Illiterate Think of Writing," in *Literacy and Society,* eds. Karen Schousboe and Mogens Trolle Larsen (Copenhagen: Akademisk Forlag, 1989), 183–96.

2. Ibid., 191.

3. Robert R. Wilson, "Prophecy in Crisis: The Call of Ezekiel," in *Interpreting the Prophets,* ed. James L. Mays and Paul J. Achtemeier (Philadelphia: Fortress Press, 1987), 163–64.

4. Contrast Davis, *Swallowing the Scroll,* 51, who implies that things are clearer.

5. Ibid., 37, 39, 66, 117.

6. Michael D. Coogan, "Literacy in Ancient Israel," 437–38.

7. See Clanchy, *From Memory to Written Record,* 147.

Chapter 6: The Literate End of the Continuum

1. See Veenhof, ed., *Cuneiform Archives and Libraries,* 30, concerning sealed "clay envelopes."

2. See above, and cf. the interaction at Ruth 4:7–12.

3. See Thomas, *Literacy and Orality,* 72–73.

Chapter 7: The Interplay between Orality and Literacy: Case Studies

1. Lemaire, *Les écoles,* 59; Williams, "Writing and Writing Materials," 915.

2. For example, Millard, "The Question of Israelite Literacy," 26, 29; "An Assessment of the Evidence," 305.

3. Millard, "An Assessment of the Evidence," 308.

4. Ibid.

5. Ibid.

6. Ibid.

7. See Hicks, "Delet and Megillah," 61–62.

Chapter 8: The Oral Mentality and the Written Bible

1. See Ivan Engell, *A Rigid Scrutiny: Critical Essays on the Old Testament,* trans. and ed. by John T. Willis, with the collaboration of Helmer Ringgren. (Nashville: Vanderbilt University Press, 1969), 6, 168.

2. Yair Zakovitch, "Review of *Underdogs and Tricksters: A Prelude to Biblical Folklore," JAF* 104 (1991): 235.

3. Brian Peckham, *History and Prophecy: The Development of Late Judean Literary Traditions* (New York: Doubleday, 1993), 21.

4. Ibid., 22.

5. See the review in Douglas A. Knight, "Wellhausen and the Interpretation of Israel's Literature," in *Julius Wellhausen and His Prolegomena to the History of Israel,* ed. Douglas A. Knight, *Semeia* 25 (1982): 21–22.

6. Cross, *Canaanite Myth,* 274–89.

7. New York: Summit Books, 1987.

8. Walter Brueggemann, "David and His Theologian," *CBQ* 30 (1968): 158–59.

9. R. E. Clements, *Abraham and David* (London: SCM Press, 1967); Robert B. Coote and David Robert Ord, *The Bible's First History* (Philadelphia: Fortress Press, 1989); compare Rolf Rendtorff, "The 'Yahwist' as Theologian? The Dilemma of Pentateuchal Criticism," *JSOT* 3 (1977): 2–10.

10. See, for example, Robert B. Coote, *In Defense of Revolution: The Elohist History* (Minneapolis: Augsburg Fortress, 1991).

11. David Rosenberg and Harold Bloom, *The Book of J* (New York: Grove Weidenfeld, 1990).

12. Coote, *In Defense of Revolution,* 77.

13. So Friedman, *Who Wrote the Bible?* (New York: Summit Books, 1987), 247–48; and Coote and Ord, *The Bible's First History,* 99–109, 139–45.

14. Niditch, *War,* 90–105.

15. Westermann, *Genesis 12—36,* 30–50.

16. See Skeat, "Origin," 265.

17. David Damrosch, *The Narrative Covenant: Transformations of Genre in the Growth of Biblical Literature* (San Francisco: Harper & Row, 1987), 4.

18. Ibid., 59, 77, 116.

19. John Van Seters, *Prologue to History: The Yahwist as Historian in Genesis* (Louisville, Ky.: Westminster/John Knox Press, 1992). See for example his treatment of Noah's tale in Genesis 6—9, 160.

20. John Van Seters, *In Search of History: Historiography in the Ancient World and the Origins of Biblical History* (New Haven, Conn.: Yale University Press, 1983), 357.

21. Van Seters, *Prologue to History,* 22.

22. Van Seters, *In Search of History,* 355–57.

23. Ben-Amos, "Analytical Categories and Ethnic Genres."

24. Van Seters, *Prologue to History,* 20, 40.

25. Van Seters, *In Search of History,* 248, 215.

26. Ibid., 258, 292.

27. Ibid., 361.

28. Van Seters, *Prologue to History,* 332.

29. Ibid., 123–24, 128.

30. R. N. Whybray, *The Making of the Pentateuch: A Methodological Study,* JSOT-Sup 53 (Sheffield: Sheffield Academic Press, 1987), 129–31, 170, 215–19.

31. See also Niditch, *Underdogs and Tricksters,* 8–9; and Patricia G. Kirkpatrick, *The Old Testament and Folklore Study,* JSOTSup 62 (Sheffield: Sheffield Academic Press, 1988).

32. Whybray, *The Making of the Pentateuch,* 142–58.

33. Robert R. Wilson, *Sociological Approaches to the Old Testament* (Philadelphia: Fortress Press, 1984), 54; Burke O. Long, "Recent Field Studies in Oral Literature and the Question of *Sitz im Leben,*" *Semeia* 5 (1976): 192, 198; Whybray, *The Making of the Pentateuch,* 165.

34. Whybray, *The Making of the Pentateuch,* 242.

35. Mabel L. Lang, *Herodotean Narrative and Discourse* (Cambridge Mass.: Harvard University Press, 1984), 13–14.

36. Ibid., 39, 41–43, 51.

37. Ibid., 17. See also pp. 52 and 58 for a discussion of other devices.

38. Ibid., 17.

39. See Niditch, "Composition," 518–20.

40. See ibid., 523–27.

41. Niles, "Understanding *Beowulf:* Oral Poetry Acts," *JAF* 106 (1993): 133.

42. Ibid., 133–34; on the latter see Ivan Engnell, *Gamla Testamentet: En traditionshistorisk inledning* (Stockholm: Svenska Kyrkans Diakonistyrelses Bokförlag, 1945), 42; and Nielsen, *Oral Tradition,* 60–61.

43. Robert R. Wilson, *Prophecy and Society in Ancient Israel* (Philadelphia: Fortress Press, 1980), 51, 76–83.

44. Oral communication from Wilson.

45. Morton Smith, *Palestinian Parties and Politics That Shaped the Old Testament* (London: SCM Press, 1987), 17, 30–42.

46. Niles, "Understanding *Beowulf,*" 137–39.

47. Yehoshua Gitay, "Deutero-Isaiah: Oral or Written?" *JBL* 99 (1980): 191–94.

48. See Nielsen, *Oral Tradition,* 33–34.

49. Gregory Nagy, *Greek Mythology and Poetics* (Ithaca, N.Y.: Cornell University Press, 1990), 42.

50. Ibid., 37, 40–42; see Nielsen's brief allusion to rhapsodes, *Oral Tradition,* 30–31.

51. Nagy, *Greek Mythology and Poetics,* 41, quoting P. Kiparsky, "Oral Poetry: Some Linguistic and Typological Considerations," in *Oral Literature and the Formula,* eds. B. A. Stolz and R. S. Shannon (Ann Arbor, Mich.: Center for the Coordination of Ancient and Modern Studies, University of Michigan, 1976), 99–102.

52. Nagy, *Greek Mythology and Poetics,* 42.

53. Ibid., 41.

54. Niles, "Understanding *Beowulf,*" 134–35.

55. Ibid., 134.

56. Ibid., 135.

57. George A. Kennedy, *Classical Greek Rhetoric and Its Christian and Secular Tradition from Ancient to Modern Times* (Chapel Hill, N.C.: University of North Carolina Press, 1980), 110–19.

58. Ibid., 11.

59. See Niditch, *Folklore* for a fuller discussion of the use of proverbs in Ecclesiastes.

60. On the Chronicler's worldview, see J. D. Newsome, "Toward an Understanding of the Chronicler and His Purposes," *JBL* 94 (1975): 201–17; and Sara Japhet,

The Ideology of the Book of Chronicles and Its Place in Biblical Thought (Frankfurt am Main: Peter Lang, 1989).

61. The use of masculine pronouns here does not imply taking for granted that the Chronicler was a man. Matters of gender, voice, and author's identity are devilishly difficult to decode in the Hebrew Bible; see S. D. Goitein, "Women as Creators of Biblical Genres," *Prooftexts* 8 (1988): 1–33; and Athalya Brenner and Fokkelien Van Dijk-Hemmes, *On Gendering Texts: Female and Male Voices in the Hebrew Bible* (Leiden: E.J. Brill, 1993). It seems likely that some women of particular classes or occupations, like some men, in the time of the Chronicler had access to skills of writing and reading.

62. On the question of the text quoted by the Chronicler, see Steven L. McKenzie, *The Chronicler's Use of the Deuteronomistic History,* HSM 33 (Atlanta: Scholars Press, 1984).

Conclusion

1. Denise A. Troll, "The Illiterate Mode of Written Communication: The Work of the Medieval Scribe," in *Oral and Written Communication: Historical Approaches,* ed. Richard Leo Enos (Newbury Park, Calif.: Sage Publications, Inc., 1990), 97–98.

2. Ibid., 98.

3. Ibid., 111.

4. Ibid., 118–20

5. George C. Heider, *The Cult of Molek: A Reassessment,* JSOTSup 43 (Sheffield: JSOT Press, 1985); John Day, *Molech: A God of Human Sacrifice in Old Testament,* University of Cambridge Oriental Publications, 41 (Cambridge: Cambridge University Press, 1989); Susan Ackerman, *Under Every Green Tree: Popular Religion in Sixth-Century Judah,* HSM 46 (Atlanta: Scholars Press, 1992).

6. Theodore J. Lewis, *Cults of the Dead in Ancient Israel and Ugarit,* HSM 39 (Atlanta: Scholars Press, 1989).

7. Niditch, *War.*

Bibliography

Ackerman, Susan. *Under Every Green Tree: Popular Religion in Sixth-Century Judah*. HSM 46. Atlanta: Scholars Press, 1992.

Alster, Bendt. "Interaction of Oral and Written Poetry in Early Mesopotamian Literature." In *Mesopotamian Epic Literature: Oral or Aural?* edited by Marianna E. Vogelzang and Herman L. J. Vanstiphout, 23–55. Lewiston, N.Y.: Edwin Mellen Press, 1992.

Alter, Robert. *The Art of Biblical Narrative*. New York: Basic Books, 1981.

Andersen, Øivind. "The Significance of Writing in Early Greece: A Critical Appraisal." In *Literacy and Society*, edited by Karen Schousboe and Mogens Trolle Larsen, 73–91. Copenhagen: Akademisk Forlag, 1989.

Avigad, N. *Bullae and Seals from a Post-Exilic Judean Archive*. Qedem 4. Jerusalem: The Institute of Archaeology, The Hebrew University of Jerusalem, 1976.

———. "The Epitaph of a Royal Steward from Siloam Village." *IEJ* 3 (1953): 137–52.

———. "The Second Tomb-Inscription of the Royal Steward." *IEJ* 6 (1955): 163–66.

Avrin, Leila. *Scribes, Script, and Books: The Book Arts from Antiquity to the Renaissance*. Chicago/London: American Library Association and the British Library, 1991.

Baines, J., and C. J. Eyre. "Four Notes on Literacy." *Göttingen Miszellen* 61 (1983): 65–96.

Bar-Adon, P. "An Early Hebrew Inscription in a Judean Desert Cave." *IEJ* 25 (1975): 226–32.

Barkay, Gabriel. "The Iron Age II–III." In *The Archaeology of Ancient Israel*, edited by Amnon Ben-Tor, 302–73. New Haven, Conn.: Yale University Press for The Open University of Israel, 1992.

———. *Ketef Hinnom: A Treasure Facing Jerusalem's Walls*. Israel Museum Catalogue, 274. Jerusalem, 1986.

Barrera, Julio Trebolle. "The Authoritative Functions of Scriptural Works at Qumran." In *The Community of the Renewed Covenant: The Notre Dame Symposium on the Dead Sea Scrolls*, edited by Eugene Ulrich and James VanderKam, 95–110. Notre Dame, Ind.: University of Notre Dame Press, 1993.

Beit-Arieh, Itzhaq. "A First Temple Period Census Document." *PEQ* 115 (1983): 105–8.

———. "A Literary Ostracon from Ḥorvat ʿUza." *Tel Aviv* 20 (1993): 55–65.

Ben-Amos, Dan. "Analytical Categories and Ethnic Genres." In *Folklore Genres*, edited by Dan Ben-Amos, 215–42. Austin: University of Texas Press, 1976.

Biran, Avraham, and Joseph Naveh. "An Aramaic Stele Fragment from Tel Dan." *BAR* 43 (1993): 81–98.

———. "The Tel Dan Inscription: A New Fragment." *IEJ* 45 (1995): 1–18.

Botha, P.J.J. "Greco-Roman Literacy as Setting for New Testament Writings." *Neotestamentica* 26 (1992): 195–215.

Brenner, Athalya, and Fokkelien Van Dijk-Hemmes. *On Gendering Texts: Female and Male Voices in the Hebrew Bible.* Leiden: E.J. Brill, 1993.

Brueggemann, W. "David and His Theologian." *CBQ* 30 (1968): 156–81.

Clanchy, M. T. *From Memory to Written Record: England 1066–1307.* Cambridge, Mass.: Harvard University Press, 1979.

Clements, R. E. *Abraham and David.* London: SCM Press, 1967.

Conrad, Edgar. "Heard But Not Seen: The Representation of 'Books' in the Old Testament." *JSOT* 54 (1992): 45–59.

Coogan, Michael D. "Canaanite Origins and Lineage: Reflections on the Religion of Ancient Israel." In *Ancient Israelite Religion: Essays in Honor of Frank Moore Cross,* edited by Patrick D. Miller, Jr., Paul D. Hanson, and S. Dean McBride, 115–24. Philadelphia: Fortress Press, 1987.

———. "Literacy in Ancient Israel." In *The Oxford Companion to the Bible,* edited by Bruce M. Metzger and Michael D. Coogan, 437–38. New York: Oxford University Press, 1993.

Cooper, Jerrold S. "Babbling on Recovering Mesopotamian Orality." In *Mesopotamian Epic Literature: Oral or Aural?* edited by Marianna E. Vogelzang and Herman L. J. Vanstiphout, 103–22. Lewiston, N.Y.: Edwin Mellen Press, 1992.

Coote, Robert B. *In Defense of Revolution: The Elohist History.* Minneapolis: Augsburg Fortress, 1991.

Coote, Robert B., and David Robert Ord. *The Bible's First History.* Philadelphia: Fortress Press, 1989.

———. *In the Beginning: Creation and the Priestly History.* Minneapolis: Fortress Press, 1991.

Crenshaw, James. "Education in Ancient Israel." *JBL* 104 (1985): 601–15.

Cross, Frank Moore, Jr. *Canaanite Myth and Hebrew Epic: Essays in the History of the Religion of Israel.* Cambridge, Mass.: Harvard University Press, 1973.

———. "The Cave Inscriptions from Khirbet Beit Lei." In *Near Eastern Archaeology in the Twentieth Century: Essays in Honor of Nelson Glueck,* edited by James A. Sanders, 299–306. Garden City, N.Y.: Doubleday, 1970.

———. "Papyri of the Fourth Century B.C. from Daliyeh." In *New Directions in Biblical Archaeology,* edited by David Noel Freedman and Jonas C. Greenfield, 41–62. Garden City, N.Y.: Doubleday, 1969.

Culley, Robert C. "An Approach to the Problem of Oral Tradition." *VT* 13 (1963): 113–25.

———. *Oral Formulaic Language in the Biblical Psalms.* Near and Middle East Series, 4. Toronto: University of Toronto Press, 1967.

———. "Oral Tradition and Biblical Studies." *Oral Traditions* 1 (1986): 30–65.

———. "Oral Tradition and Historicity." In *Studies on the Ancient Palestinian World,* edited by J. W. Wevers and D. B. Redford, 102–16. Toronto: University of Toronto Press, 1972.

———. "Oral Tradition and the OT: Some Recent Discussion." *Semeia* 5 (1976): 1–33.

———. *Themes and Variations.* Semeia Studies. Atlanta: Scholars Press, 1992.

Dalley, Stephanie. *Myths from Mesopotamia.* New York: Oxford University Press, 1989.

Damrosch, David. *The Narrative Covenant: Transformations of Genre in the Growth of Biblical Literature.* San Francisco: Harper & Row, 1987.

Davies, G. I. *Ancient Hebrew Inscriptions: Corpus and Concordance.* Cambridge: Cambridge University Press, 1991.

Davis, Ellen F. *Swallowing the Scroll: Textuality and the Dynamics of Discourse in Ezekiel's Prophecy.* Sheffield: Almond Press, 1989.

Dawson, Doyne. *Cities of the Gods: Communist Utopias in Greek Thought.* New York: Oxford University Press, 1992.

Day, John. *Molech: A God of Human Sacrifice in Old Testament.* University of Cambridge Oriental Publications, 41. Cambridge: Cambridge University Press, 1989.

Dearman, J. Andrew, ed. *Studies in the Mesha Inscription and Moab.* Atlanta: Scholars Press, 1989.

Demsky, A. "Education in the Biblical Period." *Encyclopedia Judaica* (1971): 6:382–98.

———. "Writing." *Encyclopedia Judaica* (1971), 16:654–72.

Demsky, A., and M. Kochavi. "An Alphabet from the Days of the Judges." *BAR* 4 (1978): 23–30.

Doane, A. N. "The Ethnography of Scribal Writing and Anglo-Saxon Poetry: Scribe as Performer." *Oral Tradition* 9 (1994): 420–39.

Drinkard, Joel. "The Literary Genre of the Mesha Inscription." In *Studies in the Mesha Inscription and Moab,* edited by A. Dearman, 131–54. Atlanta: Scholars Press, 1989.

Engnell, Ivan. *Gamla Testamentet: En traditionshistorisk inledning.* Stockholm: Svenska Kyrkans Diakonistyrelses Bokförlag, 1945.

———. *A Rigid Scrutiny: Critical Essays on the Old Testament.* Translated and edited by John T. Willis, with the collaboration of Helmer Ringgren. Nashville: Vanderbilt University Press, 1969.

Enos, Richard Leo, ed. *Oral and Written Communication: Historical Approaches.* Written Communication Annual, 4. Newbury Park, Calif.: Sage Publications, Inc. 1990.

Eyre, Christopher, and John Baines. "Interactions between Orality and Literacy in Ancient Egypt." In *Literacy and Society,* edited by Karen Schousboe and Mogens Trolle Larsen, 91–119. Copenhagen: Akademisk Forlag, 1989.

Finnegan, Ruth. "How Oral Is Oral Literature?" *Bulletin of the School of Oriental and African Studies* 37 (1974): 52–64.

———. *Literacy and Orality.* Oxford: Basil Blackwell, 1988.

———. "Literacy Versus Non-Literacy: The Great Divide?" In *Modes of Thought,* edited by Robin Horton and Ruth Finnegan, 112–44. London: Faber & Faber, 1973.

———. *Oral Poetry: Its Nature, Significance, and Social Context.* Cambridge: Cambridge University Press, 1977.

———. "Oral Literature and Writing in the South Pacific." In *Oral and Traditional Literatures,* edited by Norman Simms, 22–36. Colorado Springs, Colo.: Three Continents Press, 1982.

———. *Oral Literature in Africa.* Oxford: Clarendon Press, 1970.

Fishbane, Michael. *Text and Texture.* New York: Schocken Books, 1979.

Foley, John Miles. *Immanent Art: From Structure to Meaning in Traditional Oral Epic.* Bloomington, Ind.: Indiana University Press, 1991.

———. "The Oral Theory in Context." In *Oral Traditional Literature: A Festschrift for Albert Bates Lord,* edited by John Miles Foley, 27–122. Columbus: Slavica, 1980.

———. *The Singer of Tales in Performance.* Bloomington, Ind.: Indiana University Press, 1995.

———. *The Theory of Oral Composition: History and Methodology.* Bloomington, Ind.: Indiana University Press, 1988.

———. *Traditional Oral Epic: The Odyssey, Beowulf, and the Serbo-Croatian Return Song.* Berkeley, Calif.: University of California Press, 1990.

———. "Word-Power, Performance, and Tradition." *JAF* 105 (1992): 275–301.

Foley, John Miles, ed. *Comparative Research on Oral Traditions: A Memorial for Milman Parry.* Columbus: Slavica, 1980.

———. *Oral Tradition in Literature: Interpretation in Context.* Columbia: University of Missouri Press, 1986.

———. *Oral Traditional Literature: A Festschrift for Albert Bates Lord.* Columbus: Slavica, 1980.

Fontaine, Carole R. *Traditional Sayings in the Old Testament: A Contextual Study.* The Bible and Literature, 5. Sheffield: Almond Press, 1982.

Friedman, Richard E. *Who Wrote the Bible?* New York: Summit Books, 1987.

Geller, Stephen A. *Parallelism in Early Biblical Poetry.* HSM 20. Missoula, Mont.: Scholars Press, 1979.

Gevirtz, Stanley. *Patterns in the Early Poetry of Israel.* Studies in Ancient Oriental Civilization, 32. Chicago: University of Chicago Press, 1963.

Gitay, Yehoshua. "Deutero-Isaiah: Oral or Written?" *JBL* 99 (1980): 185–97.

Gledhill, J. B., B. Bender, and M. T. Larson, eds. *State and Society: The Emergence and Development of Social Hierarchy and Political Centralization.* London: Unwin Hyman, 1988.

Goody, Jack, ed. *Literacy in Traditional Societies.* Cambridge: Cambridge University Press, 1968.

Goitein, S. D. "Women as Creators of Biblical Genres." *Prooftexts* 8 (1988): 1–33 (translation of "Našim k'yosrot Sugey Sifrut Bammiqra." In *Iyyunim Bammiqra,* Tel Aviv: Yavneh Press, 1957).

Goodman, Martin. "Sacred Scripture and 'Defiling the Hands.'" *JTS* 41 (1990): 99–107.

Graham, M. Patrick. "The Discovery and Reconstruction of the Mesha Inscription." In *Studies in the Mesha Inscription and Moab,* edited by A. Dearman, 41–92. Atlanta: Scholars Press, 1989.

Greenfield, Jonas C. "Aspects of Archives in the Achaemenid Period." In *Cuneiform Archives and Libraries: Papers Read at the 30th Rencontre assyriologique inter-*

nationale, Leiden, 4–8 July 1983, edited by Klaas R. Veenhof, 289–95. Leiden: Nederlands Historisch Archaeologisch Institut, 1986.

Gunkel, Hermann. *The Folktale in the Old Testament.* Sheffield: Almond Press, 1987. Originally published as *Das Märchen im Alten Testament.* Tübingen: J.C.B. Mohr, 1917.

————. *Genesis.* 3d ed. Göttingen: Vandenhoeck & Ruprecht, 1910.

————. *The Legends of Genesis.* New York: Schocken Books, 1966.

Gunn, David. "The 'Battle Report': Oral or Scribal Convention?" *JBL* 93 (1974): 513–18.

————. "Narrative Patterns and Oral Tradition in Judges and Samuel." *VT* 24 (1974): 286–317.

————. "On Oral Tradition: A Response to John Van Seters." *Semeia,* 5 1976): 155–61.

Hackett, Jo Ann. *The Balaam Text from Deir 'Alla.* HSM 31. Chico, Calif.: Scholars Press, 1980.

————. "Religious Traditions in Israelite Transjordan." In *Ancient Israelite Religion: Essays in Honor of Frank Moore Cross,* edited by Patrick D. Miller, Jr., Paul D. Hanson, and S. Dean McBride, 125–36. Philadelphia: Fortress Press, 1987.

Halpern, Baruch. *The First Historians: The Hebrew Bible and History.* San Francisco: Harper & Row, 1988.

Hanson, Paul D. "Rebellion in Heaven, Azazel, and Euhemeristic Heroes in 1 Enoch 6–7." *JBL* 96 (1977): 195–233.

————. "Zechariah 9 and the Recapitulation of an Ancient Ritual Pattern." *JBL* 92 (1973): 37–59.

Haran, Menahem. "Archives, Libraries, and the Order of the Biblical Books." *JANESCU* 22 (1993): 51–61.

————. "Book-Scrolls at the Beginning of the Second Temple Period: The Transition from Papyrus to Skins." *HUCA* 54 (1983): 111–22.

Harris, William V. *Ancient Literacy.* Cambridge, Mass.: Harvard University Press, 1989.

Heidel, Alexander. *The Babylonian Genesis.* Chicago: University of Chicago Press, 1951.

Heider, George C. *The Cult of Molek: A Reassessment.* JSOTSup 43. Sheffield: JSOT Press, 1985.

Hendel, Ronald S. *The Epic of the Patriarch: The Jacob Cycle and the Narrative Traditions of Canaan and Israel.* HSM 42. Atlanta: Scholars Press, 1987.

Hicks, Lansing R. "Delet and Megillah: A Fresh Approach to Jeremiah *xxxvi.*" *VT* 33 (1983): 46–66.

Holbek, Bengt. "What the Illiterate Think of Writing." In *Literacy and Society,* edited by Karen Schousboe and Mogens Trolle Larsen, 183–96. Copenhagen: Akademisk Forlag, 1989.

Holladay, John S., Jr. "Religion in Israel and Judah under the Monarchy: An Explicitly Archaeological Approach." In *Ancient Israelite Religion: Essays in Honor of Frank Moore Cross,* edited by Patrick D. Miller, Jr., Paul D. Hanson, and S. Dean McBride, 249–99. Philadelphia: Fortress Press, 1987.

Hymes, Dell. "Ethnopoetics, Oral-Formulaic Theory, and Editing Texts." *Oral Tradition* 9 (1994): 330–70.

Irvin, Dorothy. "The Joseph and Moses Stories as Narrative in the Light of Ancient Near Eastern Narrative." In *Israelite and Judaean History,* edited by John H. Hayes and J. Maxwell Miller, 180–209. Philadelphia: Westminster Press, 1977.

———. *Mytharion: The Comparison of Tales from the Old Testament and the Ancient Near East.* Veröffentlichungen zur Kultur und Geschichte des Alten Testaments, 32. Neukirchen-Vluyn: Neukirchener Verlag, 1978.

Izre'el, Shlomo. "The Study of Oral Poetry: Reflections of a Neophyte." In *Mesopotamian Epic Literature: Oral or Aural?* edited by Marianna E. Vogelzang and Herman L. J. Vanstiphout 155–225. Lewiston, N.Y.: Edwin Mellen Press, 1992.

Jacoby, Felix. *Atthis: The Local Chronicles of Ancient Athens.* Oxford: Clarendon Press, 1949.

Jamieson-Drake, David W. *Scribes and Schools in Monarchic Judah: A Socio-Archaeological Approach.* JSOTSup 109. Sheffield: Sheffield Academic Press, 1991.

Japhet, Sara. *The Ideology of the Book of Chronicles and Its Place in Biblical Thought.* Frankfurt am Main: Peter Lang, 1989.

Jolles, André. *Einfache Formen.* Halle: Niemeyer, 1929.

Kennedy, George A. *Classical Rhetoric and Its Christian and Secular Tradition from Ancient to Modern Times.* Chapel Hill, N.C.: University of North Carolina, 1980.

Kiparsky, P. "Oral Poetry: Some Linguistic and Typological Considerations." In *Oral Literature and the Formula,* edited by B. A. Stolz and R. S. Shannon, 73–106. Ann Arbor, Mich.: Center for the Coordination of Ancient and Modern Studies, University of Michigan, 1976.

Kirk, G. S. *Myth: Its Meaning and Functions in Ancient and Other Cultures.* Berkeley, Calif.: University of California Press, 1970.

Kirkpatrick, Patricia G. *The Old Testament and Folklore Study.* JSOTSup 62. Sheffield: Sheffield Academic Press, 1988.

Knight, Douglas A. "Wellhausen and the Interpretation of Israel's Literature." In *Julius Wellhausen and His Prolegomena to the History of Israel,* edited by Douglas A. Knight, 21–36. *Semeia* 25 (1982).

———. *Rediscovering the Traditions of Israel.* SBLDS 9. Missoula: Scholars Press, 1975.

Kselman, John R. "The Recovery of Poetic Fragments from the Pentateuchal Priestly Source." *JBL* 97 (1978): 161–73.

Kugel, J. "The Adverbial Use of *kî tôb.*" *JBL* 99 (1980): 433–35.

———. *The Idea of Biblical Poetry: Parallelism and Its History.* New Haven, Conn.: Yale University Press, 1981.

Lang, Mabel L. *Herodotean Narrative and Discourse.* Cambridge, Mass.: Harvard University Press, 1984.

Larsen, Mogens Trolle. "What They Wrote on Clay." In *Literacy and Society,* edited by Karen Schousboe and Mogens Trolle Larsen, 121–48. Copenhagen: Akademisk Forlag, 1989.

Lemaire, André. *Les écoles et la formation de la Bible dans l'ancien Israël.* OBO 39. Fribourg: Editions Universitaires; Göttingen: Vandenhoeck & Ruprecht, 1981.

———. *Inscriptions hébraïques I: Les ostraca.* Littératures anciennes du Proche-Orient, 9. Paris: Cerf, 1977.

———. "Une inscription paléo-hébraïque sur granade en ivoire." *RB* 88 (1981): 236–39.

———. "Sagesse et écoles." *VT* 34 (1984): 270–81.

———. "Writing and Writing Materials." *ABD* (1992): 6:999–1008.

Lewis, Naphtali. *Papyrus in Classical Antiquity.* Oxford: Clarendon Press, 1974.

Lewis, Theodore J. *Cults of the Dead in Ancient Israel and Ugarit.* HSM 39. Atlanta: Scholars Press, 1989.

———. "Death Cult Imagery in Isaiah 57." *HAR* 11 (1987): 267–84.

Lieberman, Stephen J. "Canonical and Official Cuneiform Texts: Towards an Understanding of Assurbanipal's Personal Tablet Collection." In *Lingering over Words: Studies in Ancient Near Eastern Literature in Honor of William L. Moran,* edited by Tzvi Abusch, John Huehnergard, and Piotr Steinkeller, 305–36. Atlanta: Scholars Press, 1990.

Lindenberger, James M. *Ancient Aramaic and Hebrew Letters.* Edited by Kent Harold Richards. Atlanta: Scholars Press, 1994.

Long, Burke O. "Recent Field Studies in Oral Literature and Their Bearing on Old Testament Criticism." *VT* 26 (1976): 187–98.

———. "Recent Field Studies in Oral Literature and the Question of *Sitz im Leben.*" *Semeia* 5 (1976): 35–49.

———. "The Social Function of Conflict Among the Prophets." In *Anthropological Perspectives on Old Testament Prophecy,* edited by Robert C. Culley and Thomas Overholt, 31–53. Chico, Calif.: Scholars Press, 1982.

Lord, Albert B. "Characteristics of Orality." *Oral Tradition* 2 (1987, A Festschrift for Walter J. Ong): 54–72.

———. "Memory, Fixity and Genre in Oral Traditional Poetries." In *Oral Traditional Literature: A Festschrift for Albert Bates Lord,* edited by John Miles Foley, 451–561. Columbus: Slavica, 1980.

———. "The Merging of Two Worlds: Oral and Written Poetry as Carriers of Ancient Values." In *Oral Tradition in Literature: Interpretation in Context,* edited by John Miles Foley, 19–64, Columbia, Mo.: University of Missouri Press, 1986.

———. "Patterns of the Lives of the Patriarchs from Abraham to Samson and Samuel." In *Text and Tradition: The Hebrew Bible and Folklore,* edited by Susan Niditch, 7–18. Atlanta: Scholars Press, 1990.

———. *The Singer of Tales.* New York: Atheneum Publishers, 1968.

Machinist, Peter. "Assyrians on Assyria in the First Millennium B.C." In *Anfänge politischen Denkens in der Antike: Die nahöstlichen Kulturen und die Griechen,* edited by Kurt Raaflaub, 77–104. Munich: R. Oldenbourg, 1993.

Margueron, Jean. "Quelques remarques concernant les archives retrouvés dans le palais de Mari." In *Cuneiform Archives and Libraries: Papers Read at the 30th Rencontre Assyriologique Internationale, Leiden, 4–8 July 1983,* edited by Klaas R. Veenhof, 149–52. Leiden: Nederlands Historisch Archaeologisch Institut, 1986.

Matthiae, P. "The Archives of the Royal Palace G of Ebla: Distribution and Arrangement of the Tablets According to Archaeological Evidence." In *Cuneiform Archives and Libraries: Papers Read at the 30th Rencontre Assyriologique Internationale, Leiden, 4–8 July 1983,* edited by Klaas R. Veenhof, 53–71. Leiden: Nederlands Historisch Archaeologisch Institut, 1986.

Mazar, Amihai. *Archaeology of the Land of Israel.* New York: Doubleday, 1992.

McCarter, P. Kyle. "Aspects of the Religion of the Israelite Monarchy: Biblical and Epigraphic Data." In *Ancient Israelite Religion: Essays in Honor of Frank Moore Cross,* edited by Patrick D. Miller, Jr., Paul D. Hanson, and S. Dean McBride, 137–55. Philadelphia: Fortress Press, 1987.

——— "The Balaam Texts from Deir 'Alla: The First Combination." *BASOR* 239 (1980): 49–60.

McKenzie, Steven L. *The Chronicler's Use of the Deuteronomistic History.* HSM 33. Atlanta: Scholars Press, 1984.

Metzger, Bruce M. *The Text of the New Testament: Its Transmission, Corruption, and Restoration.* New York: Oxford University Press, 1992.

Meyers, Carol. *Discovering Eve: Ancient Israelite Women in Context.* New York: Oxford University Press, 1988.

Michalowski, Piotr. "Presence at the Creation." In *Lingering over Words: Studies in Ancient Near Eastern Literature in Honor of William L. Moran,* edited by Tzvi Abusch, John Huehnergard, and Piotr Steinkeller, 381–96. Atlanta: Scholars Press, 1990.

Millard, Alan R. "An Assessment of the Evidence for Writing in Ancient Israel." In *Biblical Archaeology Today: Proceedings of the International Congress on Biblical Archaeology, Jerusalem, April 1984,* 301–12. Jerusalem: Israel Exploration Society, 1985.

———. "The Question of Israelite Literacy." *Bible Review* 3 (1987): 22–31.

———. "Were Words Separated in Ancient Hebrew Writing?" *Bible Review* 3 (1992): 44–47.

Miller, Patrick D., Jr. "Animal Names as Designations in Ugaritic and Hebrew." *UF* 2 (1970): 177–86.

Miller, Patrick D., Jr., Paul D. Hanson, and S. Dean McBride, eds. *Ancient Israelite Religion: Essays in Honor of Frank Moore Cross.* Philadelphia: Fortress Press, 1987.

Nagy, Gregory. *Greek Mythology and Poetics.* Ithaca, N.Y.: Cornell University Press, 1990.

Naveh, J. "A Fragment of an Ancient Hebrew Inscription from the Ophel." *IEJ* 32 (1982): 195–98.

———. "Old Hebrew Inscriptions in a Burial Cave." *IEJ* 13 (1963): 74–92.

———. "A Palaeographical Note on the Distribution of the Hebrew Script." *HTR* 61 (1968): 68–74.

Newsom, Carol A. "A Maker of Metaphors: Ezekiel's Oracles against Tyre." In *Interpreting the Prophets,* edited by James Luther Mays and Paul J. Achtemeier, 188–99. Philadelphia: Fortress Press, 1987.

Newsome, J. D. "Toward an Understanding of the Chronicler and His Purposes." *JBL* 94 (1975): 201–17.

Niditch, Susan. *Chaos to Cosmos: Studies in Biblical Patterns of Creation.* Chico, Calif.: Scholars Press, 1984.

———. "The Composition of Isaiah 1." *Biblica* 61 (1980): 509–29.

———. "Ezekiel 40–48 in a Visionary Context." *CBQ* 48 (1986): 208–24.

———. *Folklore and the Hebrew Bible.* Minneapolis: Fortress Press, 1993.

————. "Samson as Culture Hero, Trickster, and Bandit: The Empowerment of the Weak." *CBQ* 52 (1990): 608–24.

————. *The Symbolic Vision in Biblical Tradition.* HSM 30. Chico, Calif.: Scholars Press, 1980.

————. *Underdogs and Tricksters: A Prelude to Biblical Folklore.* San Francisco: Harper & Row, 1987.

————. *War in the Hebrew Bible: A Study in the Ethics of Violence.* New York: Oxford University Press, 1993.

Niditch, Susan, and Robert Doran. "The Success Story of the Wise Courtier." *JBL* 96 (1977): 179–93.

Nielsen, Edward. *Oral Tradition: A Modern Problem in Old Testament Introduction.* London: SCM Press, 1954.

Niles, John D. "Editing *Beowulf:* What Can Study of the Ballads Tell Us?" *Oral Tradition* 9/2 (1994): 440–67.

————. "Understanding *Beowulf:* Oral Poetry Acts." *JAF* 106 (1993): 131–55.

Noth, Martin. *A History of Pentateuchal Traditions.* Translated with an introduction by B. W. Anderson. Englewood Cliffs, N.J.: Prentice-Hall, 1972.

Nyberg, H. S. *Studien zum Hoseabuche.* Uppsala: Almqvist & Wiksell, 1935.

O'Connor, M. *Hebrew Verse Structure.* Winona Lake, Ind.: Eisenbrauns, 1980.

O'Keeffe, Katherine O'Brien. *Visible Song: Transitional Literacy in Old English Verse.* Cambridge: Cambridge University Press, 1990.

Olrik, Axel. "Epic Laws of Folk Narrative." In *The Study of Folklore,* edited by Alan Dundes, 129–41. Englewood Cliffs, N.J.: Prentice-Hall, 1965.

Ong, Walter. "Literacy and Orality in Our Times." In *Oral and Traditional Literatures,* edited by Norman Simms, 8–20. Colorado Springs, Colo.: Three Continents Press, 1982.

————. *Orality and Literacy: The Technologizing of the Word.* London: Methuen, 1982.

————. "Text as Interpretation: Mark and After." In *Oral Tradition in Literature: Interpretation in Context,* edited by John Miles Foley, 147–69. Columbia, Mo.: University of Missouri, 1986.

Pardee, Dennis. *Handbook of Ancient Hebrew Letters: A Study Edition.* Chico, Calif.: Scholars Press, 1982.

————. "Letters." *ABD* (1992): 4:282–85.

Parker, Simon B. "Siloam Inscription Memorializes Engineering Achievement." *BAR* 20 (1994): 36–38.

Parpola, Simo. "Assyrian Library Records." *JNES* 42 (1983): 1–29.

Peckham, Brian. *History and Prophecy: The Development of Late Judean Literary Traditions.* New York: Doubleday, 1993.

Pedersén, Olaf. *Archives and Libraries in the City of Assur: A Survey of the Material from the German Excavations.* Part II. Uppsala: Almqvist & Wiksell, 1986.

Pope, Marvin H. *Job.* Garden City, N.Y.: Doubleday, 1965.

Posner, Ernst. *Archives in the Ancient World.* Cambridge, Mass.: Harvard University Press, 1972.

Rad, Gerhard von. "The Joseph Narrative and Ancient Wisdom." Reprinted, in *Studies in Ancient Israelite Wisdom,* edited by James L. Crenshaw, 439–47. New York: KTAV Publishing House, 1976.

Rendtorff, Rolf. *The Old Testament: An Introduction*. Philadelphia: Fortress Press, 1986.

———. "Pentateuchal Studies on the Move." *JSOT* 3 (1977): 43–46.

———. *Das überlieferungsgeschichtliche Problem des Pentateuch*. Berlin: de Gruyter, 1977.

———. "The 'Yahwist' as Theologian? The Dilemma of Pentateuchal Criticism." *JSOT* 3 (1977): 2–10.

Rosenberg, Bruce A. "The Complexity of Oral Tradition." *Oral Tradition* 2 (1987): 73–90.

Rosenberg, David, and Harold Bloom. *The Book of J*. New York: Grove Weidenfeld, 1990.

Rosenberg, Joel. "Bible." In *Back to the Sources: Reading the Classic Jewish Texts*, 31–81. New York: Summit Books, 1984.

Schousboe, Karen, and Mogens Trolle Larsen, eds. *Literacy and Society*. Copenhagen: Akademisk Forlag, 1989.

Skeat, T. C. "The Origin of the Christian Codex." *Zeitschrift für Papyrologie und Epigraphik* 102 (1994): 263–68.

Smelik, Klaas A. D. *Writings from Ancient Israel*. Louisville, Ky.: Westminster/John Knox Press, 1991.

Smith, Morton. *Palestinian Parties and Politics That Shaped the Old Testament*. London: SCM Press, 1987.

Speyer, Wolfgang. *Die literarische Fälschung im heidnischen und christlichen Altertum: Ein Versuch ihrer Deutung*. Munich: Beck, 1971.

Street, Brian. *Literacy in Theory and Practice*. Cambridge: Cambridge University Press, 1984.

Thomas, Rosalind. *Literacy and Orality in Ancient Greece*. Cambridge: Cambridge University Press, 1992.

———. *Oral Tradition and Written Record in Classical Athens*. Cambridge: Cambridge University Press, 1989.

Tigay, Jeffrey H. "Israelite Religion: The Onomastic and Epigraphic Evidence." In *Ancient Israelite Religion: Essays in Honor of Frank Moore Cross*, edited by Patrick D. Miller, Jr., Paul D. Hanson, and S. Dean McBride, 157–94. Philadelphia: Fortress Press, 1987.

Tov, Emanuel. "Biblical Texts as Reworked in Some Qumran Manuscripts with Special Attention to 4QRP and 4QPara Gen-Exod." In *The Community of the Renewed Covenant: The Notre Dame Symposium on the Dead Sea Scrolls*, edited by Eugene Ulrich and James VanderKam, 111–34. Notre Dame, Ind. University of Notre Dame Press, 1993.

Trible, Phyllis. "Depatriarchalizing in Biblical Interpretation." In *The Jewish Woman*, edited by Elizabeth Koltun, 217–40. New York: Schocken Books, 1976.

———. *God and the Rhetoric of Sexuality*. Philadelphia: Fortress Press, 1978.

Troll, Denise A. "The Illiterate Mode of Written Communication: The Work of the Medieval Scribe. In *Oral and Written Communication: Historical Approaches*, edited by Richard Leo Enos, 96–125. Newbury Park, Calif.: Sage Publications, 1990.

Ulrich, Eugene. "The Bible in the Making: The Scriptures at Qumran." In *The Community of the Renewed Covenant: The Notre Dame Symposium on the Dead Sea*

Scrolls, edited by Eugene Ulrich and James VanderKam, 77–93. Notre Dame, Ind.: University of Notre Dame Press, 1993.

Ulrich, Eugene, and James VanderKam, eds. *The Community of the Renewed Covenant: The Notre Dame Symposium on the Dead Sea Scrolls.* Notre Dame, Ind.: University of Notre Dame Press, 1993.

Van Seters, John. *Abraham in History and Tradition.* New Haven, Conn.: Yale University Press, 1977.

———. *In Search of History: Historiography in the Ancient World and the Origins of Biblical History.* New Haven, Conn.: Yale University Press, 1983.

———. *Prologue to History: The Yahwist as Historian in Genesis.* Louisville, Ky.: Westminster/John Knox Press, 1992.

Van Soldt, W. H. "The Palace Archives at Ugarit." In *Cuneiform Archives and Libraries: Papers Read at the 30th Rencontre Assyriologique Internationale, Leiden, 4–8 July 1983,* edited by Klaas R. Veenhof, 196–204. Leiden: Nederlands Historisch Archaeologisch Institut, 1986.

Vanstiphout, Herman L. J. "Repetition and Structure in the Aratta Cycle: Their Relevance for the Orality Debate." In *Mesopotamian Epic Literature: Oral or Aural?* edited by Marianna E. Vogelzang and Herman L. J. Vanstiphout, 247–64. Lewiston, N.Y.: Edwin Mellen Press, 1992.

Veenhof, Klaas R., ed. *Cuneiform Archives and Libraries: Papers Read at the 30th Rencontre assyriologique internationale, Leiden, 4–8 July 1983.* Leiden: Nederlands Historisch Archaeologisch Institut, 1986.

Vogelzang, Marianna E. "Some Aspects of Oral and Written Tradition 1992 in Akkadian." In *Mesopotamian Epic Literature: Oral or Aural?* edited by Marianna E. Vogelzang and Herman L. J. Vanstiphout, 265–78. Lewiston, N.Y.: Edwin Mellen Press, 1992.

———. "Some Questions about the Akkadian Disputes." In *Dispute Poems and Dialogues in the Ancient and Mediaeval Near East: Forms and Types of Literary Debates in Semitic and Related Literatures,* edited by G. J. Reinink and H. L. J. Vanstiphout, 47–57. Leuven: Department Orientalistiek, 1991.

Vogelzang, Marianna E., and Herman L. J. Vanstiphout, eds. *Mesopotamian Epic Literature: Oral or Aural?* Lewiston, N.Y.: Edwin Mellen Press, 1992.

Weitemeyer, Mogens. "Archives and Library Technique in Ancient Mesopotamia." *Libri* 6 (1956): 217–38.

Wellhausen, Julius. *Prolegomena to the History of Israel.* With Preface by W. Robertson Smith. Edinburgh: Adam and Charles Black, 1885. Reprinted, Atlanta: Scholars Press, 1994. (Translation of *Geschichte Israels. In zwei Bänden. Erster Band.* Berlin: G. Reimer, 1878. 2d ed., *Prolegomena zur Geschichte Israels.* Berlin: G. Reimer, 1883.)

Westenholz, Joan Goodnick. "Oral Traditions and Written Texts in the Cycle of Akkade." In *Mesopotamian Epic Literature: Oral or Aural?,* edited by Marianna E. Vogelzang and Herman L. J. Vanstiphout, 123–54 Lewiston, N.Y.: Edwin Mellen Press, 1992.

Westermann, Claus. *Genesis 12—36.* Minneapolis: Augsburg Publishing House, 1985.

———. *Genesis 37—50.* Minneapolis: Augsburg Publishing House, 1986.

Whallon, William. *Formula, Character, and Context: Studies in Homeric, Old*

English, and Old Testament Poetry. Washington, D.C.: The Center for Hellenic Studies, 1969.

Whybray, R. N. *The Making of the Pentateuch: A Methodological Study.* JSOTSup 53. Sheffield: Sheffield Academic Press, 1987.

Williams, R. J. "Writing and Writing Materials." *IDB* (1962): 4:909–21.

Wilson, Robert R. "Prophecy in Crisis: The Call of Ezekiel." In *Interpreting the Prophets,* edited by James L. Mays and Paul J. Achtemeier 157–69. Philadelphia: Fortress Press, 1987.

————. *Prophecy and Society in Ancient Israel.* Philadelphia: Fortress Press, 1980.

————. *Sociological Approaches to the Old Testament.* Philadelphia: Fortress Press, 1984.

Yoder, Perry Bruce. "A–B Pairs and Oral Composition in Hebrew Poetry." *VT* 21 (1971): 470–89.

Zakovitch, Yair. "Review of *Underdogs and Tricksters: A Prelude to Biblical Folklore.*" *JAF* 104 (1991): 233–35.

Index of Ancient Sources

BIBLICAL TEXTS CITED

ANCIENT NEAR EASTERN AND EPIGRAPHIC SOURCES

Index of Names and Subjects